AF633050

The Engagement of India

South Asia in World Affairs Series

T. V. Paul, *Series Editor*

Editorial Advisory Board

Rajesh Basrur
Maya Chadda
Stephen P. Cohen
C. Christine Fair
Timothy Hoyt
Paul Kapur
Rajesh Rajagopalan
Aseema Sinha

Titles in the Series

Afghan Endgames: Strategy and Policy Choices for America's Longest War
Hy Rothstein and John Arquilla, Editors

Pakistan's Counterterrorism Challenge
Moeed Yusuf, Editor

Vying for Allah's Vote: Understanding Islamic Parties, Political Violence, and Extremism in Pakistan
Haroon K. Ullah

THE ENGAGEMENT OF INDIA

Strategies and Responses

IAN HALL, Editor

GEORGETOWN UNIVERSITY PRESS
Washington, DC

FOUNDATION
BOOKS

FOUNDATION
BOOKS

Foundation Books is an imprint of Cambridge University Press, India.

Cambridge House, 4381/4 Ansari Road, Daryaganj, New Delhi 110 002

www.cambridgeindia.org

© Georgetown University Press, 2014
This edition is published by arrangement with Georgetown University Press, Washington DC, USA.

This publication is in copyright. Subject to statutory exception and to the provisions of relevant collective licensing agreements, no reproduction of any part may take place without the written permission of Cambridge University Press, India.

First South Asia edition 2015

Printed in India at AnVi Composers, New Delhi - 110063

ISBN 978-93-84463-42-7 Hardback

Cambridge University Press, India has no responsibility for the persistence or accuracy of URLs for external or third-party internet websites referred to in this publication, and does not guarantee that any content on such websites is, or will remain, accurate or appropriate.

CONTENTS

PREFACE

INDIA'S EMERGENCE as a significant global power is one of the most striking developments of the post–Cold War era. This book explores the strategies that other states have employed to try to shape the foreign and domestic policies of India as a "rising power." It also examines Indian responses—positive, ambivalent, and sometimes hostile—to the engagement strategies used by other states, as well as India's own attempt to engage states in its region. It argues that India's "rise" cannot be understood just in terms of Indian actions but rather as a dynamic process of domestic change and foreign engagement.

This book is the product of a workshop held at the Australian National University (ANU) in Canberra in November 2011. As the workshop convener and now as editor of this volume, I am grateful for the financial support of the Australia India Institute in Melbourne, as well as the continuing encouragement of its director, Professor Amitabh Mattoo, and his staff, especially Souresh Roy. I am also grateful to Happymon Jacob of Jawaharlal Nehru University and Rory Medcalf of the Lowy Institute for International Policy for their insightful contributions to the workshop. Thanks are due to the ANU for hosting the event, to Satomi Ono for coordinating the logistics, and to Mary-Louise Hickey, whose editorial acumen was invaluable in pulling the final book together. I would also like to express my thanks to Donald Jacobs and the staff of Georgetown University Press.

ABBREVIATIONS

ADMM	ASEAN Defence Ministers Meeting
ADMM + 8	ADMM plus defense ministers or secretaries of Australia, China, India, Japan, New Zealand, Russia, South Korea, and the United States
ALP	Australian Labor Party
ANZUS	Australia, New Zealand, United States
APEC	Asia-Pacific Economic Cooperation
ARF	ASEAN Regional Forum
ASEAN	Association of Southeast Asian Nations
ASEAN + 3	China, Japan, and South Korea
BASIC	Brazil, South Africa, India, and China
BIMSTEC	Bay of Bengal Initiative for Multi-Sectoral Technical and Economic Cooperation
BJP	Bharatiya Janata Party
BRICS	Brazil, Russia, India, China, and South Africa
CAR	Central Asian Republic
CECA	comprehensive economic cooperation agreement
CEPA	comprehensive economic partnership agreement
CSTO	Collective Security Treaty Organization
CTBT	Comprehensive Test Ban Treaty
DFAT	Department of Foreign Affairs and Trade
DPJ	Democratic Party of Japan
EU	European Union
FDI	foreign direct investment
G2	Group of Two
G8	Group of Eight
G20	Group of Twenty
G77	Group of Seventy-Seven
GDP	gross domestic product
GLONASS	Global Navigation Satellite System

IBSA	India, Brazil, and South Africa
IFS	Indian Foreign Service
IMF	International Monetary Fund
INSTC	International North-South Transport Corridor
ISAF	International Security Assistance Force
JWG	Joint Working Group
LAC	Line of Actual Control
MFN	most-favored nation
NAM	Non-Aligned Movement
NATO	North Atlantic Treaty Organization
NPT	Nuclear Non-Proliferation Treaty
ODA	official development assistance
ONGC	Oil and Natural Gas Corporation
OVL	ONGC Videsh Ltd.
PLA	People's Liberation Army
SCO	Shanghai Cooperation Organization
SLOC	sea lane of communication
TAPI	Turkmenistan, Afghanistan, Pakistan, and India
UN	United Nations
UNSC	United Nations Security Council
WTO	World Trade Organization

CHAPTER 1

THE ENGAGEMENT OF INDIA

Ian Hall

FOR MUCH OF THE COLD WAR, most of the major powers could safely neglect India. India had friends in the developing world, but relations with most of the industrialized world were often strained. In its immediate region, India met with persistent "sibling rivalry" from Pakistan and remained locked in a "protracted contest" with China.[1] While India forged a mutually beneficial relationship with the Soviet Union after 1971, its ongoing economic woes and rhetorical commitment to nonalignment "estranged" the country from Western states and other major Asian states, including Japan.[2]

The end of the Cold War, however, brought change. Initially India found itself in a difficult position. In the early 1990s, it was isolated and insecure, as its economy teetered on the brink of crisis, its Soviet sponsor fragmented and then disappeared, and its Chinese neighbor continued its rise. But only a decade later, India's fortunes appeared to have been transformed. The country had emerged from isolation and gained in confidence. By the early 2000s, India was increasingly acknowledged as an "emerging" or "rising" power of consequence in regional and world politics.[3]

This dramatic shift in India's position in the international order is normally attributed largely to Indian actions, particularly to three sets of changes made by successive Indian governments to its economic, foreign, and security policies.[4] The first set of changes were the economic reforms precipitated by an acute balance-of-payments crisis in 1991 and 1992, itself brought about by the oil price rises caused by the 1991 Gulf War and exacerbated by the decline and eventual demise of the Soviet Union. These reforms are widely credited with laying the foundation for the high rates of economic growth experienced by India in the 1990s and 2000s.[5] The second set of changes concerned foreign policy. In the early to middle 1990s, India reoriented the Ministry of External Affairs and its wider foreign policy establishment to "Look East," aiming to improve relations with states in East Asia and to locate new sources of knowledge and foreign direct investment (FDI).[6] The third set of changes—this time to strategic policy—was symbolized most clearly by India's five nuclear tests at Pokhran in the Rajasthan desert in May 1998. This move, born of acute security concerns about India's relative weakness compared to an interventionist America with global reach and an increasingly assertive rising China, initially led to India's further isolation, sanctioned and shunned by a number of states.[7] Over time, however, these changes helped to kick-start India's economy and to give the country greater diplomatic weight and momentum, and in turn this transformation in India's position required or tempted states outside India's erstwhile inner circle to engage with the country once more.

This book examines how these various engagements were conducted—what strategies were put in place, what was put on the table for India and why, and how successful they have been. It argues that India's rise in contemporary international relations cannot be attributed solely to Indian actions but rather is best understood in terms of a dynamic process of interactions between India and other states within equally dynamic international contexts. External events as much as domestic policy reforms have played their part in transforming India's standing in world politics. The rise of China, the emergence of militant Islamist terrorism, and the global financial crisis have concerned the West and Asian states, prompting them, as many have noted, to seek better relations with India. The various engagement strategies employed have created opportunities for India that India might not otherwise have had. US diplomatic and military engagement has clearly been instrumental here, but other states have also aided India's rise in ways that might not have been anticipated at the close of the Cold War.

But what is "engagement," and what kinds of engagement strategy can be employed in international relations? Which particular strategies have been used in engaging India? And which strategies have worked, and which have not? This book addresses these various questions. While much work has been done on strategies that employ coercion of various kinds to try to shape the policies of other states—from the use of military force to economic embargoes—comparatively little has been done on engagement and still less on the engagement of India.

Strategies of Engagement

This book explores the various modes of engagement employed in the Indian case, their uses, and their limits. It follows the growing consensus in the literature that defines engagement as any strategy that employs "positive inducements" to influence the behavior of states.[8] It acknowledges that various, different engagement strategies can be utilized. In particular, as Miroslav Nincic argues, we can distinguish between "exchange" strategies and "catalytic" ones. With the first type of strategy, positive inducements are offered to try to "leverage" particular quid pro quos from the target state.[9] An investment might be canvassed, a trade deal promised, or a weapons system provided in return for a specific concession. With the second type of strategy, inducements are offered merely to catalyze something bigger, perhaps even involving the wholesale transformation of a target society.[10] In this kind of engagement, many different incentives might be laid out for many different constituencies, from educational opportunities for emerging leaders to new terms of trade for the economic elite.

The objects of engagement can include changing specific policies of the target state or transforming the wider political, economic, or social order of a target society. Both of these objectives could be pursued with coercive strategies employing either compellence or deterrence—or indeed with a mixture of both engagement and coercion.[11] But much recent research has argued that the evidence for the efficacy of both compellence and deterrence in changing target state policies is inconclusive.[12] Both military and economic sanctions have been shown to have mixed results, and many scholars argue that coercion rarely works.[13] By contrast, there is some considerable evidence that engagement strategies can both elicit discrete quid pro quos from states and generate wider political and social change within them that might in the medium to long term lead to changed behavior at home or in international relations.[14] Moreover, it is clear that engagement is both more commonly utilized than often recognized by scholars of international relations and that it is generally considered more politically accepted to politicians and publics in both engaging states and in the states they seek to engage.[15]

Engagement strategies take different forms depending on their objectives. They can emphasize diplomacy, aiming at the improvement of formal, state-to-state contacts, and be led by professional diplomats, special envoys, or politicians. Alternatively, they can emphasize military ties, utilizing military-to-military dialogues, exchanges, and training to build trust, convey strategic intentions, or simply foster greater openness in the target state's defense establishment.[16] They can be primarily economic in approach, using trade, investment, and technology transfer to engender change in the target society and perhaps to generate greater economic interdependence, constraining a target state's foreign policy choices.[17] Finally, they can seek to create channels for people-to-people contact through state-driven public diplomacy, business forums and research networks, aid and development assistance, and so on.

These strategies are sometimes used in isolation but are often employed in combination. Diplomatic engagement normally precedes other forms of engagement, especially in cases in which states are highly estranged from other states or in which relatively quick changes in target state policies are desired. Henry Kissinger's secret contacts with China in 1970 and 1971 and Richard Nixon's subsequent visit in 1972 provide the most obvious and dramatic recent examples of diplomatic engagement that transformed the relations between two states. In this case, diplomatic engagement involved the establishment of full diplomatic relations as well as the recognition of China's claim to its seat on the United Nations Security Council (UNSC). The United States also mixed Nincic's "exchange" and "catalytic" strategies but was much more heavily weighted to the former than the latter. In the short term, China secured recognition, the UNSC seat, and a tacit ally against the Soviet Union. In return, the United States secured Chinese help in bringing the Vietnam War to a close and a changed Eurasian balance of power.[18]

The United States did not rely solely on diplomatic engagement in this particular episode—indeed, the other forms of engagement involved point to a longer-term "catalytic" strategy in operation. Nixon attempted also to use military means to engage China, exploring the option of supplying weapons to the People's Liberation Army (PLA) in order to change the regional military balance in China's favor. This military engagement was, however, stymied by bureaucratic and congressional opposition. Nixon's successor, Gerald Ford, succeeded in providing other technologies, including airliners and computers, which might have had some military utility.[19] In the mid-1980s under Ronald Reagan, military engagement was approved and attempted, first with a round of military-to-military dialogues and with a limited number of arms transfers to the PLA.[20]

This kind of military engagement can have short- or long-term aims. A one-off arms sale might be intended to influence a particular decision; a series of military-to-military talks or joint exercises might seek to build trust as much as to exchange information or test capabilities. By its very nature, military engagement can also be more controversial both within the engaging state and the target state and indeed with neighboring or other concerned states. Arms transferred, for example, might be used for purposes other than the ones specified by the supplier, as India knows only too well from past confrontations with a Pakistani army replete with American weapons.[21]

In the post–Cold War period, diplomatic and military engagement gave way to economic and public approaches. In the 1970s and 1980s, Western states became increasingly reliant upon economic coercion to achieve foreign policy objectives, especially the promotion of human rights and democratic politics. Sanctions were imposed to deter and compel states to change their policies.[22] After 1989, economic engagement, sometimes backed up with public diplomacy and especially civil society engagement, began to supplement diplomatic, military, and economic coercion. In the wake of the Cold War, this became the dominant approach employed by Western states to bring about political change and to entrench preferred political options in the former communist Eastern Bloc nations and other states in transition.[23] In contrast to diplomatic or military engagement, economic and public engagement generally employs long-term catalytic strategies, aimed at incremental change in the preferences and policies of target states over time. They were employed to great success by the United States in Western Europe after the Second World War, with the economic engagement of the Marshall Plan supplemented by extensive public and cultural diplomacy.[24]

In the 1990s, therefore, Western states moved rapidly from exchange engagement—involving the normalization of diplomatic relations and the redeployment of military forces—to catalytic strategies for change in target states. As in the period after 1945, from 1989 this economic and public engagement aimed at the longer-term objectives of entrenching liberal democratic norms and the rule of law while deepening interdependence.[25] Postcommunist states in Eastern Europe were thus given access to Western markets and investment; they were also provided with Western economic advice to aid reform of their economies—although not always to good effect.[26] All of the successor states to the Soviet Union, for example, were given "most-favored nation" (MFN) status by the United States in 1992. China, to which the United States had granted MFN status in 1980, had the designation withdrawn after the Tiananmen Square killings in 1989 but had it restored in 1992.[27] In parallel, the European Community / European Union (EU) extended similar privileges to the fifteen post-Soviet republics and former Warsaw Pact states, while Japan and the Association of Southeast Asian Nations (ASEAN) members pursued their own economic engagement strategies with China throughout the 1990s with similar objectives in mind.

Public engagement was also employed extensively during the post–Cold War period by Western states, especially after 9/11.[28] Like economic engagement, public engagement aims to bring about long-term shifts in preferences and policies, cultivating both public and elite opinion. Educational and cultural exchanges, old-fashioned books and magazines, plus new social media can all be used to convey ideas and values with the aim of reducing mistrust and improving understanding.[29]

In the case of Eastern Europe, as Nincic points out, the objectives of political and social change sought through catalytic engagement were conceived not just as goods in themselves but as integral parts of what Bill Clinton's administration called, in 1994, *A National Security Strategy of Engagement and Enlargement*.[30] And what began with the engagement of former communist states was soon extended to other target states, with the aim of bringing about similar transitions and behavioral change. In one combination or another, diplomatic, military, economic, and public engagement strategies, whether exchange or catalytic, have been employed by Western states to engage rising, transitioning, or rogue states to one degree or another since the early 1990s. Most obviously they have been utilized in the attempt to improve relations with China. But they have also been used by the West to try to bring about change in Iran, Libya, North Korea, Syria, and most recently Myanmar.[31]

In the post–Cold War period, engagement strategies have also been employed—with varying effects—by non-Western states. South Korea, for example, attempted to use economic engagement to bring about improved relations with North Korea from 1998 to 2008.[32] More successfully, India and the ASEAN members—individually and collectively—have used diplomatic engagement to try to bring about political change in Myanmar.[33] And China has used a variety of means to attempt to engage states in Asia,[34] as well as in Africa and Latin America,[35] mostly by utilizing exchange strategies to realize its economic interests rather than with strategies designed to catalyze large-scale social or political change in target states.

Engaging India

On the face of it, India might appear an odd candidate for engagement. As we have seen, engagement is a term historically associated with attempts to bring about changes in the policies of authoritarian, transitioning, or "rogue" states. India hardly falls into any of these categories: It is a relatively stable democracy with no particular tradition of military adventurism or systematic political repression. What made it a candidate for engagement, as Strobe Talbott observed in *Engaging India*, was not these attributes but rather the growing evidence that it was beginning to "rise" in world politics and that its relative isolation was no longer sustainable.[36] This evidence took time to emerge after 1991 and to be acknowledged as significant by major powers. Even in the mid-1990s, some in the United States continued to regard India as an economic basket case, while many in India continued to portray the United States as an imperialistic bully.[37] Relations with Western Europe were marginally better; ties with China were attenuated and difficult, at best. With much of the rest of Asia, India's relations were dominated by the export of labor and the remittance of wages earned. Only with Russia and with parts of the developing world did India have close or constructive ties.

The problematic nature of Indian relations with much of the developed world thus made engagement necessary after 1991. But it was India's economic and military rise that made it desirable. Its economic success after the reforms of 1991 and its nuclear tests in 1998 prompted many prominent actors to reassess their approaches to India. What they aimed to achieve with India, however, was not always clear. As we have seen, engagement is normally used to try to change the policies of target states—to open up markets or to discourage certain patterns of behavior, such as weapon proliferation or the state-sponsorship of terrorism. In the Indian case, it is clear that some important actors have wanted India to change some policies, notably when it came to further economic liberalization and the security of its nuclear weapons. But other actors wanted other things. Some pursued engagement as a means of encouraging India to carry on as before or merely to help it realize its latent potential, without substantive shifts in policy.

This kind of engagement is unusual, making India a special case. Generally, rising powers are met with balancing coalitions threatening sanctions, not sympathetic potential partners promising inducements. Historically this was the way in which most rising powers were managed, at least in the European experience. Far less often were they accommodated or appeased, either with changes to the rules of international society or with material concessions, and even rarer are the cases of rising powers being helped on their way.[38] To aid a rising power with the objective of actually speeding its rise as well as shaping that power's policies deviates from the norm. Yet, as Daniel Twining argues in his chapter, this is precisely what the United States has tried to do with India, and, as H. D. P. Envall suggests in his chapter, this is what Japan has also attempted to achieve with its engagement strategy.

There can be no doubt that America's engagement with India after 1991—especially after 1998—looms largest in the literature on India's foreign relations in the post–Cold War world.[39] But US engagement really began with military rather than diplomatic approaches back in the 1980s. The Reagan administration's decisions to offer American weapons (antitank missiles and howitzers) to India and then to allow more technology transfers are credited by Teresita C. Schaffer as laying the groundwork for what emerged in the late 1990s. In the early 1990s, military-to-military dialogues were followed by an Agreed Minute on Defense Relations between India and the United States in 1995.[40] But, as Twining argues, only in the aftermath of the 1998 nuclear tests did the diplomats enter the game with serious intent.

Particularly significant were Talbott's talks with Jaswant Singh (between 1998 and 2001) about India's nuclear weapons, but a wider diplomatic engagement was also initiated after the tests. Talbott characterized this "engagement" as involving both "conciliation and contest" on the nuclear issue but one in which both sides had a "desire to fix something that had been broken for a long time."[41] On the American side, this meant pulling back from positions it had once defended with some force. The most obvious change, as Twining notes, was the modification of the American stance on India's nuclear status. After initially condemning the 1998 tests with some force and pushing hard during the Talbott-Singh negotiations for India to sign and ratify at least the Comprehensive Test Ban Treaty (CTBT), if not the Nuclear Non-Proliferation Treaty (NPT), the United States under President George W. Bush abandoned both positions in favor of a bilateral deal on nuclear energy in 2005 and a special waiver from the Nuclear Suppliers Group in 2008.[42]

This was only the most obvious reversal of American policy that worked clearly in India's favor.[43] There were others, each significant less in terms of substance than symbolism. Although the United States was forced by circumstance to bolster its aid to Pakistan after 9/11, it also strove hard to "dehyphenate" its approach to South Asia, attempting to reassure India it did not see regional international relations as a zero-sum game. The United States also changed positions on a range of issues sensitive to India but of marginal concern to American domestic opinion and key foreign policy stakeholders. It dropped export controls on high-technology items used in India's space program—and therefore also in its ballistic missile programs—and concluded a cooperation agreement between the National Aeronautics and Space Administration and the Indian Space Research Organisation in 2008.[44]

Perhaps the most important symbolic shift was that the United States ceased to hector India and, moreover, decided to accept a series of rebuffs from the Indian side on issues of considerable significance to America. After 2001, the United States simply stopped criticizing its new strategic partner, whether over Kashmir or economic development or indeed its management of its relations with Pakistan. It muted calls for an internationally mediated settlement in Kashmir and criticism of the behavior of India's security forces, arguably creating a space in which India could reengage in negotiations with both Pakistan and indeed Kashmir on the issue. And the United States went further, tolerating a series of "noes" from India on issues of considerable significance to America: on the CTBT, on the idea of Indian military involvement in Afghanistan, on India's support for a climate change treaty at Copenhagen,[45] and on India's acquiescence in Western military action in support of Libya's revolution.[46] All these noes affected US interests, but the Americans responded only privately or meekly, if at all.

The aims of this American engagement were both short- and long-term, mixing exchange and catalytic strategies. Immediately after the nuclear tests, the United States was clearly concerned to ensure the security of the weapons and the stability of the South Asian region, to gain—if possible—Indian agreement to accede to the CTBT, and to shape Indian nuclear strategy.[47] Under the George W. Bush administration, however, America evolved more toward a longer-term catalytic strategy that sometimes involved the sacrifice of small immediate "wins" in favor of future, potentially larger successes. The curiosity is that this strategy united two groups within the administration usually at loggerheads but both willing to bet on India's rise as a positive force for international relations in the "Asian century" and both willing to back the catalytic dimension of US engagement. Neoconservatives concentrated more on the promise they thought latent in India's democratic politics than on its present social or economic ills. They also overlooked the deep-seated, anti-American sections of the Indian elite. Realists looked to India's potential as a counterweight to China.

To these ends, once the immediate phase of diplomatic engagement had done its work, America returned to military engagement as a short-term expression of goodwill and slowly built its economic or public engagement to catalyze longer-term change. In 2005, the United States concluded a ten-year defense partnership agreement with India that opened the way to the sale, among other things, of ballistic missile defense systems and fourth-generation fighter aircraft.[48] At the same time, it worked more slowly—using government and nongovernment agents—toward building trade in the nuclear industry and to other changes, including the further opening of the Indian economy to foreign direct investment in a range of sectors.[49]

Compared to the United States, the engagement strategies employed toward India by other states have been less overt, but they are no less significant. Western European states have focused, for example, more on economics and public engagement than high-profile diplomatic or military strategies.[50] This makes sense in terms of their capabilities and their interests. The EU is, after all, one of India's top three trading partners, alongside China and the states of the Gulf Cooperation Council. But, this said, European states in general were slow to react to India's rise in the 1990s, despite an increase in EU-Indian trade at a rate more rapid than any other bilateral economic relationship.[51] Significant political differences continued to cause friction, especially concerning India's nuclear arms. Many European states strongly condemned its tests in 1998—some even suspended the provision of development aid and assistance—and many continue to profess concerns.[52]

As with the US-Indian relationship, however, the nuclear tests proved a turning point in relations. Since 2000, the EU and India have held annual summits with the objective of developing a "strategic partnership," although without much of a substantive sense of what that partnership might mean in practice.[53] On too many issues, the two sides have divergent interests and principles. India resents EU tariff barriers and obstacles to the mobility of Indian labor. The two hold radically divergent views on global trade.[54] India resents European protectionism and subsidies with regard to the agricultural sector; the EU dislikes the barriers India still has in other sectors of its economy. Moreover, for various reasons European states have also found it harder than the Americans to stop criticizing or even hectoring India—notably, in recent years, over the NPT, Kashmir, and climate change—and this has continued to complicate relations with an Indian elite highly sensitive to criticism on these issues. The fact that some of this hectoring has been done at the high-profile and public EU-India summits can hardly be said to have helped.[55] Together it has also fostered the impression that the EU—unlike the US—is unwilling to countenance any significant changes to the rules of the prevailing international order that might be in India's interests.[56]

But problems in the EU-Indian relationship are not just the products of EU actions. The Europeans have voiced concerns that India simply does not take the EU seriously, either as a major power in its own right or as a counterweight to the United States or China, despite the size of Europe's economy.[57] Probably correctly, India views enterprises such as the Common Foreign and Security Policy with considerable skepticism, calculating that EU international relations are less than the sum of its parts. The confused response of EU states to the 1998 nuclear tests must have reinforced this impression, with German hostility contrasting with French and Spanish ambivalence.[58] As a consequence, and in line with long-standing preferences, India prefers instead to deal with individual state governments, with some of which—for example, Britain and France—it has strong and long-standing diplomatic, military, and economic relationships.

For all these reasons, this book sets aside Indo-European engagements in favor of closer examination of more proximate states to India. Envall analyzes the complex and rapidly deepening engagements between Japan and India, and Lavina Lee examines the equally complicated engagement of India by Russia. Consistent with Japan's earlier, self-defined role as an "aid great power,"[59] Japanese engagement began in the 1990s with substantial increases in aid, official development assistance (ODA), and infrastructure consistent with the use of a catalytic rather than an exchange strategy.[60] Since 2003, India has accounted for more than half of Japan's total ODA budget, but more striking is the way in which Japan has moved into new areas of investment in Indian infrastructure. In 2006, Japan signed a major deal to develop a road-and-rail-linked industrial corridor between New Delhi and Mumbai worth some US$90 billion, which would connect a series of special industrial zones. The Japan International Cooperation Agency has also supplied more than half the finance for the New Delhi Metro system in the form of soft loans. More recently, Japan has been in negotiations to provide nuclear technology to India, including up to three new reactors. At the same time, and following their government's lead, Japanese firms have begun to invest more in India, despite relatively low levels of trade between the two (about US$10 billion per annum, compared to Sino-Indian trade of around US$60 billion in 2010). Business surveys indicate that Japanese firms intend to disburse more foreign direct investment to India over the coming decade, shifting away from China.[61]

Perhaps most significant, however, is Japan's burgeoning diplomatic, military, and public engagement of India. Japan was initially very concerned about India's nuclear tests in 1998 but within two years reassessed its position, coming to the view that India could be a "global partner" to Japan. In 2005, the two declared that they wished to forge a "strategic partnership," beginning with maritime security issues. In 2007, the relationship was deepened further. India and Japan achieved agreement on nuclear issues in the wake of the US-Indian deal, Japanese prime minister Shinzō Abe included India in his proposal for a "quadrilateral initiative," and the two states conducted extensive joint naval exercises. As David Brewster has noted, not all of the aspirations expressed came to be realized, partly because of Chinese hostility and partly because of American and Australian ambivalence. In 2008, in a less ambitious mood, India and Japan signed a joint security declaration that tried to regain some of the lost momentum.[62] That declaration aimed to generate greater military-to-military dialogue and cooperation, annual joint naval exercises, and better coordination on other security issues, including money-laundering and disaster management.

As Envall shows, Japan's engagement has been almost wholly catalytic in intent—it aims at cultivating India over the medium to long term as an alternative destination for investment capital, as well as a putative political and even military ally. By contrast, as Lee argues, Russia's post–Cold War engagement of India has concentrated more on exchange, aiming less at policy change than policy continuity and mutual advantage. Building on historical ties, perceptions of overlapping interests, and especially military ties, Russia has succeeded in reviving a partnership with India that provides it with access to a key market for arms and a key player in the global information-technology industry, as well as a prospective customer for Russian hydrocarbons.

China has taken a rather different approach to engaging India, as the chapters by Louise Merrington and Harsh V. Pant demonstrate. China has relied almost completely on economic engagement and on exchange approaches, apparently in the belief that its sheer economic weight will eventually convince India to compromise with it on other issues in the medium to long term.[63] China's diplomatic, military, and public engagement of India has, by contrast, moved very slowly. Although full diplomatic relations between the two states were restored in 1976 after a hiatus of fourteen years, little progress was made on settling territorial disputes or initiating trade until the mid-2000s. In 2005, a framework was set out for negotiation on the border issue, and in 2006 a "strategic partnership" was declared, but the wording of what this would entail in practice was vague.[64] Similarly, military confidence-building measures were initiated but were tightly bounded. Substantive progress was made only on the economic front. In 2000, cross-border trade in goods stood at only US$1 billion, but by 2010, thanks to committed action on both sides, this had grown to some US$60 billion. Both sides have stated their aspiration to grow this trade to US$100 billion by 2015. If this occurs, China will then become India's biggest trading partner, at least in goods.

China's engagement of India by diplomatic, military, or public means has been much less active. Unlike America, China has not attempted any grand diplomatic gestures, nor has it reversed any significant or contentious positions. As Merrington shows, China's economics-first engagement is not just directed at India but rather is a well-worn strategy for dealing with neighboring states, including those of Central Asia. Rather than moving to diplomatic, military, or public engagement, China seems to prefer to maintain this approach and to retain extensive flexibility when it comes to dealing with India, avoiding commitment on a range of issues, from the border to Tibet and from Pakistan to the nuclear balance. When it comes to military diplomacy, little has also been offered or agreed. In public diplomacy, admittedly, efforts have been made, but little progress achieved. China has tried, for example, to establish its Confucius Institutes in Indian universities,[65] but such moves have been resisted, despite agreements having been signed with Jawaharlal Nehru University in 2005 and the Vellore Institute of Technology in 2007. By contrast, it has opened seven such institutes in Indonesia and eighteen in Japan. In sum, China's engagement of India has been one-dimensional and, as Pant argues, has generated very mixed results.

Much the same could be said of Australia's fitful engagements of India, the subject of Ian Hall's chapter 7. Estranged for much of the Cold War, Australia employed catalytic strategies of public and economic diplomacy episodically during the 1970s, the 1980s, and again in the 1990s, not always to good effect. India's nuclear tests of 1998 and Australia's harsh reaction undid much of what had been achieved, but in the mid-2000s Canberra began once again to try to engage New Delhi. This time, however, it decided to focus on security issues, alongside the building of public and business ties, to forge closer relations. While this approach has been only partially successful, the bilateral relationship has been strengthened as a consequence of this change in direction.

In chapter 8, Brewster turns to India's own strategies of engagement and their effects on its relations with Southeast Asia. Since the early 1990s, India has attempted first to rebuild links long broken, initially with economic and public engagement, especially of diaspora communities resident in the region, and then to broaden relations with Southeast Asian states with improved diplomatic and military ties. Brewster finds that although these engagements have been uneven, India seems to be succeeding in building a role for itself as an influential partner to states in the region.

Conclusion

Whether engagement succeeds or fails depends on the receptivity of the target state, the selection and the implementation of the correct strategy, and the appeal of the engager to the engaged. These rules apply in the Indian case as well. It must be observed at the outset that since the end of the Cold War, India has not always been the most welcoming state to budding engagers. As Amrita Narlikar rightly notes, India's politicians and diplomats remain wary of concluding binding agreements with other states, especially multilateral instruments.[66] India continues to prefer bilateral deals to multilateral conventions. Significant sections of the foreign policy establishment—even some of the self-styled realists—remain highly suspicious of Western and indeed Chinese motives. It is apparent too that India continues to place great stock in symbolic gesture in its international relations, especially those gestures that indicate India is being taken seriously as an interlocutor. The Americans have been particularly astute on this point, having learned that staying quiet on sensitive issues may bring greater dividends than public denunciations of Indian actions.

In his chapter, Rajesh Basrur examines some of the possible consequences of these engagements. He observes, in particular, the growing confidence of India's foreign and strategic policymaking elite, which appears to be moving from thinking best seen as revisionist, with regard to the international system, to positions that favor the status quo. Engagement by the major powers—especially by the United States—seems to have played a major part in this modification, since other significant variables, including India's economic and military power, have not witnessed the kind of change sufficient to generate such a transformation.

The final chapter by Nick Bisley reflects upon the lessons that might be learned from the various engagement strategies practiced by different states and the wider implications of these engagements of India for the contemporary international order. What is clear from the chapters in this book is that diplomatic and military engagement has so far worked better with India than economic and public engagement and that exchange strategies have worked much better in the past than catalytic ones. Russian arms and Japanese assistance appear to have generated significant dividends.[67] But neither the United States nor China has so far derived significant policy changes in India as a result of economic engagement. Contrary to the views of some on the Indian Left, the United States has not yet succeeded in persuading India to liberalize its economy in any significant way—the liberalization that has occurred happened in the early 1990s, when US-Indian relations remained strained. Nor has China seemingly gained any tangible diplomatic benefit from its own strategy of economic engagement. China's elite may think that China's sheer economic power will eventually shape its neighbors' diplomatic preferences, but in India—as elsewhere in Asia—there is little evidence that this strategy is working. Indeed, the contrary appears to have occurred, for as Sino-Indian trade grows, so too does Indian concern about Chinese intentions in Asia.[68]

At the outset of this chapter, I suggested that India's rise was as much a product of engagement as of Indian actions. Notwithstanding the fact that India's economic success is more a product of liberalization and domestic demand rather than foreign investment and trade, it is apparent that US efforts in particular have aided India's wider diplomatic success in international relations, even if they have not produced the kind of domestic socioeconomic reform some Americans might seek. It is difficult to see that India would have the place that it now does in the Group of Twenty (G20) or the East Asia Summit without American help, if only in terms of bringing India in from the cold after the Pokhran II nuclear tests. The difficulties that the Europeans and China have had in formulating and implementing successful engagement strategies highlights in this regard the success of aspects of America's engagement of India, as well as India's receptiveness to American entreaties. Whether others can learn from this experience will be evident as India continues its rise.

Notes

1. The phrase "sibling rivalry" is in common use, and I have not been able to locate who first used it, when, or where. The second phrase comes from the title of John W. Garver's book *Protracted Contest: Sino-Indian Rivalry in the Twentieth Century* (Seattle: University of Washington Press, 2001). For an assessment of recent developments in this contest, see Ian Hall, "China Crisis? Indian Strategy, Political Realism and the Chinese Challenge," *Asian Security* 8, no. 1 (2012): 84–92.

2. On Indo-American "estrangement," see Strobe Talbott, *Engaging India: Diplomacy, Democracy, and the Bomb* (Washington, DC: Brookings Institution, 2004), 6.

3. See especially James Manor and Gerald Segal, "Taking India Seriously," *Survival: Global Politics and Strategy* 40, no. 2 (1998): 53–70, and Stephen P. Cohen's *India: Emerging Power* (Washington, DC: Brookings Institution Press, 2001), as well as Baldev Raj Nayar and T. V. Paul, *India in the World Order: Searching for Major Power Status* (Cambridge: Cambridge University Press, 2003), and Ashley J. Tellis, *India as a New Global Power: An Action Agenda for the United States* (Washington, DC: Carnegie Endowment for International Peace, July 2005).

4. See, for example, C. Raja Mohan's *Crossing the Rubicon: The Shaping of India's New Foreign Policy* (New York: Palgrave, 2003).

5. See Arvind Panagariya, *India: The Emerging Giant* (New York: Oxford University Press, 2008), especially chapter 5.

6. The early reforms are discussed in J. N. Dixit, *My South Block Years: Memoirs of a Foreign Secretary* (New Delhi: UBS Publishers, 1996). The Look East policy is outlined in

Christophe Jaffrelot, "India's Look East Policy: An Asianist Strategy in Perspective," *India Review* 2, no. 2 (2003): 35–68.

7. On India's motives, see George Perkovich, *India's Nuclear Bomb: The Impact on Global Proliferation*, updated ed. (Berkeley: University of California Press, 2001), 404–43. On Indo-American relations after the tests, see Teresita C. Schaffer, *India and the United States in the 21st Century: Reinventing Partnership* (Washington, DC: Center for Strategic and International Studies, 2009).

8. See especially Miroslav Nincic, *The Logic of Positive Engagement* (Ithaca, NY: Cornell University Press, 2011), 1.

9. Ibid., 59–72.

10. Ibid., 73–87. Marc Lynch has also proposed a concept of "communicative engagement" that might transform both the engager and the engaged. See his "Why Engage? China and the Logic of Communicative Engagement," *European Journal of International Relations* 8, no. 2 (2002): 187–230.

11. The classic work on compellence and deterrence is Thomas C. Schelling, *Arms and Influence* (New Haven, CT: Yale University Press, 1966). Clearly, states often combine engagement strategies with coercive strategies. The American "congagement" of China is a case in point. See Aaron L. Friedberg, *A Contest for Supremacy: China, America, and the Struggle for Mastery in Asia* (New York: Norton, 2011), 88–119.

12. For an overview, see Nincic, *Logic of Positive Engagement*, 1–31.

13. On the (apparent) failures of military compellence, see especially Robert A. Pape, *Bombing to Win: Air Power and Coercion in War* (Ithaca, NY: Cornell University Press, 1996). On those of economic sanctions, see T. Clifton Morgan and Valerie L. Schwebach, "Fools Suffer Gladly: The Uses of Economic Sanctions in International Crises," *International Studies Quarterly* 41, no. 1 (1997): 27–50.

14. See Michael Mastanduno, "The Strategy of Economic Engagement: Theory and Practice," in *Economic Interdependence and International Conflict: New Perspectives on an Enduring Debate*, ed. Edward D. Mansfield and Brian M. Pollins (Ann Arbor: University of Michigan Press, 2003), 175–86.

15. In his *Logic of Positive Engagement*, it should be noted that Nincic is mostly concerned with the engagement of such controversial states, including Libya (under Muammar Gaddafi), Cuba, Syria, North Korea, and Iran.

16. See Carol Atkinson, "Constructivist Implications of Material Power: Military Engagement and the Socialization of States, 1972–2000," *International Studies Quarterly* 50, no. 3 (2006): 509–37, and Derek S. Reveron, *Exporting Security: International Engagement, Security Cooperation, and the Changing Face of the US Military* (Washington, DC: Georgetown University Press, 2010).

17. See Miles Kahler and Scott L. Kastner, "Strategic Uses of Economic Interdependence: Engagement Policies on the Korean Peninsula and across the Taiwan Strait," *Journal of Peace Research* 43, no. 5 (2006): 523–41.

18. See the contemporary analyses by Lucian W. Pye, "China and the United States: A New Phase," *Annals of the American Academy of Political and Social Science* 402 (1972): 97–106, and Stanley Hoffmann, "Weighing the Balance of Power," *Foreign Affairs* 50, no. 4 (1972): 618–43.

19. Friedberg, *Contest for Supremacy*, 74–75.

20. Ibid., 84.

21. In 1965, both India and Pakistan used American-supplied weapons against each other, but Pakistan's M47 and M48 tanks aroused the ire of Indian observers. See Stephen P. Cohen, "US Weapons and South Asia: A Policy Analysis," *Pacific Affairs* 49, no. 1 (1976): 49–69.

22. David C. Hendrikson, "The Democratist Crusade: Intervention, Economic Sanctions, and Engagement," *World Policy Journal* 11, no. 4 (1994/1995): 18–30.

23. On the wider context, see especially G. John Ikenberry, *After Victory: Institutions, Strategic Restraint, and the Rebuilding of Order after Major Wars* (Princeton, NJ: Princeton University Press, 2001), 215–56. On economic engagement in particular, see Ian Clark, *The Post–Cold War Order: The Spoils of Peace* (Oxford: Oxford University Press, 2001), 167–92.

24. On economic engagement, see Nincic, *Logic of Positive Engagement*, 75. On US public diplomacy, see especially Nicholas J. Cull, *The Cold War and the United States Information Agency: American Propaganda and Public Diplomacy, 1945–1989* (Cambridge: Cambridge University Press, 2009).

25. See James F. Hollifield and Calvin Jillson, eds., *Pathways to Democracy: The Political Economy of Democratic Transitions* (London and New York: Routledge, 2000).

26. Mastanduno, "Strategy of Economic Engagement."

27. For a forensic examination of America's engagement strategy with China, see Michael D. Swaine, *America's Challenge: Engaging a Rising China in the Twenty-First Century* (Washington, DC: Carnegie Endowment for International Peace, 2011).

28. See especially Joseph S. Nye Jr., *Soft Power: The Means to Success in World Politics* (New York: PublicAffairs, 2004).

29. Ian Hall and Frank Smith, "The Struggle for Soft Power in Asia: Public Diplomacy and Regional Competition," *Asian Security* 9, no. 1 (2013): 1–18.

30. Nincic, *Logic of Positive Engagement*, 77.

31. Ibid., 91–168. On North Korea, see John S. Park, "Inside Multilateralism: The Six-Party Talks," *Washington Quarterly* 28, no. 4 (2005): 73–91. On Libya, see Randall Newnham, "Carrots, Sticks, and Bombs: The End of Libya's WMD Program," *Mediterranean Quarterly* 20, no. 3 (2009): 77–94. On Myanmar, see Tan Seng Chye, "Changing Global Landscape and Enhanced US Engagement with Asia: Challenges and Emerging Trends," *Asia-Pacific Review* 19, no. 1 (2012): 108–29.

32. Jim Hoare, "Does the Sun Still Shine? The Republic of Korea's Policy of Engagement with the Democratic People's Republic of Korea," *Asian Affairs* 39, no. 1 (2008): 69–82.

33. See C. Raja Mohan, "Embracing Myanmar: India's Foreign Policy Realism," *RSIS Commentaries* 86/2010, August 2, 2010, http://dr.ntu.edu.sg/bitstream/handle/10220/6647/RSIS0862010.pdf?sequence=1 (accessed October 29, 2012), and Jürgen Haacke, "'Enhanced Interaction' with Myanmar and the Project of a Security Community: Is ASEAN Refining or Breaking with Its Diplomatic and Security Culture?" *Contemporary Southeast Asia* 27, no. 2 (2005): 188–216.

34. David Shambaugh, "China Engages Asia: Reshaping the Regional Order," *International Security* 29, no. 3 (2004/2005): 64–99.

35. Ian Taylor, *China and Africa: Engagement and Compromise* (London and New York: Routledge, 2006), and Frank O. Mora, "The People's Republic of China and Latin America: From Indifference to Engagement," *Asian Affairs: An American Review* 24, no. 2 (1997): 35–58.

36. Talbott, *Engaging India*, 1–22.

37. For an overview, see S. Paul Kapur, "India and the United States from World War II to the Present: A Relationship Transformed," in *India's Foreign Policy: Retrospect and Prospect*, ed. Sumit Ganguly (New Delhi: Oxford University Press, 2010), 252–60.

38. For contrasting reflections on this issue, see A. F. K. Organski and Jacek Kugler, *The War Ledger* (Chicago: University of Chicago Press, 1980), and Amrita Narlikar, *New Powers: How to Become One and How to Manage Them* (London: Hurst, 2010).

39. See especially Sumit Ganguly, Brian Shoup, and Andrew Scobell, eds., *US-Indian Strategic Cooperation into the 21st Century: More Than Words?* (London and New York: Routledge, 2006); Lloyd I. Rudolph and Susanne Hoeber Rudolph, eds., *Making US Foreign Policy toward South Asia: Regional Imperatives and the Imperial Presidency* (Bloomington: Indiana University Press, 2008); Schaffer, *India and the United States in the 21st Century*; and Raymond E. Vickery Jr., *The Eagle and the Elephant: Strategic Aspects of US-India Economic Engagement* (Baltimore: Johns Hopkins University Press, 2011).

40. Schaffer, *India and the United States in the 21st Century*, 74.

41. Talbott, *Engaging India*, 4.

42. See inter alia Schaffer, *India and the United States in the 21st Century*, 89–117, and Harsh V. Pant, *The US-India Nuclear Pact: Policy, Process, and Great Power Politics* (New Delhi: Oxford University Press, 2011).

43. There is a very lively debate in India about how far the deal works in India's favor. I simply assert here that it was highly advantageous, since without American help the standoff between other Western states and India over its nuclear weapons would likely have made it harder for New Delhi to pursue its wider foreign policy interests. Recent arguments about the Australian Labor Party's ban on uranium sales to India illustrate the extent of lingering resentment in other Western capitals on this question. See especially David Brewster, "Australia and India: The Indian Ocean and the Limits of Strategic Convergence," *Australian Journal of International Affairs* 64, no. 5 (2010): 549–65.

44. Schaffer, *India and the United States in the 21st Century*, 102–4, 109–13.

45. On Copenhagen, see J. Timmons Roberts, "Multipolarity and the New World (Dis)-order: US Hegemonic Decline and the Fragmentation of the Global Climate Regime," *Global Environmental Change* 21, no. 3 (2011): 776–84.

46. Ian Hall, "'Tilting at Windmills?' The Indian Debate on Responsibility to Protect after UNSC 1973," *Global Responsibility to Protect* 5, no. 1 (2013): 84–108.

47. See Talbott, *Engaging India*, as well as Jaswant Singh's *In Service of Emergent India: A Call to Honor* (Bloomington: Indiana University Press, 2007).

48. Baldev Raj Nayar, "India in 2005: India Rising, but Uphill Road Ahead," *Asian Survey* 46, no. 1 (2006): 96.

49. See especially Vickery, *Eagle and the Elephant*.

50. Ummu Salma Bava, "India and the European Union: From Engagement to Strategic Partnership," *International Studies* 47, nos. 2–4 (2010): 373–86.

51. Saponti Baroowa, "The Emerging Strategic Partnership between India and the EU: A Critical Appraisal," *European Law Journal* 13, no. 6 (2007): 738.

52. Ibid., 736.

53. The "Joint Action Plan" is strong on "dialogue" across a wide range of areas but short on concrete proposals for cooperation, except in space technology, research collaboration, and development assistance. See Council of the European Union, "The India-EU Strategic Partnership Joint Action Plan," 11984/05 (Presse 223), Brussels, September 7, 2005, www.consilium.europa.eu/ueDocs/cms_Data/docs/pressData/en/er/86130.pdf (accessed October 29, 2012). For a wider assessment of Indo-European relations, see David M. Malone, *Does the Elephant Dance? Contemporary Indian Foreign Policy* (Oxford: Oxford University Press, 2011), 224–48.

54. Nayar, "India in 2005," 100.

55. Rajendra K. Jain, "India, the European Union and Asian Regionalism," paper presented at the EUSA-AP Conference, Tokyo, December 8–10, 2005, www.eusa-japan.org/download/eusa_ap/paper_RajendraJain.pdf (accessed October 29, 2012).

56. Ibid., 6.

57. Ibid.

58. Baroowa, "Emerging Strategic Partnership," 736.

59. Dennis T. Yasutomo, "Why Aid? Japan as an 'Aid Great Power,'" *Pacific Affairs* 62, no. 4 (1989/1990): 490–503.

60. Japan has provided ODA to India since 1958. See Ministry of Foreign Affairs of Japan, "Outline of Japan's ODA to India," www.mofa.go.jp/region/asia-paci/india/pmv0504/oda_i.pdf (accessed October 29, 2012).

61. Nagesh Narayana, "India Tops Japan's FDI Destination Survey," *International Business Times*, January 6, 2011.

62. David Brewster, "The India-Japan Security Relationship: An Enduring Security Partnership?" *Asian Security* 6, no. 2 (2010): 95–120.

63. See Alka Acharya, *China and India: Politics of Incremental Engagement* (New Delhi: Har-Anand, 2008).

64. "China-India Joint Declaration," New Delhi, November 21, 2006, http://in.china-embassy.org/eng/sgxw/2006en/t282045.htm (accessed October 29, 2012).

65. Confucius Institutes, which are funded in part by the Chinese state via a nonprofit organization affiliated with the Ministry of Education and in part by the host institution, promote China's culture and languages to foreigners and people of Chinese origin overseas.

66. Narlikar, *New Powers*, 29–68.

67. See especially Deepa M. Ollapally, "The Evolution of India's Relations with Russia: Tried, Tested, and Searching for Balance," and Harsh V. Pant, "India-Japan Relations: A Slow, but Steady, Transformation," in Ganguly, *India's Foreign Policy*, 226–50, 206–25.

68. Nayar, "India in 2005," 98. See also Ian Hall, "China Crisis?," and Harsh V. Pant, ed., *The Rise of China: Implications for India* (New Delhi: Cambridge University Press, 2012).

CHAPTER 2

THE US ENGAGEMENT OF INDIA AFTER 1991

Transformation

Daniel Twining

US-INDIAN RELATIONS in the two decades following the Cold War offer a useful case study into strategies of engagement between previously alienated great powers. Following four decades of cool-to-adversarial relations, India and the United States redefined their relationship in light of structural changes to the international system. Unlike changes in other key international relationships, however, this transformation did not begin in 1989. Indeed, Washington and New Delhi spent much of the 1990s feuding—over India's opposition to American hegemony in the international system, the role of humanitarian intervention in the post–Cold War era, and India's development of nuclear weapons. The United States maintained sanctions against India throughout this period for its internal proliferation activities. In short, the demise of the Soviet Union and the onset of unipolarity do not explain the transformation of US-Indian relations, which began nearly a decade after these strategic shifts.

By the late 1990s, both Washington and New Delhi reassessed their interests in ways that drew them more closely together and created a foundation for the strategic partnership they built in the 2000s. There was both a structural and an ideational logic to these mutual reassessments. First, China's rise threatened to transform the wider Asian balance of power in ways that undermined the core interests of both the United States and India. Second, the United States came to appreciate India's concerns about this shifting balance after India tested nuclear weapons in 1998—and cited the danger from China as the primary driver of this decision. Third, India's nuclear tests, combined with its economic takeoff following liberalization in the 1990s, transformed India's identity in the eyes of American leaders: It was now a nuclear weapons state on track to become, within a few decades, one of the world's largest economies, with a power potential that could reshape the Asian balance in ways that supported US interests. Fourth, the authoritarian qualities of China's ascendance, combined with an ideological concern for democratic legitimacy in the international system, created a values-based calculus for closer ties between the world's largest democracies—which was substantially reinforced by the US recognition after September 11, 2001, that India and the United States faced the same jihadist adversaries.

As US leaders reached out to India from the late 1990s to build a new relationship, Indian leaders found their own reasons to reciprocate enhanced American engagement. India, with more poor people than in all of Sub-Saharan Africa, needed international technology and capital to steepen its development trajectory; the United States (which had organized the international sanctions regime on India from 1974 in response to concerns over Indian nuclear development) was the key to unlocking Indian access to these markets. Indian leaders, faced with extraordinary developmental challenges as well as dangers emanating from China, Pakistan, and international terrorism, understood that the sponsorship of the world's primary power for India's geopolitical rise could catalyze their own aspirations for their country and help them better manage a complex security environment. Indian leaders also understood that the gatekeeper role of the United States in international institutions could assist them in their fifty-year quest to sit at the "high table" of world politics as a great power with a voice and a vote, rather than protesting from outside the club as leader of a powerless Non-Aligned Movement.

In short, the US engagement strategy toward India was encouraged by Indian leaders: It was Indian prime minister Atal Bihari Vajpayee in 1998 who first made the case that the United States and India were "natural allies." But the US pivot toward intimate engagement with India was decisive. Given the imbalance of power between the two countries and the American role at the top of the global hierarchy, a true transformation in relations was only possible through US leadership. Reciprocal engagement transformed the logic and character of US-Indian relations in the 2000s. The two countries went from being "estranged democracies" during the Cold War to building a comprehensive strategic partnership that both American and Indian officials believed could recast the global balance of power in the twenty-first century. Yet despite the balance-of-power logic that animated the transformation in Indo-American ties, the new relationship between Washington and New Delhi is impossible to fully explain without reference to the ideational connection between the world's biggest and oldest democracies.

This chapter proceeds as follows. The first section describes independent India's alienation from the United States through the late 1990s. The second section assesses the origins of the Indo-American rapprochement around the turn of the century. The third section explains how, under multiple administrations in both countries, the United States and India worked to build a transformative strategic partnership. The fourth section highlights difficulties the relationship has encountered, perhaps not unexpectedly given how far and fast it has moved over the previous decade. The fifth section assesses the logic of engagement from a US perspective. The sixth section highlights areas on which New Delhi and Washington are focusing to deepen their partnership in ways that benefit the interests of both, using exchange and catalytic engagement strategies. The concluding section discusses the ideational foundations of closer Indo-American ties and the possibilities for values-based collaboration between the world's largest democracies.

Independent India's Strategic Alienation from the United States

India's low international profile during the second half of the twentieth century was a historical anomaly: During the British colonial period, the Raj was the strategic keystone of a global empire.[1] Under the British Empire, Indian armies served in Europe, North Africa, the Middle East, Southeast Asia, and China. Indian wealth—India's economy was the world's second largest, after only China's, until the early nineteenth century—underwrote Britain's imperial ambitions in far-flung corners of the globe and fueled British industrial development in ways that ultimately made it possible for a small island nation to stand down a more powerful Germany in two world wars.[2] Indeed, in the early 1940s, Prime Minister Winston Churchill was convinced that Britain could keep up the fight against the Axis powers even if German forces occupied England—thanks to the manpower, materiel, and geopolitical reach of its Indian empire.[3]

India helped the Allies win the Second World War, although the ideals of freedom for which they fought catalyzed the Indian independence struggle. From 1947, independent India pursued its own course of Soviet-style economic centralization at home and "nonalignment" abroad. Nonalignment later morphed into tacit alliance with the Soviet Union as Washington tied up with Indian adversaries Pakistan (from 1954) and China (from 1971) and New Delhi pursued foreign policies that isolated it from the world's developed democracies.

For half a century, the American and Indian governments were alienated by India's refusal to sign on as one of Washington's Cold War allies, by the US military alliance with Indian rival Pakistan forged in 1954, and later by America's tacit alliance with Indian rival China, countered by India's tacit alliance with Moscow. Following wars with both Pakistan and China, India launched a covert nuclear weapons program, leading the United States to muster its allies to impose sweeping sanctions on technology trade with India—stifling its development after state socialism had already undercut India's growth potential.

India was further alienated by Western support for a global order that appeared to discriminate against it. Unlike China, India was excluded from membership in the United Nations Security Council (UNSC). Because China tested nuclear weapons before the international nonproliferation regime took effect while India did not, China's nuclear arsenal was legitimized, and its right to nuclear weapons and trade affirmed, by the Nuclear Non-Proliferation Treaty (NPT). By contrast, India's later nuclear tests rendered it a "rogue state" under international law, subjecting it to sanctions on technology trade that undercut its security and limited its economic prospects.

Even after the Cold War, Washington and New Delhi spent the 1990s feuding over proliferation, which culminated in the imposition of even more US sanctions following India's 1998 nuclear weapons test. China's supplying of advanced nuclear and missile components to Pakistan, contravening Beijing's NPT obligations while Western powers looked the other way, reinforced Indian perceptions of the great powers' hypocrisy and hostility to India's legitimate security requirements. This sentiment was crystallized when US president Bill Clinton and Chinese president Jiang Zemin, meeting in Beijing, jointly condemned India's 1998 nuclear weapons tests and called for tough international sanctions to punish it. That India's leaders justified the tests with reference to the growing threat they perceived from China, which Clinton's 1997 *Quadrennial Defense Review Report* had identified as a potential peer competitor to the United States, only intensified the irony of the American position.[4]

The Origins of the Indo-American Rapprochement

In light of their complicated history, the transformation of US-Indian relations over the past fifteen years has in fact been extraordinary. Conflicts deriving from Washington's status as the ringleader of what Indians called an international "technology apartheid" designed to keep India down formed the legacy both countries began working together to overturn a decade ago.[5] New hopes for the relationship were symbolized by Vajpayee's declaration that India and America were natural allies, a formulation embraced by President Clinton in 2000 when he became the first American head of state to visit India since Jimmy Carter. In fact, India's 1998 nuclear tests had awakened Washington to the potential of Indian power, a converging threat assessment of China's growing strength, and the possibilities for Indo-American cooperation to shape a balance of power that might restrain it.

It was Indian, not American, leaders who then suggested that India and the United States should break from a half-century of discord to transform their relations for a new era. According to its leaders, India had tested nuclear weapons in response to existential threats from China and the ally it had helped to develop nuclear weapons, Pakistan. India was the world's largest democracy, and its people had friendly views toward the United States. Converging threat perceptions and common values meant that India and the United States could forge a partnership to manage the dangers of the twenty-first century and to amplify the strengths of the world's biggest open, pluralistic societies. President Clinton's unprecedented support for India over Pakistan in their near war of 1999, followed by his 2000 trip to India in which he echoed Vajpayee's call for an alliance of interests and values—examples of exchange engagement in the diplomatic realm—made possible the breakthroughs that came later.

President George W. Bush assumed office with a view of India as a future world power, a frontline Asian balancer, and a pluralistic democracy with which America should naturally cooperate in world affairs. But New Delhi's exclusion from an international nuclear order constructed by Washington and its allies to contain India stood in the way of normal relations. India's change of administrations in 2004 did not change New Delhi's support for developing a new partnership with the United States. But Bush administration officials who worked with both Indian governments faced a stark challenge. Not only did the Indian and US bureaucracies have no tradition of working together, but the international sanctions regime the United States had put in place following India's 1974 "peaceful" nuclear explosion remained in place.

The answer was the 2005 US-India Civil Nuclear Agreement. Under its terms, India would separate its civil and its military nuclear reactors, submit the former to international monitoring, make a series of binding commitments not to proliferate nuclear materials or technologies, and in return secure the support of the United States–led international cartel governing trade in civil nuclear components for India's access to these materials on the international market. The judgment of not just the Bush administration but of the US Congress, the International Atomic Energy Agency, and the Nuclear Suppliers Group was that the nuclear nonproliferation regime would be stronger if India were a part of it on these terms—rather than remaining excluded and untethered as a nuclear weapons state not bound by the NPT. The Civil Nuclear Agreement, in other words, combined exchange and catalytic engagement: Significant mutual concessions were made but with a view to bringing India out of the cold and transforming it into a long-term stakeholder in the international nuclear order.

Building a Strategic Partnership for a New Century

With support from Congress, the Bush administration elevated India to a top US foreign policy position from 2005 to 2008, upending four decades of Western policy by working systematically to support India's entry into the international nuclear club, with its ensuing rights and responsibilities. India's normalization as a nuclear power gave it access to the international trade in civil nuclear components. It promised to substantially boost India's energy production in ways that would fuel long-term economic development. It also made possible dramatically expanded high-technology trade and cooperation with the United States in civil space, defense, and other areas.

For all the attention garnered by the civil nuclear agreement, the first long-term partnership agreement between Washington and New Delhi was actually a ten-year defense cooperation agreement signed in June 2005. Many countries without a long history of partnership often begin their engagement with trade and diplomatic agreements and only after building trust move on to military cooperation. The opposite held true between the United States and India, in part because of the compelling security threats—from China, Pakistan, and terrorism—that drew them together. The defense agreement was a particularly radical step for India to take. Having allied with the United States' primary competitor during the Cold War and condemned America's military primacy in the international system throughout the 1990s, Indian leaders decided by the mid-2000s that the United States was the partner of choice in helping to modernize the Indian military and supply the needs of the world's biggest arms importer.

The success of US and Indian policy from 1998 to 2008 lay in creating a transformed basis for relations between the world's largest democracies for the new century. The United States would secure not just an ally but an independent partner that could help anchor an Asian balance of power otherwise at risk from growing Chinese strength. Washington would be able to point to India's model of democratic development as an alternative to the "Beijing consensus" of authoritarian development that otherwise might appeal to swathes of the developing world. The complementarities between America's high-technology economy and India's rich human capital would spur growth in both countries. India would secure as a sponsor for its rise and development the international system's predominant power.

Although often difficult to work with, India proved itself worthy of this sea change in its relations with America and the world. To overcome parliamentary opposition to the nuclear deal, Prime Minister Manmohan Singh submitted his government to a high-stakes confidence vote—the first time an Indian government had put its survival on the line over a question of foreign policy, no less one involving strategic partnership with India's old rival, the United States. Singh and his allies argued that India's future prosperity, security, and prestige hinged on this strategic opening to the West.[6] By enacting the nuclear deal, they argued, India would finally assume its seat at the top table of world politics—with American sponsorship. They prevailed and in doing so sharpened India's trajectory into the first tier of great powers.

After a difficult first year and a half in office in which relations between Washington and New Delhi seemed adrift, President Barack Obama ultimately followed in the footsteps of presidents Clinton and Bush in embracing India as an indispensable American partner in an emerging multipolar world and employing a catalytic strategy of engagement. During his November 2010 trip to New Delhi, Obama put to bed a notion that held sway earlier in his administration that a United States–China "Group of Two" (G2) could jointly manage Asia and the world, rejected a rehyphenation of Indo-Pakistani relations that many misguidedly had urged on him, and took ownership of a relationship with New Delhi that had been on the rocks since he took office.

President Obama's vision of a transformative partnership with India—to manage global diplomatic and security challenges, catalyze prosperity in both countries, and promote good governance in Asia and beyond—was bracing. It helped mitigate concerns in Washington that Obama did not care about the balance of power in Asia. His first administration clearly did—thanks largely to China's new assertiveness in relation to the United States and its friends in Asia. Obama's passage to India also underlined a historic and bipartisan American belief that democracies make the best allies in world affairs.

In New Delhi, President Obama made a strong case for the exceptionalism of Indo-American ties—and for a far-reaching partnership that would help chart the course of the twenty-first century: "Now, India is not the only emerging power in the world. But relationships between our countries is [*sic*] unique. . . . We are two great republics dedicated to the liberty and justice and equality of all people. And we are two free market economies where people have the freedom to pursue ideas and innovation that can change the world. And that's why I believe that India and America are indispensable partners in meeting the challenges of our time."[7] This made Obama the third successive US president to express America's core interest in India's rise and success as a future democratic superpower. As US Deputy Secretary of State William Burns said in 2011 in a major statement of the Obama administration's policies toward India, "America's vision of a secure, stable, prosperous 21st century world has at its heart a strong partnership with a rising India."[8] In 2012, Secretary of Defense Leon Panetta called defense cooperation with India a "linchpin" of the US strategic rebalance to Asia.[9]

Bumps on the Road to True Partnership

Critics of the civil nuclear deal between the United States and India have charged that its supporters oversold the broader benefits of Indo-American strategic partnership. Their critique has been given unearned momentum by the

Indian parliament, which passed nuclear liability legislation that does not meet international standards, effectively making it impossible for American companies to build civil nuclear power plants in India. Critics have also been emboldened by a certain drift in US-Indian relations since 2009—for which both sides bear responsibility—and by India's own lackluster economic performance, which diminishes its attractiveness as the pivotal US partner in twenty-first-century Asia. But these developments do not mean the relationship was oversold. The more accurate charge is that it has not yet been fully consummated.

Although its position evolved over time, the Obama administration sent decidedly mixed messages to New Delhi upon taking office in 2009. Bush administration officials had argued convincingly that a shared appreciation for managing the balance of power in Asia was at the core of the US-Indian entente—music to the ears of leaders in a country that has still not recovered from the psychological scars of a war with China in 1962. However, early in their tenure, senior Obama administration officials reportedly told Indian counterparts that the United States was no longer "doing balance of power in Asia," while senior US officials, including the president and secretary of state, gave credence for a time to the notion of a Sino-American G2 condominium in Asian and global affairs.

This unnerved Indian officials who believed Washington had chosen New Delhi—not Beijing—as its privileged partner in rising Asia. Spurned Indian officials fell back on old nonalignment instincts and began speaking of "triangulating" between the United States and China. But events somewhat changed the discourse: China's militant assertiveness in 2010 and 2011 reminded officials in Washington and across Asia of the growing danger posed by budding Chinese power. President Obama's self-declared "pivot" to Asia in 2011 moved the United States much closer to the Indian position of sustaining a regional equilibrium not tilted in China's direction—a project of such immensity that India could not achieve it absent close alignment, if not alliance, with the United States. Nonetheless, the early damage to a US-Indian relationship whose central logic is rooted in the balance of power caused mistrust that still lingers. There remains an influential camp in Indian government and strategic circles that does not see the United States as a reliable partner in managing Chinese power—just as there remain skeptics in Washington who believe India's lackluster economic growth, muddled military modernization, misgovernance, and passivity in foreign policy render it an unserious partner in the near term, even if expectations for India's geopolitical emergence over a longer time frame remain intact.

More recently, Indians have been disappointed that the United States, after reassuring them for a decade that US forces would finish the job they started in Afghanistan, will draw down combat forces from Afghanistan by 2014. Beyond its intrinsic importance, Afghanistan was in fact a key test of the proposition that the United States, as a new strategic partner, could help India solve its toughest security challenge: the propensity of its neighbors to export terrorism into India, with state support. The Taliban's eventual return to control in at least parts of Afghanistan, in cooperation with Pakistan's virulently anti-Indian security services, as North Atlantic Treaty Organization (NATO) forces draw down would undermine Indian security in tangible ways. For many Indians, the United States' lack of staying power reconfirms old suspicions about American unreliability. It reinforces the conviction that India may have more to gain from collaborating with Russia and Iran to support Afghan groups committed to the Taliban's defeat than from relying on (and working with) the United States to do the job.

Americans, in turn, have been disappointed by India's apparent willingness, for a time, to risk its US relationship over energy trade with Iran. India has moved to reduce oil and gas imports from Iran, earning New Delhi a waiver from US third-party sanctions. This is particularly significant in light of India's energy-import dependence and its previous reliance on Iran as a top supplier. But American officials have spent precious time and energy over the course of several years urging India to cut back on its Iran trade—time and energy that would have been better spent forging ahead on a wider agenda for Indo-American cooperation were it not for Indian reluctance to take American appeals to heart. New Delhi would have benefited more from early movement on this issue, rather than making a show of standing up to the United States even as India, out of concern for its own interests, systematically reduced its dependence on Iranian energy supplies.

Americans excited about the rise to great-power status of the world's largest democracy have also questioned how India's passivity toward the Arab uprisings has served Indian interests, much less prospects for partnership with both Washington and reformist Arab regimes. While India's election commission assisted in organizing Egypt's first democratic elections, New Delhi has been seriously behind the curve in Libya, Egypt, and Syria (although it has not blocked UNSC actions on the latter). It is Indian interests that suffer from such passivity, in the form of cool relations with postrevolutionary countries strategically positioned on its western doorstep. Such passivity has undermined the case, not just in Washington but internationally, that India is ready to provide global public goods and assume genuine responsibilities beyond its borders as a permanent member of the UNSC.

Nonetheless, over the past few years, India and the United States have made quiet progress in consolidating their new relationship. India is the world's largest arms importer, and the United States is at the top of its list of defense suppliers—notwithstanding American disappointment that India did not choose a US fifth-generation fighter jet as part of its ongoing military modernization. India has procured American naval vessels, transport aircraft, and other platforms with growing enthusiasm, and Indian armed forces exercise more with US counterparts than those from any other country—a remarkable development for two countries that were on opposite sides of the Cold War divide. Intelligence sharing is at historic highs; Washington and New Delhi cooperate more actively on counterterrorism than ever before. The two countries are also more closely aligned on Pakistan as a result of the degeneration of the US-Pakistani alliance over the previous three years. Perhaps most important, India and postpivot America see eye to eye on the immense strategic challenge posed by China's ascendance; the Indo-American dialogue on East Asian security has been richly rewarding for both sides.

The hard truth is that Indo-American relations would be better were India and the United States each doing better. India was a most attractive partner when it was growing at nearly double-digit rates annually. For many Americans today, India is a less attractive partner as Indian economic growth slumps, the government stalls on key reforms necessary to unlock the economy's vast potential, populism trumps effective policymaking, and politicians seem unable to break partisan gridlock to govern effectively. However, India's latent and actual potential is such that a new wave of economic liberalization could yet unleash the resurgence of what had been one of the world's fastest-growing major economies.

The Logic of Indo-American Partnership: An American Perspective

What is the American interest in India's ascendance? There are several answers to this question. With a growing middle class already the size of the entire US population, India is predicted by the National Intelligence Council to become the biggest driver of middle-class growth globally by 2030.[10] As a consequence, India will likely become a primary overseas market for American goods, services, and foreign investment over the long term, as its population and trend rate of economic growth surpass those of China. This effect will be reinforced by India's "demographic dividend," which means that its young population will continue to expand its workforce for several more decades as the demographics of every other major power—including both the developed democracies and emerging powers such as China and South Korea—head in the opposite direction as their societies rapidly age.

In the realm of national security, India and the United States may have a closer convergence of interests over the long term than any other two major powers. Both countries are on the forefront of the struggle to defeat terrorism and take on the systemic causes of violent Islamic extremism. Both countries have a profound stake in the evolution of Afghanistan and Pakistan into states capable of controlling their territory, meeting their people's basic needs, and developing accountable institutions of governance that channel dissent into nonviolent political contests rather than exporting terrorism and extremism. Both the United States, as the international system's preeminent power, and India, which shares a long, disputed land border with China and will not countenance the emergence of a unipolar Asia under Beijing's suzerainty, have a profound interest in keeping China's rise peaceful and bound by a liberal international order.

But perhaps the most compelling US interest in India's rise lies in its material and normative impact on the wider international system. A global order underpinned by the dovetailing interests and common values of the world's largest democracies would be preferable to one governed by the appeal of state capitalism and Sinocentric autocracy. A future global system anchored by robust ties between a still preeminent United States and a rising India destined for greatness would be one that remains safe for open societies. Such an order would most likely be governed by a pluralism of power that unites these states with other partners—Brazil, Europe, Japan, South Korea, Indonesia—in a global balance of capabilities and ideas tilted toward freedom. China's peaceful development would be more likely in such a world than in one it was able to dominate and impose its will upon.

The United States therefore has an inherent interest in India's success as a democratic superpower—one that can shape a non-Western modernity that is inherently peaceful, pluralistic, prosperous, and attractive to its neighbors and the wider world. As the scholar Sunil Khilnani argues, political legitimacy will be the primary currency of international politics in the twenty-first century—which means the United States should be placing its bets on democratic India as a partner and model for others to follow.[11] Forget the hardening of a new global "Beijing consensus" of authoritarian development that puts the community of democracies on the defensive in a world hostile to its values and interests. If the United States can help India shape the kind of future its leaders and people envision, the emerging international order will be one in which America and its friends can thrive and prosper.

Operationalizing the Partnership

How should the United States and India further operationalize a partnership that manifestly serves their interests and, through the stability and prosperity it would engender more broadly, those of the wider world? A bilateral investment treaty laying the groundwork for a comprehensive free trade agreement would strengthen the economic foundation of the relationship. The United States could lift restrictions on high-technology workers from India who bring their talent to Silicon Valley and many other US regions, industries, and services in the vanguard of America's innovation economy. Public-private partnerships linking Indian and American innovators could explore energy and climate solutions that leverage the respective capabilities of both countries. India could expand the Fulbright Program and other educational exchanges to enlarge its talent pool and lift onerous restrictions on foreign investment to attract far more American and global capital.

Beyond expanded bilateral training and defense supply, the next stage in rapidly growing defense ties is to multilateralize Indo-American security cooperation with other strategic partners of the two countries, including Australia, Indonesia, Japan, Singapore, South Korea, Thailand, and NATO. Perhaps most important in the long term is deepening US-Japanese-Indian trilateral cooperation, given the countries' vast combined capabilities, technological complementarities, and shared concern for freedom of the Indo-Pacific maritime commons. In 2011, Washington, Tokyo, and New Delhi launched a high-level trilateral security dialogue that could evolve into a critical bulwark of strategic stability in a rapidly changing Asia.

Another area for Indo-American collaboration is the promotion of good governance abroad. Indian leaders are beginning to understand that democracy within states is a source of security among states. This strategic calculus has led New Delhi to invest heavily in building the institutions of good governance in Afghanistan, as well as to help forge democratic outcomes to intractable civil conflicts in Bangladesh, Nepal, and Sri Lanka. The United States and India have cooperated to assist transitional democracies through the United Nations Democracy Fund, the Partnership for Democratic Governance, the Asia-Pacific Democracy Partnership, and other multilateral activities. Washington and New Delhi may also find common cause in working together—or independently toward similar ends—to lay the foundations for democratic consolidation in the Middle East and North Africa following the historic Arab awakening of 2011.

There are clear-eyed, realpolitik considerations that drive deepening Indo-American ties, not least of which is a shared desire to maintain a balance of power in the face of a rising China. It is also true that differences between India and the United States—on issues from climate change to the Doha trade talks to managing Iran's nuclear challenge—are real. But so is the promise, if not yet the reality, of Indo-American ideational cooperation, with common values serving as a bridge rather than a wedge between the countries as they pursue their national interests. Both the United States and India regard themselves as exceptional on the world stage as a result of their size, history, and distinctively open and diverse societies. US leaders have long justified their country's foreign policy practices with reference to the ideals of American democracy. Interestingly, what has changed over the past decade is Indian leaders' discourse about the role of democratic values in world affairs. As the pursuit of nonalignment has gradually given way to India's opening to the West and growing ambitions to assume a full role in the world's leading councils, so too have Indian statesmen grown more comfortable articulating and projecting liberal values. This development, coupled with the overall transformation of bilateral ties, suggests that an agenda of values-based cooperation is realistic—and would provide the missing piece of a relationship that has flourished in nearly all other realms.

India's Democratic Instinct in World Affairs

"If there is an 'idea of India' by which India should be defined, it is the idea of an inclusive, open, multi-cultural, multi-ethnic, multi-lingual society," Prime Minister Singh has said. "I believe that this is the dominant trend of political evolution of all societies in the 21st century. . . . Liberal democracy is the natural order of political organization in today's world. All alternate systems, authoritarian and majoritarian in varying degrees, are an aberration."[12] Standard rhetoric, perhaps, among the leaders of many democratic nations, but as C. Raja Mohan has pointed out, such words mark a major departure from the modern Indian tradition.[13] Indian foreign policy, historically characterized by a non-aligned, postcolonial, and noninterventionist mindset, has not generally been conducive to grand invocations of human rights and democracy abroad.

This has begun to change. Over the past decade, Indian leaders' discourse about the role of democratic values in world affairs has increased in frequency and depth, and Prime Minister Singh's words have become a dominant theme. Until its dramatic growth slowdown caused by the lackluster pace of economic reform and shifts in global capital flows, India branded itself on the world stage as the "fastest-growing free-market *democracy*"—drawing a none-too-subtle distinction with its Chinese rival.[14] Indian officials also understand that good governance can serve as a source of security and stability in their neighborhood, surrounded as India is by weak and failing states that export terrorism, refugees, and contraband into India. "India would like the whole of South Asia to emerge as a community of flourishing democracies," said Foreign Secretary Shyam Saran in 2005. "We believe that democracy would provide a more enduring and broad-based foundation for an edifice of peace and cooperation in our subcontinent."[15]

Acting on this belief, India has worked to strengthen democratic institutions in Bangladesh, Bhutan, Nepal, Sri Lanka, and most prominently Afghanistan.

India is Afghanistan's fourth-largest bilateral donor (having contributed over US$2 billion since 2001) and has invested significantly in training Afghan civil servants, building the Afghan parliament, constructing infrastructure around the country, and supporting Afghan elections. At the global level, India was one of ten founding members of the Community of Democracies and a leading cofounder of the United Nations Democracy Fund, dedicated to promoting good governance and human rights around the world. India has also participated in the multilateral activities of other, linked organizations, including the Center for Democratic Transitions, the Partnership for Democratic Governance, and the Asia-Pacific Democracy Partnership.

These and other endeavors suggest that India and the United States can be allies in supporting democracy and human rights, whether they are working together or independently toward similar ends. Moreover, in an era when not only the United States but also Canada, the countries of Europe, and many nations in Asia—including Australia, Indonesia, Japan, South Korea, and Taiwan—fund democracy-assistance programs overseas, it is only logical that the world's biggest democracy assume a leading place within this group and coordinate its efforts with like-minded powers.

Even where they have tactical differences over democracy assistance, the leaders of both countries have identified shared political values as the bedrock of broad Indo-American cooperation in world affairs. At their July 2005 summit, Prime Minister Singh and President Bush declared that both nations "have an obligation to the global community to strengthen values, ideals and practices of freedom, pluralism, and rule of law."[16] At their November 2009 summit, President Obama and Prime Minister Singh agreed that "the interests of both countries are best advanced through the values mirrored in their societies," defined these shared values as "democracy, pluralism, tolerance, openness, and respect for fundamental freedoms and human rights," and agreed that these "common ideals and complementary strengths of India and the United States today provide a foundation for addressing the global challenges of the 21st century."[17] And in the communiqué issued following the 2010 Obama-Singh summit, the two leaders pledged to "exercise global leadership in support of economic development, open government, and democratic values."[18]

Iran and, until recently, Myanmar have underscored the limits to the argument that India and the United States, as democracies, define their interests in similar ways.[19] But there may be special cases—for example, US alliances with nondemocracies such as Saudi Arabia and Egypt, as well as Washington's occasional support for military rule in Pakistan—that do not vitiate the possibilities for Indo-American values-based cooperation elsewhere. And Washington and New Delhi are now much more closely aligned on Myanmar as a result of that country's ongoing process of political opening and reform. Indeed, India has defined its relations with the world's leading democracies as more important than with nondemocracies such as Iran and China. A leaked Indian Ministry of External Affairs memo in 2006 identified relations with Britain, France, Germany, Japan, and the United States as being more strategically important to India's future than ties to other states—presumably not simply because of their power or wealth but because of a basic alignment of interests, reinforced by a set of common values, that India does not share with other countries.[20]

Strategically the key question is whether India and the United States can move beyond rhetoric and a limited record of cooperation to build a global partnership rooted not only in growing security and economic ties but also in a common commitment to strengthen good governance and pluralism within states as sources of security and stability. If India, like the United States, defines a world with more open societies as one that will best allow its interests to flourish, the two countries should be able to put into place a program of cooperation to work jointly toward that goal. If, by contrast, US officials choose to minimize ideational cooperation and instead treat India simply as an important rising power given its array of capabilities, they risk minimizing the qualitative differences between India and China—differences that Indians believe merit a special relationship with the United States of the kind neither Washington nor New Delhi enjoys with Beijing. In an era of diminishing Western influence and the "rise of the rest," India's success as a thriving market democracy is itself a critical US interest, in part to prove to those so enamored of the Chinese model of authoritarian development that prosperity can equally, and perhaps more durably, flourish amidst political tolerance and accountability.

Can Washington and New Delhi outline an agenda for values-based cooperation in areas where it reinforces their respective and increasingly converging national interests? The long-term future of the Indo-American strategic partnership may hinge on the answer. All of the United States' closest relationships with key powers are based on democratic affinity and some sense of shared values. Where these elements are missing—as in US relations with China—competitive pressures and mutual mistrust limit the possibilities for true partnership. Similarly, framing Indo-American relations in purely transactional terms could undermine the staying power of the relationship on the US side. This could put bilateral ties at risk should there be a political shift at home—or should a changing power balance in Asia render China, based purely on its geopolitical and economic heft, a seemingly more valuable US partner than India. From the US perspective, then, qualitatively distinguishing between Asia's rising giants on the basis of the possibilities for democratic cooperation with India in world affairs is a strategic imperative.

Developing a bilateral values-based action agenda with India is very much terra incognita. Even the Obama-Singh commitment to build a "shared international partnership for democracy" was short on specifics. At their summit, the two leaders agreed to launch an "open government" dialogue to promote using new technologies and public-private partnerships in order to make official information more widely available to publics at large. They agreed to "explore" coordinating efforts to support "elections organization and management in other interested countries."[21]

But unlike areas such as defense, trade, and the sharing of high technology, the values agenda remains nascent at best. While this raises doubts in many minds about the very feasibility of such cooperation, it also suggests a bold new direction for this deepening relationship. Following ratification of the landmark civil nuclear agreement, and at a time when policymakers on both sides are earnestly attempting to identify a new "big idea" that would drive forward the newly established bonds, ideational cooperation could provide the impetus for increasing alignment. A shared agenda could focus on coordinating democracy assistance and development aid, collaborating to create a new global regime to support internet freedom, reinforcing parallel and mutual strategies for building democratic institutions in Middle East societies touched by the "Arab Spring," deepening Asian security cooperation with like-minded democracies including Japan and Australia, and working more closely together to maintain a liberal bias in the institutions of global governance.

Conclusion

The strategic alienation of India from the United States was one of the great anomalies of the Cold War. The strategic rapprochement of the world's biggest democracies from 2000 to the present is one of the key dividends of the new world order that emerged following the end of US-Soviet rivalry and the dawning of the modern era of globalization. India, which will soon have the world's third-largest economy and its largest population, is increasingly central to the future of global order; the US National Intelligence Council has called it the decisive "swing state" in the international system and projects that it will emerge as the world's largest economy by the end of the twenty-first century.[22] India's posture is therefore also central to the long-term position of the United States and other democracies within it.

Yet India was once marginalized from the liberal international order built by the United States and its allies. From India's independence in 1947 through the end of the Cold War, structural constraints imposed by the US-Soviet global rivalry, India's pursuit of nonalignment, and internal development and security challenges made it difficult for a desperately poor country growing at only 1 percent to 2 percent annually to play a wider international role. India is therefore only now impacting world politics in systemic fashion after effectively sitting on (or being relegated to) the sidelines of great power politics. India's awakening could change the world as profoundly as has the rise of China and for the better.

For its part, the United States has pursued a revolutionary policy of engaging with India to accelerate its rise, with a view to the benefits that a partnership with a future Asian superpower could deliver to American interests and liberal order. The US approach contrasts markedly with its engagement with Asia's other rising giant, China. US engagement with China since the early 1990s has been framed by its advocates as a way of preventing the country from emerging as an all-out rival to the United States by demonstrating to it the benefits of integration into the United States–led liberal order. Yet America's engagement of China has always been accompanied by a military hedge against the possibility that China would pursue its rise in ways that undermined rather than reinforced international peace and security. By contrast, America's engagement of India has lacked such a hedge because policymakers and strategists view the cultivation of Indian power as an opportunity rather than a threat to US interests and values in the international system.

It is for this reason that India's rise, although slower and more ponderous, looks in some ways more inevitable than that of China's. Whereas the United States is preparing for a peer competition with Chinese power that could hobble the nascent authoritarian superpower's ultimate ascendance, America is at the same time investing in India in ways that will magnify its power and influence in Asia and globally. Never before has the international system's dominant power played handmaiden to the rise of another great power.[23] US engagement of India has sought to do exactly that because of the long-term strategic dividends American policymakers imagine will accrue to US interests and liberal international order from a strong and prosperous India.

Notes

1. Thomas R. Metcalf, *Imperial Connections: India in the Indian Ocean Arena, 1860–1920* (Berkeley: University of California Press, 2007).

2. Angus Maddison, *The World Economy: A Millennial Perspective* (Paris: Development Centre of the Organisation for Economic Co-operation and Development, 2001).

3. Lawrence James, *The Rise and Fall of the British Empire* (London: St. Martin's, 1997).

4. A letter from Indian prime minister Vajpayee to President Clinton justifying India's nuclear tests with reference to the threat from China was leaked to the *New York Times* and reprinted on May 13, 1998. For US identification of China as a peer competitor, see US Department of Defense, *Quadrennial Defense Review Report 1997* (Washington, DC: Department of Defense, May 1997).

5. K. Subrahmanyam, "Calling Off Deal Will Isolate India Globally," *Times of India*, August 20, 2007.

6. "Nuke Energy Must Meet Growing Demand: PM," *Times of India*, August 21, 2007, and Pranab Mukherjee, "India and the Global Balance of Power," Address by the Minister of External Affairs to the Global India Foundation, New Delhi, January 16, 2007.

7. Barack Obama, "Remarks by the President to the Joint Session of the Indian Parliament in New Delhi, India," Parliament House, New Delhi, November 8, 2010, www.whitehouse.gov/the-press-office/2010/11/08/remarks-president-joint-session-indian-parliament-new-delhi-india (accessed September 20, 2012).

8. William Burns, "Speech by Deputy Secretary Burns on US-India Partnership," Washington, DC, September 27, 2011, http://iipdigital.usembassy.gov/st/english/texttrans/2011/09/20110928101745su0.7591625.html#axzz26yiycj7z (accessed September 20, 2012).

9. Leon Panetta, "Remarks by Secretary Panetta at the Institute for Defense Studies and Analyses in New Delhi, India," news transcript, Office of the Assistant Secretary of Defense (Public Affairs), US Department of Defense, June 6, 2012, www.defense.gov/transcripts/transcript.aspx?transcriptid=5054 (accessed September 3, 2013).

10. National Intelligence Council, *Global Trends 2030: Alternative Worlds* (Washington, DC: Office of the Director of National Intelligence, 2012), www.dni.gov/index.php/about/organization/national-intelligence-council-global-trends (accessed September 3, 2013).

11. Sunil Khilnani, "Remarks at the German Marshall Fund's India Forum," Stockholm, October 1, 2010.

12. Manmohan Singh, "PM's Speech at India Today Conclave," New Delhi, February 25, 2005, http://pmindia.nic.in/speech-details.php?nodeid=73 (accessed September 20, 2012). This section of the book is drawn from Daniel Twining and Richard Fontaine, "The Ties That Bind? US-Indian Values-Based Cooperation," *Washington Quarterly* 34, no. 2 (2011): 193–205.

13. C. Raja Mohan, "Balancing Interests and Values: India's Struggle with Democracy Promotion," *Washington Quarterly* 30, no. 3 (2007): 99.

14. Emphasis added. This was the theme of India's much-noted marketing campaign at Davos in 2006. See, for instance, Fareed Zakaria, "India Rising," *Newsweek*, March 5, 2006.

15. Shyam Saran, "India and Its Neighbours," speech, India International Centre, New Delhi, February 14, 2005, http://mea.gov.in/Speeches-Statements.htm?dtl/2483/Foreign+Secretary+Mr+Shyam+Sarans+speech+on+India+and+its+Neighbours+at+the+India+International+Centre+IIC (accessed February 5, 2014).

16. US Department of State, "US-India Global Democracy Initiative," fact sheet, Washington, DC, July 18, 2005, http://2001–2009.state.gov/p/sca/rls/fs/2005/49722.htm (accessed September 20, 2012).

17. White House, "Joint Statement between Prime Minister Dr. Singh and President Obama: India and the United States: Partnership for a Better World," Washington, DC, November 24, 2009, www.whitehouse.gov/the-press-office/joint-statement-between-prime-minister-dr-singh-and-president-obama (accessed September 20, 2012).

18. White House, "Joint Statement by President Obama and Prime Minister Singh of India," New Delhi, November 8, 2010, www.whitehouse.gov/the-press-office/2010/11/08/joint-statement-president-obama-and-prime-minister-singh-india (accessed September 20, 2012).

19. For further analysis on the possibilities for Indo-American convergence on these issues, see Daniel Twining, "India's Relations with Iran and Myanmar: 'Rogue State' or Responsible Democratic Stakeholder?" *India Review* 7, no. 1 (2008): 1–37.

20. Nilova Roy Chaudhury, "India Maps Its Equation with the World," *Hindustan Times*, October 20, 2006.

21. White House, "Joint Statement by President Obama," November 8, 2010.

22. Cited in Ashley J. Tellis, *India as a New Global Power: An Action Agenda for the United States* (Washington, DC: Carnegie Endowment for International Peace, July 2005), 30; US National Intelligence Council, *Global Trends 2030.*

23. Edward Luce, *In Spite of the Gods: The Strange Rise of Modern India* (London: Abacus, 2006).

CHAPTER 3

JAPAN'S INDIA ENGAGEMENT

From Different Worlds to Strategic Partners

H. D. P. Envall

IN SMALL STEPS AT FIRST, and notwithstanding some significant setbacks, Japan has sought to engage more strongly with India since the end of the Cold War. Exemplified by the 2006 "strategic and global partnership," which encompassed both economic and security relations, Japan's new engagement with India raises some important questions.[1] What has Japan sought to achieve, and how has it sought to achieve it? And what factors have shaped Japan's approach? The demise of the Soviet Union, China's rise, Japan's economic decline, the globalization of the US-Japanese alliance, and India's own receptiveness to deeper engagement have all played a part in pushing Japan toward closer engagement with India. Trade and commercial opportunities have also become more obvious over the years, both as India itself has developed and opened up its economy and as opportunities for trade growth elsewhere have diminished. But the more significant part of this transformation is the strategic dimension, which has evolved rapidly since the mid-2000s.

While it is possible to see this transformation as the result of Japan's belated recognition of India's growing strategic weight in the Asia-Pacific region, it is a mistake to see Japan's engagement of India as just a response to the latter's rising profile. Japan's engagement of India is in fact highly dependent on the important changes that have been taking place in Japan's own strategic environment. Two such changes have been especially important. The first was the strategic approach adopted by the United States toward the region over the past decade, including its relations with India. The second was the rapid rise of China's economic and military power in Asia, its troubled relationship with Japan over the past decade, and ongoing questions about its intentions regarding the regional order. For Japan, engaging India is part of a wider adjustment to these systemic pressures.

This chapter begins by providing some historical background on the factors impeding Japan's engagement of India during the Cold War, before showing how these impediments were removed or diminished during the 1990s. Because the changes to the relationship during this decade were only modest, the chapter examines suggestions that Japan's post–Cold War engagement of India rests on more than trade opportunities or changing ideologies. Significant consideration is given to the 1998 nuclear crisis, which from the Japanese perspective was arguably more important for revealing Japan's strategic weaknesses than for demonstrating the rise of India as a major power. The chapter then examines how this period of adversity was overcome, leading to the implementation of a mixed strategy of exchange and catalytic engagement, especially from 2005–6 onward, demonstrating in the process how these changes were connected to Japan's shifting strategic circumstances.

Different Cold War Worlds

After establishing diplomatic relations in 1952, Japan and India stood apart for much of the Cold War. India's ambition of "steering a diplomatic path free from superpower dominance" meant that it sought its own path on the world stage; when it sought cooperation, it did so chiefly with other nonaligned and developing countries.[2] In keeping with its early socialist worldview and the tendency of its first prime minister, Jawaharlal Nehru, to associate capitalism with imperialism, India preferred the Soviet Union over the United States when dealing with the superpowers. By contrast, Japan could not avoid superpower dominance, first under US occupation and later as a key US ally. Although India was quick to recognize Japan after the war, this ideological divide, as K. V. Kesavan points out, created a "psychological barrier between the two countries that saw them taking diametrically opposite positions on a range of regional and global issues."[3] The Cold War relationship was shaped by the different choices the two countries made in response to their respective economic and strategic challenges. Japan's choices were limited but focused on building a new partnership with the United States and developing itself as an international trading economy, whereas India chose nonalignment (albeit oriented toward the Soviet Union) and economic self-sufficiency.

Politically Indian elites were notably disappointed at Japan's lack of support for its pan-Asianism and anticolonial enthusiasms. But if India considered Japan as something of an American "client state" or "satellite state," Japan saw its own strategic objectives very differently.[4] It deliberately pursued a strategy of dependence on the United States for its security needs in order to concentrate the country's resources and energies on economic development. Under the Yoshida Doctrine (named after Prime Minister Shigeru Yoshida), Japan was able to "look to its long-range interests by assuming . . . a subordinate role within the US international order."[5] When it came to the Soviet Union, Japan's perceptions ran counter to India's more benign views of that superpower. In terms of relations with the Soviet Union, India's close relationship with it as the Cold War progressed ran counter to Japanese views. Where India came to see the Soviet Union as a friendly power, Japan saw it as a threat. Indeed this perception became particularly prominent in the 1980s as a result of the Soviet military buildup in East Asia, described as "extraordinary" by some Japanese analysts.[6]

Japan and India also adopted different approaches to the global economy and to trade. Japan signed various trade and aid agreements with India in 1958, and by the early 1960s, more than 27 percent of the country's iron ore imports came from India.[7] But the trade relationship remained relatively small and grew only modestly during the 1960s and 1970s.[8] The substantial barriers the Indian government placed around its economy limited Japan's ability to sell into the Indian market. India's commitment under Nehru and his successors to a "socialist pattern of society" meant almost by definition that there was little prospect for a strong trading relationship between the two.[9]

As the Cold War progressed, both India and Japan tended also to focus their attentions on their immediate regions. David Brewster observes that Japan saw its interests during this period as "ending at Burma"—it did not want to become entangled in the troubled politics of South Asia, and in any case it viewed India as a potential rival rather than partner in wider Asian affairs.[10] So rather than engaging India and its region, Japan concentrated on its East Asian neighborhood. Closer links were pursued with Northeast Asian states, through engagement with South Korea and China. Greater attention was also paid to Southeast Asia, for instance through the provision of aid to Indonesia. Gradually Japan broadened its relations with the region by increasing its economic development and aid activities and by linking up with the Association of Southeast Asian Nations (ASEAN). This occurred in particular following Japan's adoption of the Fukuda Doctrine, named after Prime Minister Takeo Fukuda. In Manila in August 1977, on the last stop of his prime ministerial visit through Southeast Asia, Fukuda announced the basic principles of Japan's new approach to its relationships in the region. Japan would henceforth remain peaceful, contribute to the region's peace and prosperity, deal with ASEAN as an equal, and seek a closer relationship with the nations of Indochina.[11]

In the early 1980s, Japan's relationship with South Asia slowly began to change. New Japanese investment in India—illustrated by the establishment of the joint venture between the Indian government's Maruti Udyog and Suzuki

Motors in 1982—coincided with an increase in shuttle diplomacy between the two countries. Japanese prime minister Yasuhiro Nakasone visited India in 1984 and emphasized the importance of better relations between the "two most prominent democracies in Asia."[12] Indian prime minister Rajiv Gandhi also visited Japan in 1985, 1987, and 1988.[13] Japan steadily increased its foreign aid to India, a shift that certainly followed the two countries' more active economic relationship but that was also a result of Japan's wider ambitions to become an international "aid great power."[14] By 1986, although India took up only a modest share of Japan's official development assistance (ODA)—much less, for instance, than Indonesia or China—Japan had become India's largest ODA donor, contributing US$230 million or some 22 percent of India's total ODA receipts.[15]

Necessary but Not Sufficient

The end of the Cold War removed many obstacles to improved relations between India and Japan. For India the demise of the Soviet Union made developing relationships with capitalist or Western countries more desirable, if not downright necessary. With the collapse of government finances in 1991, India was forced to abandon its goal of economic self-sufficiency and begin opening its economy to the wider world, albeit slowly and partially.[16] India's Look East policy of consciously modeling its economy more on the East Asian (Japanese) economic "miracle" and developing closer economic links with the region also made the country more appealing to Japan.[17]

For Japan the end of the Soviet "threat" raised key questions for policymakers, notably about the meaning and purpose of its alliance with the United States.[18] In the early 1990s, Japan cautiously attempted to improve relations with the new Russia, while its strategic discussions focused on whether or to what extent the country should loosen some of the self-imposed restrictions on its international role, particularly in terms of security.[19] One consistent Japanese policy was the decision to continue pursuing its "aid great power" ambitions through the 1990s. Having become the world's major aid donor in 1989, Japan set about establishing a more thorough framework for its aid program in the form of an ODA charter. Released in 1992, it prioritized the environment, democracy, the restriction of military expenditures, and market reform as considerations when determining ODA policy. As a result, an increasingly open, reformist India appealed as an ODA recipient to both the mercantilist and humanitarian streams within Japan's ODA institutions, opening the door to the possibility of both exchange and catalytic engagement strategies being employed toward India by Japan.[20]

However, this engagement—especially in the economic realm—developed very slowly during the 1990s. Mutual trade was encouraged, but the total of imports and exports between the two countries remained relatively steady from 1990 until 1993 at US$3.7 billion before increasing more rapidly to over US$5 billion in 1995 and 1996.[21] But this trading relationship soon stalled. In 1999, total imports and exports between Japan and India equaled only US$4.7 billion. By contrast, the equivalent figures for Japan's trade with China had risen by around 365 percent from a base of approximately US$18.1 billion to just under US$66.2 billion.[22] Foreign firms entered the Indian economy during this period, including Japanese companies Sony, Toyota, Fujitsu, Toshiba, and Nippon Cement, among others. Yet foreign direct investment declined from the late 1980s and early 1990s and only started picking up again in the mid-1990s. Overall, Japanese firms appeared reluctant to enter the Indian market.[23]

Why did the end of the Cold War bring about only modest change? That India did not rapidly liberalize its economy goes some way to explain this, but Japanese woes were also significant. The bursting of Japan's "economic bubble" in late 1989 and the "lost decade" that followed lessened Japan's capacity and willingness to engage globally, including with India. In the mid-1980s, Japan's "developmental state" model, which held great appeal for many countries in the Asia-Pacific region, was receiving high praise all over the world. Yet after 1989, Japan's role as an exemplar began to decline. Consequently, while the end of the Cold War can be seen as necessary for change to occur in Japan's economic engagement of India, this change alone was not sufficient for a fuller transformation in that dimension of their relationship.

In terms of ODA, by contrast, Japan substantially increased its involvement in India during the decade. Its share of India's total ODA was only 7.6 percent across the second half of the 1980s, but this figure quickly rose to more than 20 percent in 1990 and even reached 38.3 percent in 1995–96.[24] However, it should be remembered that Japan's total ODA rose from US$9.1 billion to US$14.5 billion during this period, representing an increase in its overall ODA of nearly 60 percent. By comparison, American ODA fell by approximately 35 percent during the same period, while other key donors, France and Germany, only increased their ODA by 17 percent and 19 percent, respectively. Greater ODA to India was, therefore, less the product of any "special relationship" between the two countries and more the result of Japan's growing ODA ambitions and declining ODA from other developed countries.[25] And what drove this new push for ODA to India was an exchange strategy concerned with key

Japanese objectives in another realm of policy: security and particularly nuclear weapons.

The 1998 Nuclear Shock

A key feature of Japan's attempt to diplomatically engage India, and Pakistan, during the 1990s was the considerable effort made to persuade both countries to sign the Nuclear Non-Proliferation Treaty (NPT) and the Comprehensive Test Ban Treaty (CTBT). Japan's nonproliferation agenda was reflected in its ODA policies, which were deliberately tied to that agenda in an exchange strategy. Japan's ODA charter focused explicitly on restraining the development of weapons of mass destruction and the spread of weapon trafficking. The charter noted that "full attention should be paid to trends in recipient countries' military expenditures, their development and production of mass destruction weapons and missiles, their export and import of arms, etc., so as to maintain and strengthen international peace and stability."[26] The engagement of India through ODA was thus targeted at gaining specific concessions. In June 1992, Prime Minister Kiichi Miyazawa urged Indian prime minister P. V. Narasimha Rao to sign and ratify the NPT; in December, he asked the same of Pakistani prime minister Mohammad Nawaz Sharif. However, while Rao agreed to hold talks with Japan on nuclear disarmament, he rejected the request to sign the NPT.[27] A series of meetings followed during the mid-1990s in which the Japanese pushed the two countries to sign the NPT, although with little effect. According to Japanese officials, during meetings held in 1993 Japan explicitly linked the charter's principles with its ongoing ODA to India.[28]

Consequently, India's 1998 nuclear tests produced a strong reaction from Japan and led to a crisis in relations. In responding to the tests, Japan initially focused its efforts on the United Nations Security Council (UNSC), of which Japan was then a nonpermanent member, and the Group of Eight (G8). It sought an emergency UNSC meeting and cosponsored a resolution condemning both India's and Pakistan's tests. The resolution also expressed the UNSC's grave concern at the "challenge" the tests presented to global efforts to strengthen the international nuclear nonproliferation regime.[29] Japan then set about establishing a task force of officials drawn from the G8 countries, as well as Argentina, Australia, China, and South Korea, to consider how to proceed with nonproliferation efforts as well as reduce Indo-Pakistan tensions. It established a "track two" process to promote nuclear disarmament and announced that it would seek to reduce tensions in the region unilaterally. It also proposed that the international community become more involved in the dispute and focus more closely on questions of maintaining security in South Asia. On the economic front, Japan froze new grants and loans to both India and Pakistan and withdrew a previous offer to host development conferences with India.[30] The lost funds were substantial, amounting to $133 billion in grants and $3.5 billion in loans to India alone.[31] Finally, at the regional level, Japan pushed the ASEAN Regional Forum (ARF) to criticize the nuclear tests and provide a venue for resolving not only the nuclear crisis but also the dispute between India and Pakistan over Kashmir.[32]

Yet Japan's response had very little effect, with the greatest impact being on global perceptions of Japan's diplomatic weight.[33] Its failure to shift policy or affect the region dealt a serious blow to the country's post–Cold War emphasis on multilateralism. Why then did Japan pursue such a forthright but ultimately fruitless policy? Satu Limaye argues that the country's "major power ambitions" rather than its famous "nuclear allergy" were a "decisive" cause of Japan's tough response to the tests.[34] In particular, Japan's hope to become a permanent member of the UNSC was fueled by what seemed to be a perfect opportunity to buttress the country's peaceful, internationalist credentials. However, it is also important to remember that the government's strategy was initially made possible by a strong domestic antipathy toward the tests, which then made it difficult for the government to retreat from its hardline stance. As Limaye observes, with citizens and the press arguing that the foreign ministry should take an even tougher position, there was soon a momentum pushing the government toward stricter disarmament and nonproliferation policies.[35]

The dampening effect of Japan's diplomatic failure provides a partial explanation for why Japan quickly sought to patch up the relationship with India and move to new modes of engagement. The other important factor was the rising specter of global terrorism in the wake of the 9/11 attacks on the United States. In late 1999, Japan still maintained that the measures it had taken against India after the nuclear tests would be reviewed once India decided to sign the CTBT, and several rounds of mostly ineffective fence-mending diplomacy ensued.[36] However, even as little progress was being made on the CTBT issue, Japanese prime minister Yoshirō Mori visited New Delhi in August 2000 and began the substantive process of conceding ground in order to catalyze better relations in the future. According to Michael Green, Mori recognized the role that India might play in enhancing Japan's capacity to balance China in conjunction with the still central US-Japanese alliance.[37] Mori's concession was to recognize that "the Kashmir problem must be solved through bilateral dialogue."[38] Then, in October 2001, a little more than a month after the 9/11 attacks, and only two weeks following the US invasion of Afghanistan, a further breakthrough was achieved in the lead-up to Prime Minister Atal Bihari Vajpayee's planned visit to Japan. The Japanese government announced that the various measures it had implemented following the nuclear tests would be discontinued, since India and

Pakistan had maintained their moratoriums on nuclear tests since 1998 even though neither had signed the CTBT.[39] With this decision, the major source of bitterness in the relationship had been removed.

To what extent did the 1998 crisis drive Japan's engagement of India? Strategically the crisis revealed Japan's diplomatic deficiencies at the United Nations, particularly its limited prospects for permanent UNSC status, and at the ARF, which Japan had emphasized as part of its multilateral diplomacy. Brewster contends that in this context, it led "to a major realignment of Japanese strategic thinking about India." Newly aware of its weaknesses, Brewster argues, Japan was now forced to deal with India as a "major strategic player" and thus give more consideration to its "place in the broader strategic environment."[40] But as the next section shows, it took time before any readjustment in Japanese policy toward India became obvious.

The Relationship Takes Off

It took until the middle of the 2000s before Japan's engagement of India began again in earnest, despite the efforts made to patch up their differences in 2000 and 2001. Economically the relationship between India and Japan continued to tell a story—clear in the 1990s—of false starts and unfulfilled promise. From 1995 to 1998, the value of bilateral trade actually fell, from a 1990s high of US$5.5 billion to US$4.6 billion. It picked up again in the next two years, rising to US$5.1 billion in 2000 but then again fell back to another low in 2003. It was diplomatic and catalytic engagement, not economic exchange engagement, that began to shift the bilateral relationship in a more positive direction. In April 2005, Prime Minister Jun'ichirō Koizumi visited New Delhi and announced that India and Japan were forming a new "global partnership."[41] In December 2006, Prime Minister Manmohan Singh visited Tokyo to meet with Prime Minister Shinzō Abe, and the two sides declared that they would now "elevate" their partnership to a "strategic and global partnership."[42]

This new strategic and global relationship was intended to involve greater coordination between India and Japan in a range of areas, including "bilateral, regional, multilateral, and global issues," as well as "comprehensive economic engagement, stronger defence relations, [and] greater technological cooperation." It also placed significant emphasis on increasing "cultural ties, educational linkages and people-to-people contacts." In 2007, the two countries issued joint statements on their strategic and global partnership, including a "roadmap" for developing the partnership.[43] Key aspects of these statements included plans to strengthen defense cooperation, such as over sea-lane security and weapon proliferation. Cooperation would also include defense force exchanges and collaboration between the two nations' coast guards. In October 2008, the two sides announced a Joint Declaration on Security Cooperation between Japan and India. In December 2009, they issued an action plan to further advance this security cooperation.[44] Although Japanese officials conceded that there was little new in each of these declarations in terms of immediate action, US officials speculated that the Japanese aim was to highlight publicly that its relationship with India was "more 'strategic' and 'global' than that between India and China."[45] By June 2012, the two countries were engaged in joint naval exercises in Sagami Bay near Kanagawa Prefecture.[46]

Wider ODA, investment, and other trade issues were also key parts of the increasingly active relationship, for which the diplomatic engagement laid the groundwork. On the aid front, Japan's ODA to India had been falling through the mid-2000s but rose again as the decade progressed. In 2006, it had fallen to around only US$29 million but then increased significantly over subsequent years to reach approximately US$981 million in 2010.[47] Japan's foreign direct investment rose eighteenfold between 2005 and 2008, reaching $543 billion.[48] Developing the trade relationship was also intended to be an important part of the new partnership. In their 2007 joint statement, Prime Ministers Abe and Singh emphasized the importance of negotiating a free-trade agreement known as a comprehensive economic partnership agreement (CEPA) and directed officials to "complete the negotiations as soon as possible." The negotiations had been delayed over a number of market access issues, notably the pharmaceuticals market, but the two sides finally reached a compromise in late 2010.[49] Negotiations were completed in October 2010, and the final CEPA came into force in August 2011. Importantly, Prime Ministers Singh and Naoto Kan, Yukio Hatoyama's successor, noted that the two countries would "explore the possibility" of cooperation on the "development, re-cycling and re-use of rare earths and rare metals."[50] In December 2011, Kan's successor, Yoshihiko Noda, visited India to celebrate the sixtieth anniversary of the establishment of bilateral diplomatic relations. Noda pushed for greater cooperation on the rare-earth trade and emphasized the vital interests that the two countries shared as "Asian maritime nations."[51]

With commercial links expanding and the CEPA completed, trade in a range of new areas such as rare earths would be likely to increase. It has been estimated that by 2011, over a thousand Japanese firms were operating in India.[52] Japan's political leaders were especially hopeful about the relationship's direction, noting the progress that had been made on the Delhi Mumbai Industrial Corridor—an industrial development project in which Japan is heavily involved—but emphasizing the need to cooperate further in manufacturing and high technology.[53] This positive picture is also reflected in overall trade figures. After the low of

US$4.6 billion in bilateral trade in 2003, the figures rose quickly in subsequent years, from US$5.6 billion in 2004 to US$10.3 billion in 2007 and then to US$17.9 billion in 2011, representing a 391 percent increase from 2003 to 2011. This brought significant benefits to Japan, which enjoyed a trade surplus of approximately US$4.3 billion in 2011.[54]

Problems and Disappointments

This revitalized engagement has not, however, been problem-free. Some comparisons between India's engagement with other countries in the region, notably with the United States and China, suggest that the Indo-Japanese relationship has developed "extremely slowly" and key initiatives have not progressed as they might.[55] The "quadrilateral initiative" pursued by the Abe government, for example, has produced few concrete results. In August 2007, Abe argued for a closer association between those countries that shared freedom, democracy, and other "fundamental values." He suggested that an "arc of freedom and prosperity"—a term that had been introduced by then Foreign Minister Tarō Asō—could be formed across Eurasia.[56] This use of "values diplomacy" was not well received in the Asia-Pacific region, while the quadrilateral aspect of the initiative was viewed by China as a form of containment.[57] What has worked is lower-level, military-to-military engagement, which can be seen to be catalyzing deeper ties in the security realm. The low-key objective of closer security cooperation (especially joint training) rather than high-profile, "values" diplomacy has become a key feature of Japan's engagement of India, central to its overall vision of regional security. In 2012, joint naval exercises and "strategic consultations" between India, Japan, and the United States were described as a new "Triple Entente," albeit one that was "not to contain" China but to better integrate it into the international community.[58]

The nuclear issue also continues to cause problems. Having resolved their immediate differences over the 1998 tests, Japan and India have since sought to negotiate an agreement on civil nuclear cooperation, following in the footsteps of India's 2005 agreement with the United States. Prior to his visit to Japan in October 2010, Prime Minister Singh stated that he was "confident that we will be able to conclude an agreement, which will be a win-win proposition for both of us."[59] In April that year, the two sides had established the Nuclear Energy Working Group held under the Japan-India Ministerial Level Energy Dialogue in order to "exchange views and information on their respective nuclear energy policies."[60] Once again, however, the two countries' fundamentally different attitudes have made such talks difficult.[61]

Japan's experience of atomic bombings during the Second World War and its hope for total nuclear disarmament have made the issue's domestic politics extremely difficult. In July 2010, the mayors of Hiroshima and Nagasaki—the two cities that suffered the atomic bombings—handed a petition to the foreign minister calling on the government to stop negotiations with India over the civil nuclear deal.[62] In August 2010, Foreign Minister Katsuya Okada noted that "Japan would have no choice but to suspend cooperation" were India to resume nuclear testing.[63] In addition, the major earthquake, tsunami, and nuclear disaster of March 2011 have not only had enormous consequences for Japanese energy policy and domestic politics but also led to rising antinuclear sentiment across the country.[64] For the time being, the domestic political stability needed for such complex bilateral negotiations will be hard to find in Japan.

Understanding Japan's Current Strategic Environment

The role played by Japan's immediate strategic environment in shaping the country's engagement of India becomes apparent when one compares this latest "elevation" of its engagement to earlier episodes. Two important factors, which were not sufficiently influential or clearly directed in past iterations of engagement, have now grown and combined to propel Japan closer to India. These are the practices and expectations of the United States in the region and the rise of China. Strategic partnerships with countries such as India, as Thomas Wilkins argues, allow Japan to hedge against worsening relations with China while reinforcing an American alliance system that is evolving into a more complex set of regional arrangements.[65]

From the early 2000s, the United States began to cooperate more closely with India over a range of strategic areas, including military training and procurement.[66] Following the launch of the Next Steps in Strategic Partnership in early 2004, the United States gradually extended the joint dialogue to include initiatives and agreements on trade, health policy, counterterrorism, and most controversially on civil nuclear cooperation. In 2005, the two governments announced an agreement that would allow for cooperation on civil nuclear power. By 2009, they had launched an even more comprehensive "strategic dialogue."[67] In June 2012, Secretary of Defense Leon Panetta described India as a "linchpin" in America's strategy to expand its presence, including militarily, in the area "extending from the Western Pacific and East Asia into the Indian Ocean region and South Asia."[68]

As noted earlier, United States–focused bilateralism has been at the core of Japan's foreign policy since the Second World War. Accordingly, this shift in America's engagement with India has impacted on Japan's own policy, with American *gaiatsu* (external pressure)—in this case, concerning US expectations of a wider Japanese role in the region—continuing to influence Japanese diplomacy. Japan's engagement of India since 2005 followed closely after America's push to promote "federated capabilities" in the Indo-Pacific.[69] Although there was opposition in Japan to the 2005 US-Indian agreement, key players, such as the North American affairs and foreign bureaus within the Japanese Ministry of Foreign Affairs, viewed the deal in the light of achieving what Green describes as a "US-led equilibrium in Asia."[70]

Put simply, the United States has been seeking to facilitate greater cooperation between its allies and partners in the region, using a range of military engagement strategies, including joint exercises and disaster-response initiatives. Where there was once merely a US "hub and spokes" system, the US expectation now appears to be for greater "intra-spoke" cooperation within a wider regional network.[71] At the time of Abe's meeting with Singh in 2006, according to US diplomatic cables, officials in the US government saw the possibilities stemming from a deepening Indo-Japanese relationship as "dazzling." The United States should "take advantage of the opportunity at hand and take steps to build closer trilateral cooperation."[72] At Trilateral Security Dialogue meetings in Australia in December the following year, US Undersecretary of State for Political Affairs Nicholas Burns conveyed to his Japanese counterpart, Assistant Vice Minister for Foreign Affairs Mitoji Yabunaka, America's desire for Japan's support on US-Indian nuclear cooperation.[73]

These developments have occurred at the same time as China has loomed ever larger in Japanese strategic thinking. In 2012 for example, Japan's annual white paper, *Defense of Japan*, made note of China's increasing influence in the region, the lack of clarity in its military modernization, and its "expanding and intensifying . . . activities in waters close to Japan."[74] In fact, while the two countries normalized relations in the 1970s, their subsequent interactions have not always been harmonious, with diplomatic feuds erupting recurrently over history textbooks, the Yasukuni Shrine, and the Diaoyu/Senkaku territorial dispute.[75] Even as they have become more interdependent since the early 2000s, they have encountered regular diplomatic and political upheavals. Anti-Japanese riots in China in 2005 followed what Christopher Hughes describes as the "worst Sino-Japanese relations since normalization."[76] The diplomatic tussle that followed the collision between a Chinese fishing vessel and Japanese coast guard patrol boats near the disputed Diaoyu/Senkaku Islands in 2010 reinforced Japanese fears about China.[77] The tensions between Japan and China over the nationalization of these islands in September 2012 are likely to have a similar effect.[78]

A "fear of China" has become a consistent feature of recent Japanese domestic debates, with the country gradually becoming more distrustful, despite the importance of the bilateral economic relationship.[79] According to Yoshihide

Soeya, Japanese conservatives, who have a strong "revisionist" agenda promoting the need for Japan to regain its independence, see China as the greatest external threat to the realization of their vision of a strong, independent, and "normal" Japan.[80] Their view is that by using the "history card" and encouraging strong anti-Japanese sentiment domestically, the Chinese government is able to marginalize and isolate Japan and prevent its move toward greater independence. When the Democratic Party of Japan (DPJ) came to government in 2009, a brief interlude in this distrust ensued; however, the 2010 Diaoyu/Senkaku incident undermined the DPJ's efforts and heightened the appeal of more assertive policies. The Japanese mainstream, it should be said, has often been conciliatory toward China—to the extent that conservatives have attacked its "kowtow diplomacy."[81] Yet ambiguities in Chinese behavior, particularly in terms of the military expansion noted in the 2012 white paper and the many domestic anti-Japanese protests that appear to be encouraged by Chinese authorities, have provided considerable opportunities for the growth of nationalist sentiment in Japan.[82]

For Japan and India, the rise of China has been a common concern and thus, as Takeshi Yūzawa notes, "one of the main causes" for why the two countries have moved closer.[83] Sino-Japanese tensions have shaped Japan's engagement of India in some specific policy areas. In 2005, Japan shifted much of its ODA away from China and toward India.[84] The tensions have also played a role more broadly. Japan's attempts to deepen its economic relationship with India have owed much to its fear that its economy relies too heavily on China. When the Indo-Japan CEPA was announced, it was publicly noted that the agreement would reduce risks associated with both countries' rising trade dependence on China.[85] In late 2007, according to US diplomatic cables, the then ambassador designate to India, Hideaki Domichi, noted that it was his dream that trade and investment between Japan and India reach the same level as that between Japan and China.[86] Similarly the Japanese decision to consider cooperation with India in the nuclear energy field, as Kumao Kaneko argues, was prompted not only by the needs of Japan's nuclear industry but also by the government's desire to widen the "breadth" of the country's diplomacy toward Asia and thereby move beyond a China-focused policy.[87]

When Japanese analysts consider India, they regularly do so by making comparisons to China or by locating India's role in the context of China's rise. Nobukatsu Kanehara, for instance, views a key factor in the changing international system in the twenty-first century to be the industrialization of the traditional Asian great powers. This includes, in particular, the "industrialization of China and India."[88] In their work on Japanese grand strategy, Yoshinobu Yamamoto and his colleagues repeatedly pair India and China when discussing the changing strategic environment. They explain how, in a world characterized by declining American power and greater multipolarity, it is countries such as China and India that are rising. They also highlight that, in response to this changing international environment, Japan is seeking to improve its defense relationships with countries such as Australia and India.[89] Likewise Takenori Horimoto notes that since the 2005 anti-Japanese demonstrations in China, the Japanese government has been pursuing a closer relationship with India. The two countries, Horimoto suggests, share common concerns about their relationships with China while also having partnerships with the United States.[90]

Officials are also reported to make similar comments behind closed doors. At the Trilateral Security Dialogue in 2007, for example, Yabunaka was reported in American diplomatic cables as observing that India provided "an important counterbalance to China."[91] A merit of the strategic and global partnership in Japanese eyes, according to US diplomatic cables, was its superiority to the strategic and cooperative partnership between India and China.[92] Certainly both India and China appear prominently in Japanese analysis of potential "concert diplomacy" in the region; India in particular constitutes a key player in a "hedging" strategy for Japan if engagement of China proves ineffective.[93]

Conclusion

Although Japan and India lived in largely different strategic worlds during the Cold War, their bilateral relationship has recently taken on greater economic and strategic value. India's economic reforms of the 1990s appealed to Japan's trade-focused approach to the region, but the results of early post–Cold War diplomatic and economic engagement were modest at best. After this limited early interaction, the crisis sparked by India's 1998 nuclear tests became an even larger obstacle to better relations. The end of the Cold War and India's rise to nuclear-power status can thus be viewed as possible factors driving Japan's subsequent attempts to engage more carefully with India. Although these events were important, however, neither can be used to fully explain why it was only from 2005 to 2006 that the relationship became truly energized.

A better explanation for the rapid emergence of the Indo-Japanese strategic and global partnership requires a closer examination of the changes that have taken place in Japan's immediate strategic environment around this time. During the Cold War, Japan's environment was centered on the immediate East Asian region and the need to concentrate the country's energies on economic development rather than security. By contrast, from the middle of the last decade, Japan's environment has increasingly been reconfigured by China's rise and America's reengagement with the wider region—notably with India itself. These two factors have in fact pushed strongly in the same direction in terms of their effect on Japanese strategy: toward ensuring that the United States stays engaged in the region by maintaining its emphasis on bilateralism and toward hedging against uncertainty over China by improving relations with Asia's other significant powers.

Japan's engagement of India, therefore, is best understood as the product of Japan's attempts, at this critical juncture in the mid-2010s, to remain "in step" with US policy and also to hedge against the rise of China.[94] Japan's approach is notably in line with American thinking in terms of the policies of its allies and partners in the region concerning the concept of "intra-hub" cooperation. As Yamamoto et alia argue, this Indo-Pacific or "greater Asia" region takes on considerable strategic importance, especially as the maritime link between Asia and the Middle East becomes more important. Capturing the region's "dynamism" while avoiding any confrontation involving the United States, China, or India thus becomes a crucial Japanese strategic objective.[95] The long-term nature of many of these trends suggests that in the coming years India—in its role as strategic counterweight and possible partner—is likely to grow in importance in Japan's strategic calculations. They also point to a continuation of a Japanese preference for catalytic over exchange engagement with India, attempting to shift the perceived interests of its elites to align them with those of Japan.

Notes

1. Japanese Ministry of Foreign Affairs, "Joint Statement towards Japan-India Strategic and Global Partnership," Tokyo, December 15, 2006, www.mofa.go.jp/region/asia-paci/india/pdfs/joint0612.pdf (accessed October 30, 2012).

2. Sumit Ganguly, "The Genesis of Nonalignment," in *India's Foreign Policy: Retrospect and Prospect*, ed. Sumit Ganguly (New Delhi: Oxford University Press, 2010), 1.

3. K. V. Kesavan, "India and Japan: Changing Dimensions of Partnership in the Post–Cold War Period," ORF Occasional Paper 14 (New Delhi: Observer Research Foundation, May 2010), 3. The already substantial cultural differences were also important. See David Brewster, *India as an Asia Pacific Power* (London: Routledge, 2012), 65.

4. Kesavan, "India and Japan," 3, and Madhuchanda Ghosh, "India and Japan's Growing Synergy: From a Political to a Strategic Focus," *Asian Survey* 48, no. 2 (2008): 285.

5. Kenneth B. Pyle, *Japan Rising: The Resurgence of Japanese Power and Purpose* (New York: PublicAffairs, 2007), 228.

6. Hisahiko Okazaki, *A Grand Strategy for Japanese Defense* (Lanham, MD: University Press of America, 1986), 126. For a review of the different Japanese perspectives on the regional security environment and the Soviet Union, see Tetsuya Kataoka and Ramon H. Myers, *Defending an Economic Superpower: Reassessing the US-Japan Security Alliance* (Boulder, CO: Westview, 1989), 25–38.

7. For more on the 1958 trade agreements, see P. A. Narasimha Murthy, "India and Japan," *International Studies* 17, nos. 3–4 (1978): 615–18. Regarding Japan's iron ore

imports, see John Welfield, *An Empire in Eclipse: Japan in the Postwar American Alliance System; A Study in the Interaction of Domestic Politics and Foreign Policy* (London: Athlone Press, 1988), 96, and Hui-Shung Chang, "Estimating Japanese Import Shares of Iron Ore," *Resources Policy* 20, no. 2 (1994): 89.

8. United Nations Statistics Division, *UN Comtrade* (United Nations Commodity Trade Statistics Database), http://comtrade.un.org/db/ (accessed October 30, 2012).

9. Ramachandra Guha, *India after Gandhi: The History of the World's Largest Democracy* (New York: HarperCollins, 2007), 215, 216.

10. Brewster, *India as an Asia Pacific Power*, 68.

11. Akiko Fukushima, "Japan's Perspective on Asian Regionalism," in *Asia's New Multilateralism: Cooperation, Competition, and the Search for Community*, ed. Michael J. Green and Bates Gill (New York: Columbia University Press, 2009), 105–6, and Charles E. Morrison, "Japan and the ASEAN Countries: The Evolution of Japan's Regional Role," in *The Political Economy of Japan, Vol. 2: The Changing International Context*, ed. Takashi Inoguchi and Daniel I. Okimoto (Stanford, CA: Stanford University Press, 1988), 420–22. On the Fukuda Doctrine in particular, see Bert Edström, *Japan's Evolving Foreign Policy Doctrine: From Yoshida to Miyazawa* (Houndmills, UK: Macmillan, 1999), 98, and Sueo Sudo, *Southeast Asia in Japanese Security Policy* (Singapore: Institute of Southeast Asian Studies, 1991), 22–25.

12. Quoted in Yoshihide Soeya, *Nihon no "Midoru Pawā" Gaikō: Sengo Nihon no Sentaku to Kōsō* [Japan's "Middle Power" Diplomacy: Postwar Japan's Choices and Conceptions] (Tokyo: Chikuma Shobō, 2005), 162–63.

13. P. G. Rajamohan, Dil Bahadur Rahut, and Jabin T. Jacob, "Changing Paradigm of Indo-Japan Relations: Opportunities and Challenges," Indian Council for Research on International Economic Relations, Working Paper No. 212 (New Delhi: Indian Council for Research on International Economic Relations, April 2008), 9. Regarding Maruti-Suzuki, see Rajaram Panda, "Application of Japanese Management Technique in Indian 365 Joint Venture: A Case Study of Maruti Udyog Limited," in *Japan-South Asia: Security and Economic Perspectives*, ed. K. V. Kesavan and Lalima Varma (New Delhi: Lancers Books, 2000), 369–73.

14. Dennis T. Yasutomo, "Why Aid? Japan as an 'Aid Great Power,'" *Pacific Affairs* 62, no. 4 (1989/1990): 490–503.

15. Saburo Okita, "Japan's Quiet Strength," *Foreign Policy* 75 (Summer 1989): 139. See also K. V. S. Rama Sarma and V. D. Chopra, *Japan: Super Economic Power* (New Delhi: Gyan, 1998), 206.

16. Guha, *India after Gandhi*, 683–84, and Rahul Mukherji, "India's Foreign Economic Policies," in Ganguly, *India's Foreign Policy*, 312–13.

17. Brewster, *India as an Asia Pacific Power*, 14–15, and Hideki Esho, "India's New Economic Policy and the Japanese Response," in Kesavan and Varma, *Japan-South Asia*, 222–24.

18. Hitoshi Tanaka, *Gaikō no Chikara* [The Power of Diplomacy] (Tokyo: Nihon Keizai Shinbun Shuppansha, 2009), 84.

19. Christopher W. Hughes, *Japan's Security Agenda: Military, Economic, and Environmental Dimensions* (Boulder, CO: Lynne Rienner, 2004), 159–65.

20. Government of Japan, "Japan's Official Development Assistance Charter," June 30, 1992, reproduced in Ministry of Foreign Affairs, *Japan's ODA 1992* (Tokyo: Association for

Promotion of International Cooperation, 1992), 193. See also Steven W. Hook and Guang Zhang, "Japan's Aid Policy since the Cold War: Rhetoric and Reality," *Asian Survey* 38, no. 11 (1998): 1056–57, and Saori N. Katada, "Japan's Two-Track Aid Approach: The Forces behind Competing Triads," *Asian Survey* 42, no. 2 (2002): 334–41.

21. United Nations Statistics Division, *UN Comtrade*.

22. Ibid.

23. Purnendra Jain, "Japan's Relations with South Asia," *Asian Survey* 37, no. 4 (1997): 346, and "Toshiba Fails to Bail Out Toshiba Anand," *Economic Times*, August 4, 1991.

24. Esho, "India's New Economic Policy," 236–41.

25. Masahiro Kawai and Shinji Takagi, "Japan's Official Development Assistance: Recent Issues and Future Directions," Asia Program Working Paper, no. 97 (Washington, DC: Woodrow Wilson International Center for Scholars, July 2001), 3. On the broad evolution of Japan's ODA policy, see Kazuhiko Togo, *Japan's Foreign Policy, 1945–2003: The Quest for a Proactive Policy* (Leiden: Brill, 2005), 316–43.

26. Government of Japan, "Japan's Official Development Assistance Charter," 193.

27. "India Agrees to Nuclear Disarmament Talks with Japan," Agence France-Presse, June 23, 1992.

28. William J. Long, "Nonproliferation as a Goal of Japanese Foreign Assistance," in *Japanese Foreign Policy in Asia and the Pacific: Domestic Interests, American Pressure, and Regional Integration*, ed. Akitoshi Miyashita and Yoichiro Sato (Houndmills, UK: Palgrave, 2001), 126–28.

29. United Nations Security Council, Resolution 1172, S/RES/1172 (1998), June 6, 1998. See also "Security Council Unanimously Adopts Antinuke Resolution," *Kyodo News*, June 7, 1998.

30. Satu P. Limaye, "Tokyo's Dynamic Diplomacy: Japan and the Subcontinent's Nuclear Tests," *Contemporary Southeast Asia* 22, no. 2 (2000): 324–27.

31. Ibid., 324.

32. Takeshi Yuzawa, *Japan's Security Policy and the ASEAN Regional Forum: The Search for Multilateral Security in the Asia-Pacific* (London: Routledge, 2007), 124–26.

33. See Brewster, *India as an Asia Pacific Power*, 70.

34. Limaye, "Tokyo's Dynamic Diplomacy," 327.

35. Ibid., 327–28.

36. Japanese Ministry of Foreign Affairs, "Press Conference by the Press Secretary 12 November, 1999," November 12, 1999, www.mofa.go.jp/announce/press/1999/11/1112.html#5 (accessed October 30, 2012). For an example of the diplomacy, see Japanese Ministry of Foreign Affairs, "Meeting between Minister for Foreign Affairs Yohei Kono and the Indian Minister of Defence (Summary and Evaluation)," June 8, 2000, www.mofa.go.jp/region/asia-paci/india/meet0006.html (accessed October 30, 2012).

37. Michael J. Green, "Japan, India, and the Strategic Triangle with China," in *Strategic Asia 2011–12: Asia Responds to Its Rising Powers: China and India*, ed. Ashley J. Tellis, Travis Tanner, and Jessica Keough (Washington, DC: National Bureau of Asian Research, 2011), 136.

38. Japanese Ministry of Foreign Affairs, "Japan-India Summit Meeting (Summary)," August 23, 2000, www.mofa.go.jp/region/asia-paci/pmv0008/india_s.html (accessed October 30, 2012), and Harsh V. Pant, "India-Japan Relations: A Slow but Steady Transformation," in Ganguly, *India's Foreign Policy*, 218.

39. Japanese Ministry of Foreign Affairs, "Announcement by the Chief Cabinet Secretary on Discontinuation of Measures in Response to Nuclear Testing Conducted by India and Pakistan," October 26, 2001, www.mofa.go.jp/region/asia-paci/india/announce0110.html (accessed October 30, 2012), and Brewster, *India as an Asia Pacific Power*, 71.

40. Brewster, *India as an Asia Pacific Power*, 71.

41. Japanese Ministry of Foreign Affairs, "Japan-India Partnership in a New Asian Era: Strategic Orientation of Japan-India Global Partnership," April 29, 2005, www.mofa.go.jp/region/asia-paci/india/partner0504.html (accessed October 30, 2012).

42. Japanese Ministry of Foreign Affairs, "Joint Statement towards Japan-India Strategic and Global Partnership," 2–3.

43. Japanese Ministry of Foreign Affairs, "Joint Statement on the Roadmap for New Dimensions to the Strategic and Global Partnership between Japan and India," August 22, 2007, www.mofa.go.jp/region/asia-paci/pmv0708/joint-2.html (accessed October 30, 2012).

44. Japanese Ministry of Foreign Affairs, "Joint Declaration on Security Cooperation between Japan and India," October 22, 2008, www.mofa.go.jp/region/asia-paci/india/pmv0810/joint_d.html (accessed October 30, 2012), and Japanese Ministry of Foreign Affairs, "Action Plan to Advance Security Cooperation based on the Joint Declaration on Security Cooperation between Japan and India," December 29, 2009, www.mofa.go.jp/region/asia-paci/india/pmv0912/action.html (accessed October 30, 2012).

45. US Embassy in Tokyo, "Japanese Pleased with Visit of Indian PM Singh," October 29, 2008, Cable ID: 08TOKYO3015 (29 October 2018 CONFIDENTIAL), www.cablegatesearch.net/cable.php?id=08TOKYO3015 (accessed November 12, 2012).

46. "Japan, India Hold Naval Exercises to 'Counter' China's Military Build-Up," *BBC Monitoring Asia Pacific*, June 11, 2012.

47. Japanese Ministry of Foreign Affairs, "Seifu Kaihatsu Enjo (ODA) Kunibetsu Dētabukku 2011" [Overseas Development Aid (ODA) Databook by Country 2011], 131, www.mofa.go.jp/mofaj/gaiko/oda/shiryo/kuni/11_databook/pdfs/02-01.pdf (accessed October 30, 2012), and Japanese Ministry of Foreign Affairs, "Kunibetsu Chiikibetsu Seisaku, Jōhō: ODA Jisseki Kensaku" [Policy and Information by Country and Region: ODA Results Search], www3.mofa.go.jp/mofaj/gaiko/oda/shiryo/jisseki/kuni/index.php (accessed May 5, 2013).

48. Green, "Japan, India, and the Strategic Triangle with China," 139–40.

49. Japanese Ministry of Foreign Affairs, "Joint Statement Vision for Japan-India Strategic and Global Partnership in the Next Decade," October 25, 2010, www.mofa.go.jp/region/asia-paci/india/pm1010/joint_st.html (accessed October 30, 2012).

50. Ibid., and P. R. Ramesh, "India to Export Rare Earths to Japan," *Economic Times*, October 26, 2010.

51. Yoshihiro Kiyonaga, "Japan, India Agree to Boost Maritime Security Cooperation," *Daily Yomiuri*, December 30, 2011, and Japanese Ministry of Foreign Affairs, "Joint Statement: Vision for the Enhancement of Japan-India Strategic and Global Partnership Upon Entering the Year of the 60th Anniversary of the Establishment of Diplomatic Relations," December 28, 2011, www.mofa.go.jp/region/asia-paci/india/pmv1112/joint_statement_en.html (accessed October 30, 2012).

52. "India, Japan to Sign Free Trade Pact Feb. 16, Newspaper Says," *Kyodo News*, January 14, 2011.

53. "Yoshihiko Noda and Kamal Nath Address India Japan Business Summit," *Indiainfoline News Service*, May 24, 2012.

54. United Nations Statistics Division, *UN Comtrade*.

55. Takeshi Yūzawa, "Nichin Kankei no Genjō to Kadai" [Indo-Japanese Relations: Current Conditions and Problems], *Kokusai Mondai* [International Affairs] 571 (2008): 43.

56. Shinzō Abe, "Confluence of the Two Seas," speech at the parliament of the Republic of India, August 22, 2007, www.mofa.go.jp/region/asia-paci/pmv0708/speech-2.html (accessed October 30, 2012), and Tarō Asō, "Arc of Freedom and Prosperity: Japan's Expanding Diplomatic Horizons," speech, Japan Institute of International Affairs seminar, November 30, 2006, www.mofa.go.jp/announce/fm/aso/speech0611.html (accessed October 30, 2012).

57. Christopher W. Hughes, "Japan's Response to China's Rise: Regional Engagement, Global Containment, Dangers of Collision," *International Affairs* 85, no. 4 (2009): 854.

58. Brahma Chellaney, "Asia's New 'Triple Entente': Together, US, India and Japan Can Check China," *Washington Times*, January 25, 2012.

59. "India Ready to Strike Civilian Nuclear Deal with Japan," *Kyodo News*, October 24, 2010.

60. Japanese Ministry of Foreign Affairs, "Joint Statement Vision for Japan-India Strategic and Global Partnership in the Next Decade." See also Green, "Japan, India, and the Strategic Triangle with China," 143–44.

61. Kumao Kaneko, "Nichi'in Genshiryoku Kyōtei o Sokushin Subeshi" [Promoting Indo-Japanese Nuclear Cooperation], *Gaikō* [Diplomacy] 8 (2011): 61.

62. "India to Send Envoy to Japan amid Opposition to Nuclear Talks," *Kyodo News*, July 5, 2010.

63. Japanese Ministry of Foreign Affairs, "Press Conference by Minister for Foreign Affairs Katsuya Okada," August 24, 2010, www.mofa.go.jp/announce/fm_press/2010/8/0824_01.html (accessed October 30, 2012). See also Kaneko, "Nichi'in Genshiryoku Kyōtei o Sokushin Subeshi," 61.

64. Kazuaki Nagata, "Protest Rally against Noda, Oi Reactor Restarts Intensifies," *Japan Times Online*, June 30, 2012, www.japantimes.co.jp/text/nn20120630a1.html#.T-_5Zl JKWIA (accessed October 30, 2012).

65. Thomas S. Wilkins, "Japan's Alliance Diversification: A Comparative Analysis of the Indian and Australian Strategic Partnerships," *International Relations of the Asia-Pacific* 11, no. 1 (2011): 145–47.

66. Evan S. Medeiros, "Strategic Hedging and the Future of Asia-Pacific Stability," *Washington Quarterly* 29, no. 1 (2005/2006): 150–51.

67. Dinshaw Mistry, "Diplomacy, Domestic Politics, and the US-India Nuclear Agreement," *Asian Survey* 46, no. 5 (2006): 681–97, and US Department of State, "Background Note: India," April 17, 2012, www.state.gov/r/pa/ei/bgn/3454.htm (accessed October 30, 2012).

68. Quoted in Gardiner Harris, "Defense Chief Shrugs Off Objections to Drones," *New York Times*, June 6, 2012.

69. Michael J. Green and Andrew Shearer, "Defining US Indian Ocean Strategy," *Washington Quarterly* 35, no. 2 (2012): 185.

70. Green, "Japan, India, and the Strategic Triangle with China," 137.

71. William T. Tow and H. D. P. Envall, "The US and Implementing Multilateral Security in the Asia-Pacific: Can Convergent Security Work?" *IFANS Review* 19, no. 2 (2011): 59–60, 68.

72. US Embassy in New Delhi, "PM Singh Visit to Japan: Time for the US to Seize the Day on Closer Trilateral Cooperation," December 5, 2006, Cable ID 06NEWDELHI8137 (3 December 2021 CONFIDENTIAL), www.cablegatesearch.net/cable.php?id = 06NEWDELHI8137 (accessed November 12, 2012).

73. US Embassy in Canberra, "U/S Burns' 12/4 Meeting with Japan Deputy Foreign Minister Yabunaka," December 20, 2007, Cable ID: 07CANBERRA1783 (3 December 2017 CONFIDENTIAL), http://dazzlepod.com/cable/07CANBERRA1783/ (accessed November 12, 2012).

74. Japanese Ministry of Defense, "Part I: Security Environment Surrounding Japan," in *Defense of Japan 2012*, 2012, www.mod.go.jp/e/publ/w_paper/pdf/2012/04_Part1_Overview.pdf (accessed October 30, 2012).

75. The Yasukuni Shrine commemorates Japan's war dead, including class A war criminals, and is controversial throughout Asia.

76. Hughes, "Japan's Response to China's Rise," 842.

77. H. D. P. Envall and Kiichi Fujiwara, "Japan's Misfiring Security Hedge: Discovering the Limits of Middle-Power Internationalism and Strategic Convergence," in *Bilateral Perspectives on Regional Security: Australia, Japan and the Asia-Pacific Region*, ed. William T. Tow and Rikki Kersten (Houndmills, UK: Palgrave Macmillan, 2012), 70–71.

78. "Protesting Too Much," *The Economist*, September 22, 2012.

79. Richard J. Samuels, *Securing Japan: Tokyo's Grand Strategy and the Future of East Asia* (Ithaca, NY: Cornell University Press, 2007), 138–43, and Tomohiko Taniguchi, "A Cold Peace: The Changing Security Equation in Northeast Asia," *Orbis* 49, no. 3 (2005): 445–57.

80. Yoshihide Soeya, "A 'Normal' Middle Power: Interpreting Changes in Japanese Security Policy in the 1990s and After," in *Japan as a "Normal Country"? A Nation in Search of Its Place in the World*, ed. Yoshihide Soeya, Masayuki Tadokoro, and David A. Welch (Toronto: University of Toronto Press, 2011), 78.

81. Ryosei Kokubun, "Changing Japanese Strategic Thinking toward China," in *Japanese Strategic Thought toward Asia*, ed. Gilbert Rozman, Kazuhiko Togo, and Joseph P. Ferguson (New York: Palgrave Macmillan, 2007), 143.

82. Tomohide Murai, "Chūgoku no Gunjiteki Kakudai to Nihon no Taiō" [China's Military Expansion and Japan's Response], in *Nichibei Dōmei to wa Nani ka* [What Is the Japan-US Alliance?], ed. Sekai Heiwa Kenkūjo (Tokyo: Chūō Kōron Shinsha, 2011), 134.

83. Yūzawa, "Nichin Kankei no Genjō to Kadai," 48.

84. Samuels, *Securing Japan*, 167. See also Gilbert Rozman, "Japanese Strategic Thinking on Regionalism," in Rozman, Togo, and Ferguson, *Japanese Strategic Thought toward Asia*, 255.

85. "Japan-India FTA May Help Japan Boost Exports, Reduce 'China Risk'," *Kyodo News*, October 25, 2010.

86. US Embassy in New Delhi, "Domichi Affirms Continued Close US-Japan Cooperation on India," December 10, 2007, Cable ID: 07NEWDELHI5258 (6 December 2012 CONFIDENTIAL), http://cables.mrkva.eu/cable.php?id = 133533 (accessed November 12, 2012).

87. Kaneko, "Nichi'in Genshiryoku Kyōtei o Sokushin subeshi," 60–61.

88. Nobukatsu Kanehara, "Atarashii Pawā Baransu to Nihon Gaikō" [The New Power Balance and Japanese Diplomacy], in *"Ronshū" Nihon no Gaikō to Sōgōteki Anzen Hoshō* ["Essays" Japanese Diplomacy and Comprehensive Security], ed. Shōtarō Yachi (Tokyo: Uejji, 2011), 80.

89. Yoshinobu Yamamoto et al., *Nihon no Gurando Sutoratejii: Rekishiteki Pawā Shifuto o Dō Norikiru ka* [Japan's Grand Strategy: How Will We Survive a Historic Power Shift?] (Tokyo: PHP Kenkyūjo, 2012), 33, 222–24.

90. Takenori Horimoto, "Taikokuka suru Indo: Chūgoku to no Taihi" [India Becoming a Great Power: The Contrast with China], *Gaikō* [Diplomacy] 6 (2011): 116.

91. US Embassy in Canberra, "U/S Burns at 12/5 TSD SOM – Afghanistan, Pakistan, India," January 3, 2008, Cable ID: 08CANBERRA4 (3 December 2032 SECRET// NOFORN), www.cablegatesearch.net/cable.php?id=08CANBERRA4 (accessed November 12, 2012).

92. US Embassy in Tokyo, "Japanese Pleased with Visit of Indian Prime Minister," December 20, 2006, Cable ID: 06TOKYO7067 (17 December 2016 CONFIDENTIAL), http://wikileaks.org/cable/2006/12/06TOKYO7067.html (accessed November 12, 2012).

93. For a discussion of "concert diplomacy," see Yamamoto et al., *Nihon no Gurando Sutoratejii*, 346–49.

94. On Japan's balancing of multilateralism and bilateralism in its diplomacy, see Hughes, "Japan's Response to China's Rise," 844–45.

95. Yamamoto et al., *Nihon no Gurando Sutoratejii*, 364–65.

CHAPTER 4

RUSSIA'S ENGAGEMENT OF INDIA

Securing the Longevity of a "Special and Privileged" Strategic Partnership

Lavina Lee

APART FROM A BRIEF DRIFT IN RELATIONS in the immediate aftermath of the Soviet collapse, the India–Soviet Union/Russia story is one of consistent engagement from the late 1960s, which over time has resulted in a relationship based on a deep level of trust unsurpassed in their relations with any other state. Despite the end of the Cold War, Indian-Russian relations have, if anything, deepened in many sectors. The questions that this chapter addresses are how has Russia sought to engage India, what objectives has it sought to achieve, and why has this proved to be so successful despite the end of the Cold War?

Russia has sought to engage India in the fields of defense, nuclear, and space cooperation as an energy supplier, as a global political partner sharing a commitment to a multipolar world, and as a geostrategic partner in Central Asia. But narrow economic engagement and withering people-to-people contacts have so far proved to be the core weaknesses in the relationship. Apart from these two areas, however, Russian engagement of India has proved to be extremely successful. Five factors, I argue, are at work.

First, India's receptiveness to deeper Russian engagement on a wide range of issues is highly influenced by history. India's political, defense, and strategic establishment remember well the Soviet Union's support for India's economic development and provision of diplomatic support and armaments at key points in its history where such support was scarce from the West. This strong track record in politico-military engagement, which mainly consisted of a straightforward strategy of exchange without any overt attempt at catalyzing substantive change in Indian domestic politics, has established Russia's reputation in the

Indian mind as a time-tested and respectful friend, and it is this deep trust that makes India receptive and responsive to further Russian engagement.

Second, Russian and Indian elites perceive that their countries have shared interests, especially in promoting "multipolarity" over American hegemony and thus expanding their respective "strategic autonomy." This again suggests, indeed, that exchange engagement can build the kind of lasting relationships that catalytic strategies of engagement are normally designed to generate.

Third, India has been receptive to Russian engagement as a geostrategic partner in Central Asia because of a shared apprehension about the impact a rising China might have on their respective spheres of influence in Central and South Asia. In contrast, both respect the other's sphere of influence and assess that they have little to fear from each other, now or in the medium to long term. Further, as multiethnic pluralistic states, both have shared interests in containing the spread of instability from Central Asia arising from fundamentalist Islamic terrorist and separatist movements.

Fourth, both states are drawn to each other in the fields of energy security and trade in oil, gas, uranium, and civil nuclear power. Russian exports of energy resources could provide India with a means to sustain the high levels of economic growth necessary to alleviate poverty and achieve great power status. Friendship with Russia is also attractive as a means to gain greater access to the energy resources of Central Asia.

Fifth, to protect its military-industrial complex and cement its strategic partnership with India, Russia has proven willing to provide cutting-edge high-technology weaponry beyond that offered by other countries, at competitive rates, and with the possibility of technology transfer through joint military production. In both energy resources and technology transfer, in other words, Russia is continuing and extending the exchange strategy that has generally ensured strong relations and will likely ensure that India will remain receptive to Russian engagement for the medium and long term.

Historical Roots of Russian-Indian Engagement

During the Cold War, the Soviet Union built a solid reputation among India's elite as a trustworthy, "respectful and reliable friend" in a sometimes hostile international system.[1] For the Soviet Union, gaining the support of India, a prominent leader of the nonaligned movement and the largest nonsocialist country in the world, lent weight to its broader ideological struggle with the United States. Toward the end of the 1960s and into the early 1970s in particular, the Soviet Union also began to appreciate the strategic value of India as a potential counterweight to China and Pakistan, America's key ally in South

Asia. In August 1971, at the initiation of the Soviet Union, the two signed a treaty of peace, friendship, and cooperation.[2] Under the treaty both sides pledged not to assist "'any third party that engages in armed conflict with the other'" and to "mutual consultations" if either party was under attack or threatened with attack in order to "remove such threat" and to take "appropriate effective measures."[3] This agreement proved its worth and demonstrated Soviet reliability to India's elite in December 1971 in the Bangladesh Liberation War. The Soviets warned China against any involvement on Pakistan's side, vetoed three United States–sponsored resolutions aimed at halting the war before India achieved its strategic objectives, and responded to the dispatch of the USS *Enterprise* to the Bay of Bengal by sending two nuclear-powered submarines to the area to ward off possible US intervention.[4]

While India's continued commitment to nonalignment meant that it was not receptive to Leonid Brezhnev's dream of a Soviet-led Asian collective security system or to the establishment of military bases on Indian territory, India was soon dependent on Soviet arms.[5] A sustained drive by the Soviet Union to employ exchange strategies of engagement in the military and economic spheres brought about this dependence. By the 1980s, the Soviets supplied 85 percent of India's military hardware and were willing to trade the most modern weapon systems for bartered Indian goods, rather than hard currency, or via low-interest loans with long repayment periods of up to fifteen years.[6] This was vitally important to India in the context of increasing American economic and military support given to Pakistan.[7]

Between 1964 and 1985, India was also the largest noncommunist recipient of Soviet aid and the USSR's largest trading partner in the developing world.[8] Soviet economic aid enabled India to develop an independent industrial capacity in steel, oil, coal, power, and machine building and from the Soviet point of view allowed India to reduce its dependence on the West. Soviet aid came in the form of low-interest loans repaid in rupees or Indian commodities that avoided the need to deplete India's meager foreign exchange reserves.[9] By the 1980s, the Soviet Union was the largest importer of Indian goods, notably importing a larger proportion of manufactured or semimanufactured goods than any other trading partner.[10]

This significant military and economic engagement was put at grave risk with the collapse of the Soviet Union in 1991. The new Russian Federation was initially in no position to offer much in terms of partnership to India, and India was no longer valued as a counterweight to China or the United States. Russia undertook a conscious reorientation toward "Atlanticism"—that is, liberal democratic, trade, and market reforms, and the formation of closer political and economic relations with the West and the North Atlantic Treaty Organization (NATO). During the January 1993 visit of Russian president Boris Yeltsin to

India, the 1971 treaty of peace, friendship, and cooperation was replaced by a new treaty of friendship and cooperation that removed any references to military support in the event of attack by a third party. Yeltsin did not offer any "special relationship" between the two countries but rather a pragmatic one "defined by the balance of power, and common interests."[11] That same month, West and South Asia were listed seventh out of ten priorities for Russian foreign policy after the United States, Europe, and the Asia-Pacific.[12]

Between 1990 and 1995, the volume of trade between the Soviet Union/Russia and India plunged from US$4.2 billion to US$2.2 billion, declining further to US$1.6 billion in 1997–98.[13] India's other major concern at this time was to ensure a reliable supply of arms and spare parts from the Russian Federation. In particular, in the early 1990s the Indian Air Force reportedly only had one year's supply of spare parts for its Soviet-supplied MiGs, which represented around three-quarters of India's military aircraft inventory.[14] By September 1992, in response to these concerns and amid indications that India was looking elsewhere for arms supplies, Russia put forward a proposal for the setting up of joint manufacturing and transfer of technology in relation to spare parts. Although no longer a strategic asset to Russia in geopolitical terms, India was still perceived as critical to keeping its military-industrial complex alive.

Russia's reputation as a dependable arms supplier was, however, severely dented in July 1993 when, under strong US pressure, it reneged on the 1990 Soviet agreement to sell India "two cryogenic rocket-engines with the corresponding technology for India's Geo-Stationary Launching Vehicle (GSLV) project."[15] In May 1992, the United States imposed technology-transfer sanctions on Glaskomos and the Indian Space Research Organisation, arguing that the sale contravened the Missile Technology Control Regime, with potential use for the development of intercontinental ballistic missiles.[16] When the Russians signed a new agreement with India in March 1994 for the supply of seven cryogenic engines, technology transfer on how to produce the engines was not included.[17] This episode demonstrated to India that it was now a much lower priority in Russian foreign policy relationships and sowed seeds of doubt about whether a Russia economically dependent on the United States was capable of an independent defense relationship with India.

The Putin Era: Renewing Engagement and the Development of a Special and Privileged Partnership

Russia's experimentation with Atlanticism and its diminished interest in India proved, however, to be short-lived. The 1994 US decision to expand NATO eastward to include former Warsaw Pact members and America's rejection of

Russia's proposal of a new collective-security organization containing all European states came to be viewed as a clear indication that Russia would never be trusted enough to join the West.[18] NATO's military action in Bosnia in 1995 and then Kosovo in 1999, in spite of Russian objections, confirmed to Russian eyes that its security concerns were being disregarded by the West.[19] Internally the mismanagement of the liberalization of the economy led to spiraling unemployment, inflation, corruption, and a dramatic drop in living standards among the Russian people, which severely undermined popular support for Yeltsin's Westernization project.

From the mid-1990s, in response to these developments, Russia's elite shifted its foreign policy from an Atlanticist to a "Eurasianist" orientation. The core of the Eurasianist school was the view that the Russian Federation, and the Soviet Union before it, had a unique cultural, ethnic, and political character that was distinct from Europe and allowed it to play a role as a bridge between Asia and Europe. Based on Russia's history and representation as a grand civilization, its foreign policy should defend the great-power status of the nation, maintain a sphere of influence over the former Soviet republics in Central Asia, and defend the national interest from Western intrusions, particularly NATO's eastward expansion. Rather than developing links with the West to the exclusion of all others, Russia's political and economic interests were better served by also developing closer links with China, India, the Middle East, and the Pacific rim countries "among whom Russia could be an ally, even a leader, while with the West, Russia would never become more than a second-class citizen."[20]

In pursuit of this Eurasian strategy, Yevgeny Primakov, who served as Russia's prime minister in the last years of Yeltsin's rule, in particular sought to pursue closer ties with rising and established Asian powers in a bid to establish a multipolar world order and rebuild Russia's global influence. Initially this engagement was principally diplomatic and symbolic, but more lasting strategies of exchange and catalytic engagement were signaled. Primakov chose India as the first stop on his inaugural foreign tour in December 1998. In New Delhi he raised the idea of a Russia-China-India strategic triangle directed toward a "multipolar world" and (implicitly) against American "hegemony."[21] The Indian response to this proposal was lukewarm, however. New Delhi viewed Russia's subdued reaction to the 1998 nuclear tests as an indication that Russia was sympathetic to its security concerns. While Moscow joined in the condemnation of the Indian and Pakistani tests, it opposed international economic sanctions. Instead, only a month after the tests, Russia signed an agreement with New Delhi to build two one-megawatt light-water nuclear reactors at Kudankulam in Tamil Nadu and in December 1998 signed a long-term military technical cooperation agreement operative until 2000.[22]

Efforts to renew the relationship with India intensified with the election of Vladimir Putin to the Russian presidency in May 2000.[23] Under Putin's direction, Russia put forward a series of initiatives to deepen and broaden cooperation between the two countries. In October 2000, Russia and India signed a declaration on strategic partnership that delineated forms of enhanced political, economic, defense, scientific, and technical cooperation. In the political realm, the system of annual summit meetings between the prime minister of India and the president of the Russian Federation was reinstated. Both agreed that neither country would participate "in any military-political or other alliances or associations or armed conflict directed against the other Side, or in any treaties, agreements or understandings infringing upon the independence, sovereignty, territorial integrity or national security interests of the other Side."[24]

Going further, under the 2002 New Delhi Declaration on Further Consolidation of Strategic Partnership, it was agreed that "neither side shall take any actions which might threaten or impair the security of the other. Both sides shall be guided by this principle in determining their security and defence policies as well as in military technical cooperation with third countries."[25] Russia thus acknowledged that assurances needed to be given that its arms sales to Pakistan and China would not threaten India's own security.

From 2000 onward, thirteen summits have taken place between Russian and Indian leaders. The visit by Russian president Dmitri Medvedev to India in December 2010 was particularly significant, resulting in the signing of twenty-nine bilateral agreements and an upgrading of the relationship to a "special and privileged strategic partnership." Efforts to deepen relations have steadily become more institutionalized at levels below that of head of state. India's national security adviser and the secretary of the Russian Security Council are in regular contact, and consultations between the National Security Council and the Russian Security Council have been institutionalized through a "joint coordination group" involving bureaucrats at the deputy national security adviser level.[26]

Russia's diplomatic engagement of India has generated, in other words, a mixed record of success. Moreover, as the next section argues, what success has been achieved has been due more to preexisting shared interests and values or to factors exogenous to the engagement itself. Russia's economic and military engagement, on the other hand, has been much more successful, for reasons explored in more detail below, while its public engagement has generally failed to achieve its objectives. The rest of the chapter examines each of these areas of engagement and asks what each side has hoped to achieve, what has been offered, accepted, or rejected as the currency of engagement, and why engagement in these areas has succeeded or failed.

Political and Diplomatic Engagement: The Global Distribution of Power, Shared Values, and Shared Interests

India's receptivity to Russian political and diplomatic engagement strategies can be explained less by the form of the strategies themselves and more by the two countries' similar positions in the global distribution of power, by shared values, and by a number of shared interests.

Although India was wary of the overtly anti-US overtones of Primakov's 1998 idea of a "strategic triangle" with China, India has not been averse to promoting normative ordering principles that support pluralism within the international system. In December 2002, in the context of the increasing likelihood of US military action against Iraq, President Putin and Prime Minister Atal Bihari Vajpayee "reaffirmed" in the Delhi Declaration that "both countries favour strengthening of UN's central role in promoting international security in a multi-polar world."[27] And in November 2003, both countries "affirm[ed] that the future international order based on multi-polarity, should be determined by collective and multilateral processes rather than unilateral ones."[28] Russia took a leading role in opposing the Iraq War in the Security Council, and Vajpayee was highly critical of the US military action, stating to the Indian parliament that "we want a multipolar (*bahurashtriya*) world. The concept of one country dictating a regime change in another doesn't fit this century."[29] In May 2003, India also rejected the George W. Bush administration's request to send seventeen thousand troops to Iraq as part of a stabilization force, on the grounds that the United States lacked a UN mandate.

Since then, both countries have reiterated these sentiments in annual declarations. India has also warmed to the Russia-India-China trilateral framework, which (by 2012) had met eleven times at the foreign minister level.[30] So far the trilateral framework has not hardened into any consistent anti-US grouping, largely because all three countries are dependent upon trade with the United States for their development needs but also because of divergent interests and unresolved bilateral disputes between India and China and between Russia and China (discussed further below). The one area that consistently brings the three states together is a broad commitment, albeit only rhetorically so far, to work toward the development of a multipolar order that mirrors their own positions within the present distribution of power, as either emerging great powers—in the case of China and India—or great powers fighting decline—in the case of Russia—seeking greater autonomy vis-à-vis the hegemonic power of the United States.

Russia and India also share a vulnerability to militant Islamist secessionist movements and terrorism—in Kashmir and Chechnya, for example—and a desire to ward off foreign intervention in these disputes by individual states or the United Nations. India and Russia have made a number of declarations, beginning with the 1994 Moscow Declaration on the Protection of the Interests of Pluralistic States, that drew attention to their common "special responsibility" as large "multiethnic, multilingual and multireligious states" to combat threats to pluralism arising from "aggressive nationalism, religious and political extremism, terrorism and separatism." Both also strongly expressed the conviction that such problems must be dealt with based on "respect for sovereignty, equality and territorial integrity of States [and] non-interference in their internal affairs." This goes some way to explaining India's and Russia's abstention on United Nations Security Council (UNSC) Resolution 1973 authorizing the use of force in Libya and criticism that the military bombing campaign undertaken by Britain, Canada, France, and the United States went beyond the purpose of protecting civilians and defending the no-fly zones.[31]

Both countries are particularly concerned about the spread of religious and political extremism, terrorism, and drug trafficking from Central Asia, Afghanistan, and Pakistan, which is directly related to domestic terrorist attacks within Russia and India. Both supported the Northern Alliance against the Taliban in the 1990s and are working to avoid the resurgence of the Taliban and al-Qaeda once US and NATO forces withdraw from Afghanistan in 2014. India signed a strategic partnership agreement with Afghanistan in 2011 and has committed around US$2 billion for infrastructure projects, including roads to connect Afghanistan to Iran, as well as training for Afghan national security forces.[32] Russia has so far held back from any significant security aid to Afghanistan while NATO and US forces remain in Afghanistan[33] but has prepared for the spread of instability from Afghanistan by leading the Collective Security Treaty Organization (CSTO) to create a rapid-reaction force in 2009 with the capability to deal with terrorism and instability in Central Asia.[34] In addition, the two countries are supportive of infrastructure and gas projects (discussed below) that will enmesh Afghanistan in the regional economy and thereby reduce potential support for anti-Afghan government forces. New Delhi and Moscow are wary of the recent US strategy of opening negotiations with the Taliban given the latter's support for al-Qaeda, as well as the direct sanctuary, training, and arms given to various Islamic terrorist groups such as the Islamic Movement for Uzbekistan in Central Asia, while they were in power.[35]

India's receptivity to Russian political engagement has undoubtedly been strengthened by Russian criticism of Pakistani support for the Taliban and terrorist groups in Afghanistan, Central Asia, and India. For example, in December 2010, both countries issued a joint statement condemning state support for terrorism, "noting that States that aid, abet or shelter terrorists are as guilty of acts of terrorism as their actual perpetrators." It "called upon Pakistan to expeditiously bring all perpetrators . . . of the November 2008 Mumbai attacks to justice."[36] From India's perspective (and others'), Pakistan's Directorate for Inter-Services Intelligence continues to support the Taliban and other Central Asian Islamic terrorist groups as part of a greater plan to achieve "territorial aggrandizement" in Central Asia in a quest for greater "strategic depth" in the event of war with India.[37] Russia's role as a security guarantor for secular Central Asian states suits India's interest in preventing Pakistan from creating a strategically integrated region united by the bonds of Islam.

India's receptivity to Russian political and strategic engagement is also explained by their shared apprehension about the geostrategic impact of a rising China. Both India (2005) and Russia (1996) concluded official strategic partnerships with China, but the potential to form a tight strategic triangle between the three has proved elusive. Apart from the fact that all three states need to maintain good relations with the United States to achieve or maintain great-power status, a more meaningful antihegemonic alliance has failed to emerge because of tension in the India-China leg but also due to emerging weaknesses in the Russia-China relationship.

Russia's relations with China have no doubt improved considerably since the mid-1990s, particularly under Putin's presidency. The Russia-China relationship has strengthened from a "constructive partnership" in 1994 to a "strategic partnership" in 1996, followed by a twenty-year renewable friendship treaty signed in 2001.[38] Apart from shared normative positions on international order, both cooperate in the Shanghai Cooperation Organisation (SCO) to limit the spread of the "three evils"—ethnic separatism, religious extremism, and terrorism—to their own territory (the Caucasus, Chechnya, and Xinjiang) and have successfully combined to pressure members of the SCO (Uzbekistan and Kyrgyzstan) to end US use of airbases for combat operations in Afghanistan.[39]

Russia also continues to be China's only major source of modern military hardware and technology. Joint military exercises were conducted in 2005 (the first ever between the two countries), 2007, and 2009 in the name of combating terrorism, and joint naval exercises were conducted for the first time in April 2012 in the Yellow Sea.[40] Border disputes that had almost brought the two countries to the brink of war in 1969 were also settled relatively quickly through mutual compromise in 1997, 1998, and 2004.[41]

Although Moscow-Beijing relations have improved considerably from a Cold War low, Russia still has cause to view China's rise with some apprehension. At core, the fundamental problem lies in the growing disparity of power between the two states that is already evident. First, demographic shifts in the Far East and weaknesses in border control have given rise to fears of uncontrolled Chinese immigration and a de facto loss of Russian sovereignty.[42] The reduction in subsidies to the area from the central government after the end of the Cold War led to a significant economic and demographic decline in the region and to the internal migration of seven to eight million Russians from the Far East seeking better prospects in Western Russia.[43] Further, both Putin (in 2001) and Medvedev (in 2008) have warned that without a development strategy for the region, the Far East would be no more than "an outpost for the export of raw material to more developed East Asian states [and] could lead to a Chinese takeover of the region, not by migration . . . but by trade and investment."[44] China has become the strongest source of food, goods, workers, and investment for major infrastructure projects in power generation and resource extraction, with the Eastern Siberia–Pacific Ocean oil pipeline as a prime example.[45]

Second, Russia is increasingly aware that China is steadily encroaching into its traditional sphere of influence in Central Asia and has the potential to displace it as the dominant power in the long term. Russia has used the CSTO to retain its position as the security provider of choice for Central Asian states; however, China has become a serious competitor as far as economic influence is concerned. In 2009 and 2010, for example, Russia's net trade with Central Asia was overtaken by China for the first time based on the export of consumer and finished goods and import of raw materials and energy resources by China.

More worrying for Russia, China has also begun to undermine its ability to control energy exports from the region and extract rents by developing alternative pipeline routes that bypass Russia.[46] The Sino-Turkmen gas pipeline (which includes Kazakhstan and Uzbekistan) and the Sino-Kazakh oil pipeline allow these states to directly sell resources to the end user (in this case China) without having to pay transit fees for use of Russian pipelines and energy infrastructure. Further, if China's present economic trajectory continues, it will be difficult for Russia to compete with the level of investment in infrastructure that China can offer to Central Asian states to develop their energy resources. Russia therefore fears the logical outcome of these trends in Central Asia. Just as Russia presently bristles against a United States–led unipolar order, so it does against the future prospect of becoming a junior partner to a regionally hegemonic China.[47]

India's conflicts with China are active, more immediate, and have historical roots. India's defeat by China in the 1962 border war firmly placed China as its primary security threat, over and above any threat from Pakistan. It was the fear of being subject to nuclear coercion by the Chinese that spurred India to conduct its first nuclear tests in 1974 and to upgrade to a thermonuclear capability with further tests in 1998.[48] India's military modernization drive is similarly in direct response to China's more advanced modernization program. Unlike Russia, India still has open and unresolved border disputes with China over Arunachal Pradesh and Aksai Chin that are, if anything, escalating. China has made stronger claims over populated areas in Arunachal Pradesh as well as Tawang, the birthplace of the sixth Dalai Lama, which India will not concede.[49] Border incursions by the Chinese across the line of control in Arunachal Pradesh and

Sikkim have been increasing, and India has responded by increasing its troop levels, which stood at around a hundred thousand in 2010.[50] China has also significantly modernized infrastructure on the Tibetan Plateau having military uses, with upgrades to airfields, railroads, and highways, as well as suspected deployments of nuclear weapons and delivery systems.[51]

From India's viewpoint, China has been unwilling to acknowledge it as a peer and has sought to ensure that it does not have the capabilities to become one in the future. India views China's military and nuclear cooperation with Pakistan and support for separatist groups within India as a means to keep it occupied in low-intensity conflicts in order to sap its economic and military strength.[52] India has also viewed with alarm China's progression toward building a blue-water navy and attempts to support naval activities in the South China Sea, the Malacca Strait, the Straits of Hormuz, and most important in the Indian Ocean through access to naval bases in Cambodia, Myanmar, Pakistan, and Sri Lanka.[53] India also sees China's overtures to its close neighbors such as Bangladesh, Myanmar, Nepal, and Sri Lanka as part of a strategy to undermine its leadership and influence in South Asia. Similarly China's opposition to India's membership in the Asia-Pacific Economic Cooperation (APEC) grouping, the Group of 8, the SCO, and the Association of Southeast Asian Nations Regional Forum, as well as its quest to be made a permanent member of the UNSC, has been interpreted as a direct attempt to prevent recognition of India's status as a great power.[54]

China too fears future encirclement and is wary of the strategic partnership between the United States and India, as well as the high-technology access that India will potentially be able to gain as a result of the US-Indian nuclear cooperation agreement and Nuclear Suppliers Group waiver of 2008. India's post–Cold War attempt to break out of the political and economic limitations of the South Asian region by "looking East" to such countries as Japan, Vietnam, and Singapore is also viewed as balancing behavior designed to contain Chinese influence in East and Southeast Asia. China is also paying increasing attention to India's military modernization program, particularly its procurement and indigenous development of power-projection capabilities (for example, ballistic missile development and naval modernization) that affects the credibility of its own nuclear deterrent capability as well as India's dominance of the Indian Ocean.[55] Further, China views India's provision of sanctuary to the Dalai Lama as an attempt to undermine its domestic stability and control over Tibet.

In light of the strategic competition and unresolved disputes between India and China and the emerging apprehension in Russia about the implications of a rising China, there is little chance that the China-India-Russia triangle will harden into any consistent anti-US alliance and stronger reasons to suspect that India and Russia will be increasingly drawn together with China in mind.

Importantly, both operate in distinct geographical areas and have long respected each other's spheres of influence in Central and South Asia, respectively. The normative convergence on ordering principles and values between Russia and India reinforces common interests between them that are likely to endure.

Energy Security and Economic Drivers of the Relationship

Russia's economic and military engagement of India has met with significant success in two areas of strategic significance—energy and arms. Overall, however, bilateral trade between the two countries is insignificant relative to other trading partners and is considered the weakest link in the relationship. Bilateral trade stood at US$8.9 billion in 2011, and despite repeated failures to meet previous trade targets, Russia and India set a target of US$20 billion in trade turnover by 2015.[56] In comparison, India's total trade with China, its second largest trading partner, stood at almost US$59 billion in 2010–11, while Russia's trade with China and the European Union stood at US$58 billion and US$271 billion, respectively, for the same year.[57] Foreign direct investment is similarly weak, with Russia ranked as India's twenty-first most important source of foreign direct investment between April 2000 and April 2011, amounting to US$467 million, while Indian investments in Russia are estimated to total US$6.5 billion, mostly in the energy sector.[58]

Russian economic engagement of India outside of energy- and defense-related trade has been slow to take off for a number of reasons. First, India's economic growth is consumption-driven rather than export-led, and private-sector firms have much less risky opportunities to invest in the domestic economy than they do in tackling entry into a Russian market that is unfamiliar and often viewed as a "hostile investment environment."[59] Second, the withering of people-to-people contacts and civil society engagement through education since the end of the Cold War has had a direct impact on the numbers of Indian businesspeople who have a direct cultural experience of Russian life, as well as requisite language skills. It is estimated that there are only forty thousand Indians in Russia, mostly medical students, who do not linger after their studies are over.[60] This lack of direct experience and understanding of each other's cultures and comparative advantage economically fuels perceptions inimical to expanding the trade and investment relationship. Indian businesspeople reportedly view the Russian economy as unstable and rife with criminality, while their Russian counterparts view India as a "poor and underdeveloped country" with meager opportunities for trade and investment.[61]

Third, on a practical level, Russia and India lack a direct and cost-competitive land route for trade in goods and services. Should the International North-South Transport Corridor be successfully developed (discussed below), which would cut ten to twenty days off the present shipment time, there is a much higher chance that broader economic engagement will succeed. Finally, Russia and India have yet to agree on a preferential trade agreement that could standardize trade relations. Both countries have been in discussion for a number of years on the formation of a comprehensive economic cooperation agreement (CECA) that will now need to encompass the customs union formed between Belarus, Kazakhstan, and Russia in 2010. Russia's entry into the World Trade Organization (WTO) in 2012 should further its attempts to more closely engage with India economically.

Although broader trade and investment is clearly the weakest link in Russia's engagement strategy, this has not had a significant impact on the relationship as a whole because trade has developed in areas of complementary and high strategic interest for the two countries—energy and defense. In relation to energy, India and Russia are drawn together by complementary interests: India's energy insecurity and need to sustain high levels of economic growth and Russia's interest in a growing market for carbon-based and nuclear energy sources. With an economy growing at 6.5 percent in 2011–12, increasing urbanization, and rising incomes, India's energy consumption could continue to expand exponentially.[62] As of 2011, India is the world's sixth largest importer of oil and imports satisfy approximately 70 percent of its oil needs.[63] The dependence on oil imports is increasing at a steady pace, with petroleum-related imports growing by 30 percent in 2006–7 and 25 percent in 2010–11.[64] Russia provides a natural fit for India's energy security needs as the world's second largest oil exporter (after Saudi Arabia) and the world's largest gas exporter in 2011.[65] Unlike China, India is a relative latecomer to the strategy of diversifying its sources of energy away from the Middle East through direct investment by state-controlled companies in oil and gas fields in Russia, the Caucasus, and Central Asia.[66] In 2010, most of its oil imports came from the Middle East (18 percent from Saudi Arabia, 11 percent from Iran, and the remaining 34 percent from other countries in the Middle East such as Iraq, Kuwait, and the United Arab Emirates).[67]

So far, India's investment in Russian oil and gas developments has been modest. As of June 30, 2009, Indian investment stood at US$1.2 billion, mainly directed toward oil and gas projects. This includes the investment of US$2.2 billion (20 percent equity) in Sakhalin I by the state-owned Oil and Natural Gas Corporation (ONGC).[68] Its subsidiary, ONGC Videsh Ltd. (OVL), also purchased in 2008 for US$2.1 billion the Imperial Energy Corporation PLC, a company that produces oil in the Tomsk region.[69] OVL has made known its interest to invest in Sakhalin III and has conducted talks with Gazprom and Rosneft about investing in projects in Siberia, North Russia, and the Yamal Peninsula gas fields.[70] Further, in December 2010, the two countries signed an intergovernmental agreement on cooperation in oil and gas, while OVL and

Sistema also signed a framework agreement on cooperation in the hydrocarbon sector to encourage joint development of energy fields in Russia, India, and elsewhere.[71] This modest level of investment in Russian oil and gas projects by India is largely explained by geography. The Middle East is simply a much closer and therefore more economically viable source of energy resources.[72]

In terms of nuclear energy, however, cooperation between India and Russia has grown significantly since the Nuclear Suppliers Group waiver of September 2008. During the December 2008 visit to New Delhi by Russian president Medvedev, the two countries signed a nuclear cooperation agreement to provide four new nuclear power plants in Kundankulam, Tamil Nadu, per a memorandum of understanding agreed upon in January 2007. This was in addition to two other Russian reactors that were under construction at the same site. In March 2010, Russia and India signed a further nuclear cooperation agreement under which Russia would provide another sixteen nuclear reactors, six of which would be built by 2017.[73] India also signed a framework nuclear agreement with France in December 2010 under which the French nuclear energy company Areva would supply two nuclear reactors and twenty-five years' worth of fuel for around US$9.4 billion, with the potential to sell four more reactors.[74] Reactor sales by American firms have been stymied by India's civil liability laws that place liability for accidents with the supplier rather than the operator of nuclear plants throughout the reactor's service life. While US nuclear suppliers are privately owned, Russian and French nuclear corporations are state-owned and have been able to commercially bear the greater risk involved.

Overall, however, Russia has been given the greatest opportunity to assist India to achieve its nuclear power expansion plans to extend capacity from 4.8 gigawatts in 2011 to 60 gigawatts by 2032.[75] Under the 2008 cooperation agreement, Russia also agreed to provide a lifetime supply of nuclear fuel for the four reactors, as well as fuel for India's nuclear reactor at Tarapur for five years under a renewable contract. The fuel supply agreement does not specify any conditions under which fuel would be withheld, including the conduct of further nuclear tests by India. This is in contrast to the US domestic legal constraints on the US-Indian nuclear cooperation deal imposed by the Hyde Act, which requires an immediate end to nuclear trade should India undertake a nuclear test.[76] For many in the Indian nuclear establishment, Russia's willingness to undertake nuclear trade unconditionally entrenches the perception that it is the more trustworthy strategic partner whose friendship should be rewarded.

Apart from direct trade in oil, gas, and nuclear energy, the Russian relationship could potentially open up greater access to energy supplies from Central Asia for India, reducing its dependence on oil supplies from the Middle East traded by sea. China too is vulnerable to blockades or disruptions to Middle

Eastern energy supplies by sea but shares land borders with Kazakhstan, Kyrgyzstan, and Tajikistan, allowing it direct access to the resources of Central Asia. China has sought to build a "pan-Asian global energy bridge from Central Asia to Iran" that would link it "to the Middle East" by land,[77] with the 2006 Kazakhstan-China oil pipeline and the 2009 Turkmenistan-China gas pipeline (which involves Turkmenistan, Uzbekistan, and Kazakhstan) forming the first steps in this strategy.[78]

India has no land borders with any Central Asian state and must negotiate access for the purposes of trade with Pakistan and Afghanistan—the first being deeply unfriendly and the second highly unstable—or via the international pariah, Iran. Some measure of progress has been made with the signing of an intergovernmental framework agreement to construct a gas pipeline between Turkmenistan, Afghanistan, Pakistan, and India (known as the TAPI pipeline) in December 2011.[79] Given that the pipeline passes through unstable parts of Afghanistan and Baluchistan, it is highly unlikely that security over its route can be maintained, and therefore it is questionable whether the TAPI pipeline is in fact feasible.[80]

In these circumstances, Iran is seen to be the only truly viable land route to Central Asia that would not involve Afghanistan and Pakistan. With this in mind, India, Russia, and Iran signed a North-South Corridor agreement in 2000 to create a multimodal transport network (known as the International North-South Transport Corridor, or INSTC) connecting fourteen countries, with the main route connecting India to Iran, Azerbaijan, Kazakhstan, and Russia. The proposed route will reportedly reduce freight transport times to Russia by twenty to thirty days.[81] Since the project has languished for many years, in 2012 India took the initiative to kick-start it, despite US advocacy for its "New Silk Road" proposal that excludes Iran and concerted pressure on India to minimize its trade relations with Iran.[82] The fourteen stakeholder countries reaffirmed their interest in participating in the project in January 2012 and sent experts to meet in New Delhi in May 2012 to identify the remaining gaps in infrastructure development along the route, as well as establish a time frame for harmonizing customs procedures.[83] Russia could play a valuable role for India by using its still considerable influence over the Central Asian republics to persuade them to look favorably on the INSTC. Without this route, India cannot even begin to compete with China for access to Central Asia's resources and for trade in goods and services more generally.

So far Russia has used its influence on India's behalf to support its application to become an official observer of the SCO, which was successful in 2005, and publicly made the case for India's full membership in 2010.[84] For Russia, full membership for India would dilute the ability of China to displace it as the dominant player in the region. As mentioned earlier, China's ability to offer financial capital to develop energy deposits and rail and other transport infrastructure to Central Asian states directly challenges the monopoly on energy-supply routes that Russia has until recently maintained since the fall of the Soviet Union. Competing Indian capital for infrastructure development would attenuate the potential for China to dominate Central Asia's resources. Apart from this, India has shared interests with Russia and other members of the SCO to ensure that Islamic radicalism does not spread from Afghanistan or that political instability and separatist tendencies in Central Asia more generally do not sabotage the growing investment in energy pipelines and infrastructure in the region.[85] The enduring military and energy links between the two countries also make it highly unlikely that India would seek to undermine Russia's influence in Central Asia.

Military Codependence

The Indian military has been undergoing a process of modernization that accelerated after the Kargil conflict with Pakistan in 1999.[86] With a total military expenditure of US$48.9 billion, in 2011 India was the ninth largest military spender in the world and the largest arms importer in the world, importing US$3.5 billion in military equipment.[87] Russia has remained the supplier of choice in this modernization process, accounting for 77 percent of India's military imports from 2005 to 2011 despite increasing competition from other countries, with purchases being made for all three branches of its armed forces.[88] In turn, India remains Russia's biggest market for arms exports, representing 28 percent of all arms sales between 2005 and 2011.[89]

Russian military engagement of India since the Putin era began has been highly successful because it has been willing to provide reliable, state-of-the-art weaponry at competitive prices, with opportunities for technology transfer and joint production of weapon systems.[90] India's post–Cold War dependence on Russian arms is also explained by inertia in the Indian military establishment and the lower costs associated with training personnel to use upgrades of existing models. The consequence has been a series of significant Indian orders for Russian arms. Of note are two orders of a total of 640 T-90 main battle tanks in 2001 and 2007, with a combined value of over US$1 billion, as well as the purchase of 98 Su-30MK long-range fighter aircraft since 1996.[91] India reportedly plans to increase this to 230 by 2015 at a cost of around US$12 billion.[92] Both these tanks and a substantial portion of the aircraft have been produced in India under license, providing significant opportunities for technology transfer to India's own defense industry.

Further, Russia has been willing to supply high-technology arms to add to India's power-projection capabilities that no other state is willing to supply, a sign of the high level of trust between the two countries. This includes an Akula-II class nuclear-powered submarine (renamed the INS *Chakra*), which was delivered in January 2012 on a ten-year lease, and a refurbished aircraft carrier, *Admiral Gorshkov* (renamed the INS *Vikramaditya*), commissioned on November 16, 2013.[93] These purchases represent high levels of military technology that the United States, with its domestic legal constraints on high-technology transfers, would find difficult to supply.

Russia too has proved to be sensitive to India's concerns about arms sales to China. Although China has been the buyer of between one-quarter and one-half of Russia's military exports over the past twenty years, sales dropped from a peak of US$3.2 billion in 2005 to US$834 million in 2011, the last year for which we have reliable data, with indications that they declined further in 2012 and 2013.[94] This has been caused by two factors. First, China has improved its indigenous capacities to produce sophisticated military hardware and simply does not need Russian products to the same extent. Second, and more important for India, Russia has declined to provide China with the same level of technology that it supplies to India. Recent arms sales, including the sale of fifteen additional S-300 surface-to-air missiles in April 2010, consist of only Soviet-era technologies.[95] Russia's refusal to part with its most advanced weapon systems stems from its sensitivities to its partners, such as India, as well as regional players, such as the United States and Japan. Russia has also become concerned about China's lack of respect for intellectual property rights to military technology, with Russian analysts reporting "past instances when Chinese technicians copied Russian weapons systems and, after making slight adjustments, sold them to third parties."[96] Russia has thus come to view China as a potential competitor in the military hardware market.

By contrast India has proved to be more trustworthy in this regard, which goes some distance to explain Russia's willingness, as compared to other arms suppliers, to move beyond the buyer-seller relationship by proposing joint development of new weapon systems. Only India has been given the opportunity to sign a military-technical cooperation agreement with Russia in 2009, which will operate between 2011 and 2020.[97] The fruit of their joint labor has thus far consisted of the BrahMos cruise missile, which has been in use by India's armed forces since 2006, and the selection in 2007 of India to be Russia's development partner for a multirole transport aircraft and a fifth-generation fighter aircraft, with the production of the Indian version of the latter to begin in 2015.[98] It has been suggested that a lack of domestic capital has encouraged Russia's openness to joint development and production with India, but regardless of possible pragmatic motives, without a high level of trust between the two states the joint development of high technologies would not be possible.[99]

The other area of significant high-technology engagement between the two countries is space research. Space research cooperation began in the 1970s with Russian assistance in the development and manufacture of Indian satellites, as well as the use of Soviet launchers to deliver these satellites into space. Since then, cooperation in the field of launchers has continued, with the cryogenic engine controversy of the 1990s part of this, but is likely to be curtailed given that India has now developed its own indigenous commercial Polar Satellite Launch Vehicle in direct competition with Russia's own commercial satellite launch services.[100] Since 2005, the Russian Federal Space Agency (Roscosmos) and the Indian Space Research Organisation have signed a number of space cooperation agreements that have so far resulted in activities such as the launch of a jointly built youth satellite for space science studies and work on a joint lunar exploration mission—Chandrayaan-2—due to be launched in 2014.

The implications of India's and Russia's 2005 agreement on the joint use of Russia's Global Navigation Satellite System (GLONASS), the Russian competitor to the US Global Positioning System, are also significant.[101] Under this agreement, India will launch GLONASS-M satellites using its own Geosynchronous Satellite Launch Vehicle and will jointly develop GLONASS-K satellites.[102] Both countries have "expressed mutual interest" in jointly developing commercial satellite-navigation equipment based on GLONASS.[103] India has also signed an agreement with the European Union for access to its Galileo system.[104] However, while Russia has signed access agreements with other states, it has reserved access to GLONASS for military applications only for India.[105] A formal agreement giving India access to the high-precision signals of GLONASS was signed in New Delhi in December 2010.[106] Here again Russia's offer of joint development of high technology in an area with very sensitive military applications demonstrates its view of India as a highly trusted partner, with common interests extending for the long term.

For Russia, military engagement is essential in order to maintain its dominant position as the supplier of choice in India's defense modernization drive and to defend this position against emerging competitors, particularly Israel, the United States, Britain, and France. The newfound competitiveness of the Indian market was made plain by the Indian government's decision to reject US and Russian bids for the estimated US$11 billion multirole combat aircraft contract and to select the French Dassault Rafale in January 2012.[107] India has stated that the decision is based purely on cost and technical fit with India's requirements.[108] However, Russia's failure to deliver the *Admiral Gorshkov* aircraft carrier on time and on budget has dented its reputation for reliability and caused many in India's Ministry of Defence to question the wisdom of being overly reliant on one arms supplier.

The *Admiral Gorshkov* was promised to be delivered by August 2008 but was only commissioned in November 2013, at a cost of US$2.33 billion (or more), as opposed to the US$947 million refit agreed upon in the original contract.[109] This has left India without an aircraft carrier for a year, as China pushes ahead with its refurbishment of the ex-Russian aircraft carrier *Varyag* (purchased from Ukraine), which took its first sea trial in August 2011.[110] India has had little choice but to accept the price revision, given the lack of alternative aircraft carriers and the large sunk costs already invested in the project. While Russia has so far been India's only partner in the joint development of high technology, any complacence on Russia's part will have been rattled by recent US statements offering India the carrot of closer high-technology cooperation. In July 2012, Deputy Secretary of Defense Ashton B. Carter stated in New Delhi that the United States "want[s] to be India's highest-quality and most trusted long-term supplier of technology" and that new "efforts will help us respond more rapidly to India's requests for US equipment and systems—particularly for more advanced technologies."[111]

While this statement portends a potential future erosion of India's dependence on Russian arms, for the United States to become high-technology partners with India the Barack Obama administration needs to complete the difficult task of removing the plethora of technology-transfer restrictions contained within domestic legislation. On a broader strategic level, Russia has demonstrated during the course of over forty years of relations that it is a reliable friend in times of crisis, while the United States has supported India's erstwhile enemies and led the world in creating a technology-denial regime directed against it. While the US-Indian nuclear cooperation agreement and progress on defense relations since then has been a circuit breaker in bilateral relations between the two countries, there is still significant skepticism, particularly among the old guard within the defense establishment, that high-technology cooperation with the United States will come with strings attached that will inevitably encroach on India's jealously guarded strategic autonomy. Until these perceptions are dispelled, it is difficult to see the United States displacing Russia as India's primary defense and strategic partner.

Conclusion: An Enduring Relationship?

India and Russia have a long history of deep engagement that, apart from a brief interlude, has remained unbroken for more than forty years. The bilateral relationship has proved to be enduring, surviving the end of the Cold War, the rise of US hegemony, and now the emerging global power shift toward Asia.

The steadfastness of this relationship is underpinned by a mix of historical sentiment, pure self-interest and pragmatism, and converging values that mirror the fact that they are both significant powers trying to oppose Western impositions on their strategic autonomy. Indeed, a key factor behind the success of the relationship is an understanding and acceptance by the Soviet Union, and now Russia, that relations with India would need to proceed on the basis of equality. As A. K. Damodaran writes, "non-alignment [was] nothing more or less than a firm assertion of sovereignty by the post-colonial state."[112] While India has abandoned nonalignment, it continues to pursue the goal of maximizing strategic autonomy by maintaining multiple alignments short of alliances, of which its partnership with Russia is one. The Russian relationship is certainly the most "special" of all India's strategic partnerships, and Moscow has worked very hard to keep it that way.

For Russia, keeping up its engagement of India is essential to ensure that India—a recognized rising great power in Asia—remains a friend with the ability to act independently of the influence of other less friendly great powers, particularly the United States and China. Russia has sought to engage India because the two countries' interests converge ideationally and strategically, even though India is an emerging great power at a time when Russia is a great power fighting decline. Their common positions on normative principles underpinning international order reflect both states' desire to defend their strategic independence in the face of US hegemony, as well as their ability to manage problems of ethnic separatism without outside intervention. Cooperation in Central Asia stems from mutual interests in containing the spread of fundamentalist Islamic terrorism and instability from the region, as well as shared suspicions of China, whose rise will inevitably impinge upon their respective spheres of influence in Central and South Asia. In contrast, neither Russia nor India has much to fear in the medium to long term from the good fortunes of each other. Just as they have combined with the fear of US dominance in mind, geostrategic cooperation in Central Asia effectively preserves and defends against the ability of a fully risen China to restrict their strategic autonomy in the future. This mutual interest is a medium- to long-term one and as such will ensure that close relations will continue for some time.

In pragmatic terms, the substantial energy and military cooperation between the two countries serves mutual interests that also bind the two together for the medium to long term. The recent reversals in Russia's economic fortunes and political influence are largely due to its emergence as an energy superpower, with India being a major export market, particularly in nuclear energy. On the defense front, India's significant military modernization program has sustained and grown Russia's military industrial complex. From India's perspective, energy security is key to sustaining the high levels of economic growth that have already begun to lift millions out of poverty and is essential to the emergence of India as a great power in years to come. Russia is able to assuage India's energy security needs as a source of oil and nuclear power and to assist in gaining access to the energy resources of Central Asia. On a broader military-strategic level, Russia's decision to offer India partnership in joint development of high-level defense and space technologies has cemented the depth of the relationship between the two countries and demonstrated the assessment that both share long-term interests and have no real conflicts of interest.

Economic engagement in areas outside of defense and energy trade has been the least successful aspect of the relationship between the two countries, largely because of a lack of efficient and cost-effective trade routes, the significant decline in people-to-people contacts between the two countries (particularly in education), and the private sectors' resultant lack of understanding of the comparative advantages and business culture of the respective economies. The potential opening of the INSTC, the accession of Russia to the WTO, and progress toward the negotiation of a CECA between the two countries should assist in boosting bilateral trade. Baleful portents of the demise of the relationship based on this lack of substantial overall bilateral trade are, however, overplayed. Russia has been able to successfully engage India diplomatically, strategically, economically (in defense and energy trade), and militarily because of the existence of a deep level of historical trust developed over the last forty years, a strong compatibility of strategic and geopolitical interests, and an absence of direct conflict of interests that will endure for the medium to long term.

Notes

1. Vojtech Mastny, "The Soviet Union's Partnership with India," *Journal of Cold War Studies* 12, no. 3 (2010): 50.
2. Peter J. S. Duncan, *The Soviet Union and India*, Chatham House Papers (London and New York: Routledge, 1989), 4, 5.
3. Mastny, "Soviet Union's Partnership," 68; Jyotsna Bakshi, *Russia and India: From Ideology to Geopolitics, 1947–1998* (Delhi: Dev Publication, 1999), 108; and Duncan, *Soviet Union and India*, 20.
4. Bakshi, *Russia and India*, 117, and Duncan, *Soviet Union and India*, 20.
5. Mastny, "Soviet Union's Partnership," 71.
6. Bakshi, *Russia and India*, 132–33, and ibid., 75.
7. Bakshi, *Russia and India*, 157, 183, 189.
8. Duncan, *Soviet Union and India*, 3.
9. Robert C. Horn, *Soviet-Indian Relations: Issues and Influence* (New York: Praeger, 1982), 7, 8, and Bakshi, *Russia and India*, 171, 188.
10. Bakshi, *Russia and India*, 132–33, 157.

11. Anita Inder Singh, "India's Relations with Russia and Central Asia," *International Affairs* 71, no. 1 (1995): 70.

12. Ibid., 72.

13. Indian Department of Commerce, "Total Trade: Top n Countries," Export Import Data Bank, http://commerce.nic.in/eidb/iecnttopnq.asp (accessed October 22, 2012).

14. Sreemati Ganguli, *Indo-Russian Relations: The Making of a Relationship, 1992–2002* (Delhi: Shipra Publications, 2009), 117.

15. Ibid., 122.

16. Singh, "India's Relations with Russia and Central Asia," 73.

17. Ganguli, *Indo-Russian Relations*, 125.

18. Yong Deng, "Remolding Great Power Politics: China's Strategic Partnerships with Russia, the European Union, and India," *Journal of Strategic Studies* 30, nos. 4–5 (2007): 875.

19. See Deborah Welch Larson and Alexei Shevchenko, "Status Seekers: Chinese and Russian Responses to US Primacy," *International Security* 34, no. 4 (2010): 79–80, 81.

20. Ganguli, *Indo-Russian Relations*, 112.

21. Thomas Ambrosio, "The Third Side? The Multipolar Strategic Triangle and the Sino-Indian Rapprochement," *Comparative Strategy* 24, no. 5 (2005): 401.

22. Bakshi, *Russia and India*, 276, 279, and Ganguli, *Indo-Russian Relations*, 131.

23. Larson and Shevchenko, "Status Seekers," and Bobo Lo, *Vladimir Putin and the Evolution of Russian Foreign Policy*, Chatham House Papers (Oxford: Blackwell Publishing for Royal Institute of International Affairs, 2003), 65–88.

24. Declaration on Strategic Partnership between the Republic of India and the Russian Federation, October 3, 2000.

25. Delhi Declaration on Further Consolidation of Strategic Partnership between Republic of India and the Russian Federation, December 4, 2002.

26. Indian Ministry of External Affairs, "India-Russia Relations," December 2012, www.mea.gov.in/Portal/ForeignRelation/Russia_-DEC_2012.pdf (accessed September 17, 2013).

27. Delhi Declaration.

28. Declaration of the Russian Federation and the Republic of India on Global Challenges and Threats to World Security and Stability, November 12, 2003.

29. Quoted in Ambrosio, "The Third Side?," 405.

30. See, for example, "Full Text of Joint Communique of Russian, Indian, Chinese Foreign Ministers' Meeting," April 14, 2012, http://news.xinhuanet.com/english/china/2012-04/14/c_122980038. htm (accessed October 22, 2012).

31. "Libya Attacks Criticised by Arab League, China, Russia and India," *The Telegraph*, March 21, 2011.

32. "US Wants 'More Active' India in Afghanistan," *The Express Tribune with the International Herald Tribune*, June 5, 2012.

33. "NATO Fails to Gain Russia Aid in Afghanistan," *BBC News*, December 17, 2009, http://news.bbc.co.uk/2/hi/8418292.stm (accessed October 22, 2012), and Ilya Arkhipov, "Russia Ready to Step Up Afghan Economic Aid, Putin Tells Karzai," *Bloomberg*, June 8, 2012, www.bloomberg.com/news/2012-06-07/russia-ready-to-step-up-afghan-economic-aid-putin-tells-karzai.html (accessed October 22, 2012).

34. "CSTO's Rapid-Reaction Force to Equal NATO's—Medvedev," *RiaNovosti*, February 4, 2009, http://en.rian.ru/russia/20090204/119984654.html (accessed October 22, 2012), and Roger N. McDermott, "CSTO Prepares for Post-2014 Afghanistan," *Central Asia-Caucasus Institute Analyst*, June 27, 2012, www.cacianalyst.org/?q=node/5805/print (accessed October 22, 2012).

35. Indian Prime Minister's Office, "Joint Statement Furthering the India-Russia Strategic Partnership to Meet the Challenges of a Changing World," press release, December 16, 2011, http://pmindia.gov.in/press-details.php?nodeid=1335 (accessed November 6, 2012).

36. Indian Ministry of External Affairs, "Joint Statement: Celebrating a Decade of the India-Russian Federation Strategic Partnership and Looking Ahead," December 21, 2010.

37. Jagannath P. Panda, "India's New Look at Central Asia Policy: A Strategic Review," in *Mapping Central Asia: Indian Perceptions and Strategies*, ed. Marlène Laruelle and Sébastien Peyrouse (Farnham, UK: Ashgate, 2011), 119.

38. Deng, "Remolding Great Power Politics," 868.

39. Ibid.

40. "China and Russia Conduct Joint Military Exercises," *China View*, July 20, 2009, http://news.xinhuanet.com/english/2009–07/20/content_11736802.htm (accessed October 22, 2012), and "China and Russia Launch Naval Exercises in Yellow Sea," *BBC News Asia*, April 22, 2012, www.bbc.co.uk/news/world-asia-17803624 (accessed October 22, 2012).

41. Deng, "Remolding Great Power Politics," 870–71.

42. Ibid., 869, and Peter Baker, "A Tense Divide in Russia's Far East," *Washington Post*, July 29, 2003.

43. Deng, "Remolding Great Power Politics," 870.

44. Stephen Blank, "At a Dead End: Russian Policy and the Russian Far East," *Demokratizatsiya* 17, no. 2 (2009): 124.

45. Gabriel Gatehouse, "Russia's Far East Looks to China," *BBC News*, June 5, 2007, http://news.bbc.co.uk/2/hi/europe/6713509.stm (accessed October 22, 2012), and ibid., 125.

46. James MacHaffie, "China's Role in Central Asia: Security Implications for Russia and the United States," *Comparative Strategy* 29, no. 4 (2010): 374.

47. Deng, "Remolding Great Power Politics," 879.

48. Lavina Lee, "The Indian Nuclear Energy Programme: The Quest for Independence," in *Nuclear Energy Development in Asia: Problems and Prospects*, ed. Xu Yi-Chong (Basingstoke, UK: Palgrave Macmillan, 2011), 74, 76.

49. Mohan Malik, "India and China: As China Rises, India Stirs," in *Indian Foreign Policy in a Unipolar World*, ed. Harsh V. Pant (New Delhi: Routledge, 2009), 175.

50. Jonathan Holslag, "The Persistent Military Security Dilemma between China and India," *Journal of Strategic Studies* 32, no. 6 (2009): 818, 819–21, and "A Himalayan Rivalry," *The Economist*, August 21, 2010, 17.

51. Lee, "The Indian Nuclear Energy Programme," 77.

52. Malik, "India and China," 171.

53. Hong Zhao, "India and China: Rivals or Partners in Southeast Asia?" *Contemporary Southeast Asia* 29, no. 1 (2007): 130–31, and ibid., 181.

54. Malik, "India and China," 172; Ambrosio, "The Third Side?," 404; and Harsh V. Pant, "China Tightens the Screws on India," *Far Eastern Economic Review* 172, no. 7 (2009): 38.

55. Jing-Dong Yuan, "The Dragon and the Elephant: Chinese-Indian Relations in the 21st Century," *Washington Quarterly* 30, no. 3 (2007): 136.

56. Indian Ministry of External Affairs, "Joint Statement: Celebrating a Decade."

57. Indian Department of Commerce, "Total Trade: Top n Countries," and EU Director General, "Russia: EU Bilateral Trade and Trade with the World," March 21, 2012, using an exchange rate of US$1 = 0.77, which was the average exchange rate for 2010.

58. Embassy of India in Moscow, "Overview of India-Russia Economic Cooperation," http://indianembassy.ru/index.php?option = com_content&view = article&id = 705&Item id = 705&lang = en (accessed August 10, 2012).

59. Pramitpal Choudhuri, "From Russia with Profit," *Hindustan Times*, December 23, 2010.

60. Ibid.

61. "Report of the India-Russia Joint Study Group," Moscow-New Delhi, 2007, www .commerce.nic.in/publications/Report_India_Russia_Joint...Study_Group_10_9_2007.pdf ?id = 15 (accessed October 22, 2012).

62. "Strains on Indian Government Grow after Sharp Economic Slowdown," *New York Times*, May 31, 2012.

63. "India," CIA World Fact Book, www.cia.gov/library/publications/the-world-fact book/geos/in.html (accessed October 22, 2012), and India Government, Planning Commission, *Eleventh Five Year Plan 2007–12: Volume I: Inclusive Growth* (New Delhi: Oxford University Press, 2008), 15.

64. Indian Government, Planning Commission, *Eleventh Five Year Plan 2007–12: Volume I*, table 13.3, 268, and India Ministry of Petroleum and Natural Gas, Economic Division, "Basic Statistics on Indian Petroleum and Natural Gas: 2010–11," October 2011, table 17, 18, http://petroleum.nic.in/petstat.pdf (accessed October 22, 2012).

65. "Russia," CIA World Fact Book, www.cia.gov/library/publications/the-world-fact book/geos/rs.html (accessed October 22, 2012).

66. Harsh V. Pant, *Contemporary Debates in Indian Foreign and Security Policy: India Negotiates Its Rise in the International System* (New York: Palgrave Macmillan, 2008), 155.

67. Energy Information Administration, "India: Country Analysis Brief," November 21, 2011, www.eia.gov/countries/cab.cfm?fips = IN (accessed October 22, 2012).

68. T. S. Subramanian, "Sakhalin Success," *Frontline* 23, no. 26 (December 30, 2006–January 12, 2007), www.hindu.com/fline/fl2326/stories/20070112001708900.htm (accessed October 22, 2012), and Embassy of India, Moscow, "Overview of India-Russia Cooperation."

69. Sergei Lavrov, "Russia and India: A Decade of Strategic Partnership," *International Affairs (Moscow)* 57, no. 1 (2011): 7; Mikhail Rapota, "Trade and Investment Cooperation between Russia and India," Embassy of the Russian Federation in the Republic of India, http://rusembassy.in/index.php?option = com_content&view = article&id = 96&Itemid = 107&lang = en (accessed September 1, 2011); and "India, Russia Can Share Innovations and Technologies: Envoy," *Russia & India Report*, August 15, 2011, http://indrus.in/articles/

2011/08/15/india_russia_can_share_innovations_and_technologies_envoy_12866.html (accessed October 22, 2012).

70. James Lamont and James Fontanella-Khan, "India's ONGC and Russia in Energy Pact Talks," *Financial Times*, March 11, 2010.

71. "India, Russia Can Share Innovations and Technologies."

72. Ambassador P. P. Shukla, Vivekananda International Foundation, New Delhi, conversation with author, August 1, 2012.

73. "Russia Signs India Nuclear Reactor Deal," *BBC News*, March 12, 2010, http://news.bbc.co.uk/2/hi/8561365.stm (accessed November 7, 2012).

74. Amol Sharma, "France, India Sign Pacts," *Wall Street Journal*, December 5, 2010, and "Nicolas Sarkozy and Manmohan Singh in Nuclear Deal," *BBC News*, December 6, 2010, www.bbc.co.uk/news/world-south-asia-11923836 (accessed October 22, 2012).

75. Indian Ministry of Power, "Power Sector at a Glance: All India," July 31, 2011, www.powermin.nic.in/indian_electricity_scenario/introduction.htm (accessed October 22, 2012), and World Nuclear Association, "Nuclear Power in India," updated September 2011, www.world-nuclear.org/info/inf53.html (accessed October 22, 2011).

76. Peter Crail, "Russia, India Ink Nuke Cooperation Deal," *Arms Control Today*, January–February 2009, www.armscontrol.org/act/2009_01-02/russiaindiacoop (accessed October 22, 2012).

77. Pant, *Contemporary Debates*, 16.

78. Bruce Pannier, "New Turkmen-China Pipeline Breaks Russia's Hold over Central Asian Gas," *Radio Free Europe Radio Liberty*, December 14, 2009, www.rferl.org/content/TurkmenistanChina_Gas_Pipeline_To_Open/1903108.html (accessed October 22, 2012).

79. Catherine A. Fitzpatrick, "Turkmenistan Keeps the Balls in the Air on Trans-Caspian, TAPI Pipelines," *Natural Gas Europe*, March 27, 2012.

80. Robert M. Cutler, "Turkmenistan-Afghanistan-Pakistan-India Gas Pipeline Gets Official Four-Way Go-Ahead," *Central Asia-Caucasus Institute Analyst*, January 19, 2011.

81. Indrani Bagchi, "India to Spread Tentacles into Central Asia via Iran," *Times of India*, March 13, 2012.

82. Rebecca Byerly, "Why India Is Trying to Expand Trade with Iran," *Christian Science Monitor*, March 30, 2012.

83. Sandeep Dikshit, "Despite US Opposition, Iran to Be Transport Hub for North-South Corridor," *The Hindu*, May 31, 2012.

84. "Russia Backs India's Case for Membership of the SCO," *Times of India*, June 12, 2010, and Lavrov, "Russia and India," 4.

85. Andrew D. Brunatti and David M. Malone, "Fading Glories? India's Relations with Western Europe and Russia," *International Relations* 24, no. 3 (2010): 359.

86. Deepa M. Ollapally, "India and Russia: Renewing the Relationship," in Pant, *Indian Foreign Policy in a Unipolar World*, 196.

87. SIPRI, "Background Paper on SIPRI Military Expenditure Data, 2011," April 17, 2012, www.sipri.org/research/armaments/milex (accessed August 30, 2012) and http://portal.sipri.org/publications/pages/transfer/tiv-data (accessed February 15, 2014)

88. SIPRI Arms Transfer Database, "TIV of Arms Exports to India, 2005–2011," http://portal.sipri.org/publications/pages/transfer/tiv-data (accessed February 15, 2014).

89. SIPRI Arms Transfer Database, "TIV of Arms Exports from Russia, 2005–2011," http://armstrade.sipri.org/armstrade/html/export_values.php (accessed November 7, 2012).

90. Ollapally, "India and Russia," 196, and Rajiv Sikri, *Challenge and Strategy: Rethinking India's Foreign Policy* (New Delhi: Sage, 2009), 158.

91. "Indian Army Wants to Add Another 1,000 T-90S Tanks by 2020," *Defense Industry Daily*, August 20, 2008, www.defenseindustrydaily.com/indian-army-wants-to-add-another-1000-t90s-tanks-by-2020-updated-02697/ (accessed October 22, 2012).

92. "Russia's Su-30 Fighter to Become World's Most Exported Jet," *Pravda,* July 13, 2009.

93. "Russian-built Nuclear Submarine Joins Indian Navy," *BBC News*, April 4, 2012, www.bbc.co.uk/news/world-asia-india-17606829 (accessed November 7, 2012), and "All Six Scorpene Subs Will Be Delivered from 2015 to 2018, Says Mazagon Dock Chief," *Times of India*, August 23, 2011.

94. SIPRI Arms Transfer Database, "TIV of Arms Exports from Russia, 2005–2011."

95. Richard Weitz, "Why China Snubs Russia Arms," *The Diplomat*, April 5, 2010.

96. Ibid.

97. Sikri, *Challenge and Strategy*, 158, and Lavrov, "Russia and India," 8.

98. Sikri, *Challenge and Strategy*, 158; Ollapally, "India and Russia," 199; and G. Ivashentsov, "India and Russia: Longstanding and Good Partners," *International Affairs (Moscow)* 56, no. 4 (2010): 64.

99. Ollapally, "India and Russia,"196.

100. Charlotte Mathieu, "Assessing Russia's Space Cooperation with China and India: Opportunities and Challenges for Europe," *Acta Astronautica* 66, nos. 3–4 (2010): 358.

101. Lavrov, "Russia and India," 9.

102. Mathieu, "Assessing Russia's Space Cooperation," 358.

103. Indian Prime Minister's Office, "Joint Statement Furthering the India-Russia Strategic Partnership."

104. Anuradha M. Chenoy, "India and Russia: Allies in the International Political System," *South Asian Survey* 15, no. 1 (2008): 58.

105. Ivashentsov, "India and Russia," 66.

106. Sandeep Joshi, "India to Get Access to GLONASS," *The Hindu*, December 22, 2010.

107. "IAF to Buy 126 Medium Multi-Role Combat Aircraft," *The Hindu*, July 1, 2012, and "India's M-MRCA Fighter Competition: Is the Deal in Trouble?" *Defense Industry Daily*, September 5, 2012, www.defenseindustrydaily.com/mirage-2000s-withdrawn-as-indias-mrca-fighter-competition-changes-01989/ (accessed October 22, 2012).

108. Nitin Gokhale, "Behind India's US Fighter Snub," *The Diplomat*, May 27, 2011.

109. "Defence Buys Lack Planning, Price Negotiations: CAG," *Times of India*, September 9, 2011; "INS Vikramaditya: Waiting for Gorshkov . . . ," *Defense Industry Daily*, August 10, 2011, www.defenseindustrydaily.com/ins-vikramaditya-may-hit-delay-cost-increases-03283/ (accessed November 7, 2012); and "INS Vikramaditya Undergoing Sea Trials," *The Hindu*, June 29, 2012.

110. "China's Aircraft Carrier 'Varyag' Sets Out for Sea Trial," *International Business Times*, August 10, 2011.

111. Ashton B. Carter, "Towards a Joint Vision for US-India Defense Cooperation," Remarks by the US Deputy Secretary of Defense at the Confederation of Indian Industry, New Delhi, July 23, 2012, http://chennai.usconsulate.gov/remarkashtonbcarter_120723.html (accessed November 7, 2012).

112. A. K. Damodaran, *Beyond Autonomy: India's Foreign Policy* (Mumbai: Somaiya Publications, 2000), 162.

CHAPTER 5

INDIA AND CHINA

Strategic Engagements in Central Asia

Louise Merrington

DISCUSSIONS OF INDIAN and Chinese interactions in Asia commonly focus on East Asia and the Indian Ocean. The vast Central Asian interior to the west, however, is becoming an increasingly important strategic playground for both countries. Home to vast reserves of oil and natural gas, as well as Islamist militants and unstable, dictatorial regimes, the five former Soviet Central Asian republics (CARs) of Kazakhstan, Kyrgyzstan, Tajikistan, Turkmenistan, and Uzbekistan are slowly being factored into both Indian and Chinese foreign policy, particularly in the context of energy security. How China and India approach this region, however, is quite different. While China has been investing heavily in Central Asian infrastructure—particularly in the energy sector—since the fall of the Soviet Union in 1991, India has come relatively late to the "New Great Game" and, apart from some ad hoc investment, has only recently begun to articulate a regional strategy with the unveiling of its 2012 Connect Central Asia policy. India has more natural advantages in the region than China: It is seen as a benign power without expansionist tendencies, has maintained a relatively good relationship with the Soviet Union/Russia throughout the twentieth century, and has significant cultural capital—mostly thanks to Bollywood—but so far has not managed to capitalize on these in any meaningful way.

This chapter compares and contrasts Indian and Chinese engagement strategies in Central Asia, drawing on a series of interviews conducted with Indian and Chinese Central Asian analysts, diplomats, policymakers, and strategists. It not only seeks to identify the strengths and weaknesses of the two countries' strategies in terms of engaging the CARs but also explores how China and India are engaging each other in the region. One of the most interesting aspects of Chinese and Indian relations in Central Asia at present is that although there are areas where their interests overlap significantly—particularly the energy sector and counterterrorism—and have the potential to result in either cooperation or competition, at this stage neither is occurring to a substantial extent. There have been isolated instances of both cooperation and rivalry, but significant differences in capacity and geography mean that China has been pursuing its interests in the region much more aggressively than India. Consequently the two countries are essentially following parallel agendas, in spite of their overlapping interests.

Energy and Afghanistan: Indian Interests in Central Asia

The imminent withdrawal of the NATO-led International Security Assistance Force (ISAF) from Afghanistan in 2014 has once again turned the spotlight on Central Asia. India, thanks to its conflict with Pakistan, has maintained an interest in Afghan stability for many years and is one of the largest donors to the reconstruction effort. It is also now realizing that engagement in the wider Central Asian region is becoming increasingly important.

In terms of strategic policy, the importance of Central Asia to India has been a matter of some debate. India's major obstacle to many forms of regional engagement is geographic—with no direct border, its land access is through either Pakistan/Afghanistan or by sea and then up through Iran—and many analysts have argued that any potential benefits are outweighed by these difficulties. There has historically also been a lack of political will in India to engage with Central Asia. Although this appears to be changing, with the announcement in June 2012 of India's comprehensive Connect Central Asia policy, it remains to be seen how effectively this can be implemented, as India's history of engagement with the region is one of missed opportunities.

Unlike China, which began developing interests in Central Asian resources from the mid-1990s, India has only recently begun its first forays into the Central Asian hydrocarbon sector. In January 2009, a deal was signed by the Indian state-owned oil and gas company ONGC Mittal Energy Ltd. (a joint venture of OVL[1] and Mittal Investments Sarl[2]) and KazMunaiGas (the national oil company of Kazakhstan), which will lead to the start of oil exploration in the Satbayev block of the Kazakhstan oil and gas sector of the North Caspian Sea.[3] Similarly, in April 2008, India and Turkmenistan signed a memorandum of understanding for cooperation in the oil and gas sector, but India is also looking to cooperate in other areas, including education, hence the establishment of an information technology center at Ashgabat State University, which would complement the research center already in operation at the Ashgabat Polytechnic Institute.[4] This is just one example of how India is attempting to deploy "soft power" in a bid to facilitate positive relations with the Central Asian states, which will in turn smooth its way into the energy sector. Politically India is interested in Central Asia not just for its hydrocarbon resources but also because it sees a need to counter Pakistani influence in the region.

Indian engagement with the CARs faces two major obstacles. The first is geographical: After Partition in 1947 and the creation of Pakistan, India lost its overland access to Afghanistan and the CARs, which has meant the distribution of Central Asian resources is much more difficult for India than for China. The second problem, however, is political: Historically Indian policy toward Central Asia has been, and continues to be, primarily reactive rather than proactive. This was evident in India's dealings with the newly created CARs in the immediate aftermath of the Soviet Union's collapse, which is now widely regarded as a missed opportunity for capitalizing on the large amount of goodwill India has and for setting up sound investments in Central Asia. Nearly two decades on, as China, the United States, and Russia battle for energy resources and political influence, India is once again finding itself left behind. Former Indian ambassador to Uzbekistan and Central Asia–watcher M. K. Bhadrakumar notes:

> The hard reality is that apart from the common bonds of history and despite having a head start over most other regional powers—India was one of only four countries permitted by the Soviet authorities to maintain a consulate in Central Asia—India's presence remains thin on the ground in economic terms. Even in political terms, if a touchstone were to be applied, it is noteworthy that the Central Asian countries have chosen to back Japan's claim to be represented in an expanded UN Security Council. This is despite the Central Asian leaderships being uniformly comfortable that India has never moralized to them on the dynamics of democratization, human rights or globalization affecting their national life. The point is India has not put much money on the table in Central Asia.[5]

Opinions on the importance of Central Asia to Indian foreign policy, however, vary widely, with those who have worked in the region, such as Bhadrakumar, often considering it vital, while other analysts believe there are more pressing priorities. Some Indian strategists, such as former ambassador Ranjit Gupta—and to a lesser extent former foreign secretary–turned–national security adviser Shivshankar Menon—believe that any focus on Central Asia apart from Afghanistan is overblown because, simply, "you can't trump geography."[6] They believe that the countries that border Central Asia, such as China, will naturally have an enormous advantage—which means that India cannot compete on a level playing field—and that in terms of hydrocarbon resources, the Persian Gulf has always been, and will continue to be, India's major source of energy.[7]

This geography argument is one that often arises. Bhadrakumar, however, who was Indian ambassador to Uzbekistan during the 1990s and also served in Afghanistan, Kuwait, Pakistan, the Soviet Union, Sri Lanka, and Turkey, argues that India's view of Central Asia is always seen through the prism of Pakistan, and as a result the ongoing conflict in Afghanistan is seen primarily as a turf war with Pakistan. Consequently, in the immediate wake of the breakup of the Soviet Union, India's regional policy was ad hoc, and this is now affecting its relationships not only with the CARs but also with Russia. The reluctance of many Indian strategists to look beyond Afghanistan, however, has meant that this facet has been left largely underexplored.[8]

According to Bhadrakumar, India had a very close relationship with the Soviet Union but failed to notice the early trend of Russia's disenchantment with the West after the breakup of the Soviet Union. Russia is now gravitating toward China, whereas India might have consolidated the relationship in the wake of the Soviet Union's collapse. Bhadrakumar believes that China is very sensitive to the relationship between Russia and the West and therefore notices how rifts in this relationship can be exploited, such as through the development of the Shanghai Cooperation Organisation (SCO). The development of the region's only multilateral forum was aimed at complementing a strong program of bilateralism on behalf of the Chinese. During the 1990s, China sent carefully selected Soviet specialists and Russian speakers to Central Asia, who worked closely in tandem with the Russians so as to avoid ruffling Russian feathers. As a result, China built strong state-to-state relations, worked against terrorism and separatism, and then began to build strong commercial linkages.[9]

India's failure to become involved in the region at this crucial time, however, was simply the latest in a litany of missed diplomatic and economic opportunities. According to Bhadrakumar, India was always projected as a benign power by the Soviet Union (unlike China) and so had huge natural advantages in Central Asia, but it neglected this region. He believes that if there had been the political will in New Delhi, energy security problems that are now plaguing India, such as access routes and pipelines, could have been solved. However, unlike China, India had no engagement plan, in spite of active overtures from the CARs.[10]

Although it is true that India's failure to capitalize on its opportunities in the early 1990s means it is at a disadvantage in Central Asia today, direct access to the region is still through Pakistan and Afghanistan. The other option that tends to surface periodically is the possibility of an Indian-built pipeline from the CARs to Iran, from which oil could then be shipped to India, and it is possibly this to which Bhadrakumar is referring when he talks about solving access problems. Indeed, with this sort of access development in mind, India has already invested in the port development of Chabahar in Iran, discussed below.

Bhadrakumar argues that India knew the area was resource-rich and that there was an opportunity in the 1990s to exploit it. In the wake of the breakup of the Soviet Union and the subsequent exodus of industry from the CARs, the new nations were desperate to attract industry and investment to the region. In addition, during the 1990s, Russia urged India to get involved and stabilize the region. Although India gave some small credit relief—around US$5 million to US$10 million—this was minuscule compared to China's US$10 billion investment in the region. Bhadrakumar also argues that China knew there was an innate suspicion and hostility toward it from Central Asia, so it used Russia to help overcome this by establishing the SCO and adopted a harmonization policy with Russia so that the SCO supplemented bilateral relations. Twenty years later, China has extensive investment in most of the CARs, particularly Kazakhstan, including access to energy resources, which India cannot hope to match.[11]

Because India missed its initial opportunity in Central Asia, in some quarters there is now a feeling of futility in regard to the region. There is a sense that, because India is not able to compete with China, Russia, and the United States in terms of investment and because India does not share a border with any of the CARs, the region should not be given very high priority. Apart from Afghanistan, to which India has been one of the largest aid donors, contributing over US$1 billion, until recently there has been little political importance attached to Central Asia. The recent unveiling of the Connect Central Asia policy—which aims to build political, security, economic, and cultural cooperation between India and the CARs—may be an indication that this is changing; the policy is certainly ambitious.[12] Whether it can be fully realized, however—and whether this surge of proactive political will toward the region can continue—remains to be seen. But throughout history, India's destiny has been linked with the fluctuations of power in Central Asia, and it would be unwise for India to turn its back on the region.

Even with the political willpower to enhance engagement, India faces considerable obstacles. As noted above, access is by far the overriding problem that currently inhibits clear policy choices. There are two main potential access routes for India: directly overland through Pakistan and Afghanistan or by sea to Iran and then overland to the CARs. Both of these, however, are problematic.

The Pakistan-Afghanistan route has obvious security issues, and indeed the so-called Af-Pak problem is an entire area of policy in India that is relatively disconnected from Central Asian engagement. India's policy toward Afghanistan is essentially aimed at denying Pakistan "strategic depth" and preventing the establishment of Muslim fundamentalist regimes in the wider region that could give haven to terrorists with their sights set on India.[13] In this ambition, however, India may yet be thwarted by the difficult dynamics of South Asian politics, particularly the need of the United States to maintain its relationship with Pakistan in order to continue prosecuting the final stages of the conflict in Afghanistan and to combat Islamist terrorism.[14] At one stage the United States was concerned that increased Indian involvement in Afghanistan could cause Pakistan to retaliate by embracing the Taliban and Kashmir-focused terrorist groups such as Lashkar-e-Taiba more closely, although this now appears to be changing.[15] In his 2012 visit to New Delhi, Defense Secretary Leon Panetta spoke clearly of American wishes for greater Indian involvement in Afghanistan after the 2014 ISAF drawdown.[16]

Pakistani objections to Indian involvement in Afghanistan, however, do not play well in India, not least because Afghanistan is seen as part of South Asia rather than Central Asia (a distinction that was made official in 2007 when Afghanistan joined the South Asian Association for Regional Cooperation). Although grouping Afghanistan with South rather than Central Asia may seem arbitrary, it is important because of the divisions between South Asian and Central Asian policy in India, where there is more emphasis on the former. South Asia is seen unequivocally as India's strategic backyard, while there is considerable vacillation on the issue of Central Asia. In addition, the linkage of Afghanistan with South Asia is used in India to highlight the long history of cultural connections between India and Afghanistan and to justify strengthening the relationship.[17]

Aside from a solid and committed foreign policy toward Afghanistan, however, Indian attitudes toward Central Asia proper are ambiguous. As noted above, the standout problem is access. With the Pakistan-Afghanistan route unviable for the present, the other option for India is through Iran. This is problematic in that the two countries have a turbulent relationship, especially since India voted in support of a resolution in the International Atomic Energy Agency in 2009 urging Iran to halt construction of a nuclear enrichment plant and to confirm that it has no more clandestine facilities, although India stopped short of supporting sanctions.[18] The relationship seems to be warming, however, with the two countries holding talks in June 2012 on how to bypass Western sanctions on Iran's oil exports and deepen their trade relationship.[19] India must also balance its relationship with Iran against that with the United States, given the animosity that exists between those two countries. Normalization of Iranian-US relations would go a long way to strengthening the Indian-Iranian relationship.[20]

There have, however, been moves to develop a trade route between India, Iran, and Afghanistan (and by extension the CARs), starting with the Indian port development of Chabahar in Iran. The proposed trade route, first discussed at a trilateral meeting in 2003, would link Chabahar (Iran), Melak (Iran), Zaranj (Afghanistan), and Dilaram (Afghanistan).[21] Iran would finance an upgrade of the road between Chabahar and Melak and a bridge linking Melak and Zaranj, thereby shortening the Iran-Afghanistan route by around a thousand kilometers, while India would build the 218-kilometer Zaranj-Dilaram road. In January

2009, India completed this latter part of the project and handed the road over to Afghanistan. Although the trade corridor will be advantageous for India, Iran, and Afghanistan, the road was built at considerable human cost—6 Indian and 129 Afghan workers were killed in Taliban attacks.[22] The death toll from the Zaranj-Dilaram highway project highlights the danger of doing business in Afghanistan. Nevertheless, the Iran-Afghanistan option remains India's best hope of establishing reliable access to the CARs and by extension to the Caspian Sea region, the Caucasus, Russia, and Europe. Assuming that the access problem can be solved, however, there is still considerable discussion over the form that Indian engagement with the region should take.

Given India's increasing domestic demand for energy resources, it is only natural that hydrocarbon acquisition should be at the forefront of India's Central Asian policy. Increasingly, however, there is discussion of how India can diversify its economic interests in the region, for example by cooperating with the CARs in areas such as pharmaceuticals, textiles, information technology, tourism, infrastructure building, and food processing or by following China's lead and exercising greater soft power through education.[23] India has some educational partnerships with various CARs, but these could be expanded, exploiting India's natural advantages—such as English, information technology, and democracy—and the goodwill it has in the region.[24]

India's priorities in Central Asia are first Tajikistan, second Kazakhstan, and third Uzbekistan.[25] While this engagement has partly to do with energy resources, there is also a growing military aspect to relations, particularly with Tajikistan, which is home to India's first (and only) overseas air base, at Farkhor. India has also discussed establishing a second base at Ayni, also in Tajikistan, although this is not without its controversies.[26]

During the overthrow of the Taliban in Afghanistan in the early 2000s, India worked with Tajikistan to support the Northern Alliance, including renovating the Ayni air base.[27] There are, however, major questions about the status of the air base, which are not helped by the murky geopolitics of the region. Although originally intended to house a squadron of Indian MiG-29 fighter jets, eight years after the expected operational start date of 2006, the base remains idle. Speculation is rife that Tajikistan is facing pressure from Russia to restrict other foreign militaries' access.[28] Another issue, however, is one that is sadly familiar: When it began its tenure at Ayni, India did not have a clear plan for the facility and has consequently been unable to properly leverage the opportunity.[29]

As a result, India has no permanent military presence in Tajikistan, and its involvement is restricted to training, language assistance, and aircraft maintenance training. There is still debate about whether Indian foreign policy should be about power projection through overseas military bases, in the same vein as the United States.[30] Given that the Indian government continues to pursue

Tajikistan in relation to Ayni, however, it seems that this policy may be changing.

India's involvement in Central Asia is hampered not only by access but by indecision about whether to engage and what strategies to pursue. Although it faces more physical obstacles than China in terms of having no land border with a Central Asian state, which makes oil and gas transportation difficult, there is also disagreement within the Indian strategic community as to what degree of importance Central Asia should be given. Some analysts argue that India does not desperately need Central Asian oil and gas, and therefore the difficulties involved with finding a solution to the access problem outweigh any potential benefits,[31] while others believe that the region is vital to India's interests, not only because of India's energy needs but because of the geostrategic importance of the CARs in relation to Afghanistan, China, Russia, and the United States.[32] At this point, India's major strategic focus is Afghanistan and denying Pakistan any strategic depth, but this issue is not generally viewed in a greater Central Asian context, in spite of India's application to join the SCO. Thus there are stark differences between China's methodical regional policy and India's ad hoc, largely exchange-driven engagement. Although the access problem is a major barrier, it is not insurmountable, provided India decides what it wishes to achieve in the region and then figures out how to get it.

Pipelines, Politics, and Terrorism: Chinese Interests in Central Asia

Since the early 1990s, Central Asia has become a plank in China's multifaceted energy-security strategy, aimed at reducing its dependence on hydrocarbons transiting through the Malacca Strait. Consequently, China has invested heavily in oil and gas pipelines across the CARs and has poured money into other infrastructure projects in the region. Yet while this extensive investment has won China friends among the governments of the CARs—mainly because it gives them an alternative export market to Russia—it has also caused some tensions. On a local level there has been concern, especially in Kazakhstan, about the influx of Chinese workers and cheap Chinese goods, while internationally the growing Chinese influence in the region has alarmed both Russia and the United States and has significantly complicated regional geopolitics. China is thus walking a delicate line between pursuing its commercial and political objectives, principally using exchange strategies to meet immediate interests, and maintaining good bilateral and multilateral relations in the region with an eye to longer-term strategic objectives.

China is aggressively pursuing Central Asian oil and gas and has already built pipelines in Kazakhstan and Turkmenistan; indeed the Kazakhstan-Xinjiang pipeline idea was initiated as early as 1993.[33] Of all the CARs, Kazakhstan arguably faces both the biggest advantages—oil, gas, and other resources, including uranium, are abundant—and the biggest hurdles, in that its sheer size and location, away from international cargo transport routes, make it very difficult for the country to capitalize on its natural wealth.[34] For this reason, Kazakhstan has been particularly keen to build pipelines, and China offers not only an unquenchable market for Kazakh oil and gas but also a strong alternative customer to Russia. Although Kazakhstan has been independent for over twenty years, its old colonial master still poses political problems; Russia's controlling oil interests are often reluctant to sell on Kazakh oil, which would turn the isolated former Russian colony into a serious competitor in the international hydrocarbon market.[35] The Kazakhstan-China route is also relatively secure, particularly in comparison to other proposed routes, such as through Afghanistan. Thus, in spite of the enormous cost and construction difficulties involved in the Kazakhstan-China pipeline, the project is seen as highly advantageous to both countries and has been fully operational since July 2010.

China still produces most of its energy (70 percent) by burning coal, which accounts for much of the country's legendary pollution, and it is trying to diversify by developing the use of natural gas.[36] China is also attempting to break its "Malacca dilemma"—80 percent of China's energy imports pass through the Malacca Strait, which, bookended as it is by a US naval presence (a US Navy base in Changi, Singapore, and US Marine Corps and Navy fleet capabilities based at the British territory of Diego Garcia in the Indian Ocean), makes China strategically vulnerable.[37]

In addition to the Kazakhstan-China oil pipeline, China has also been pursuing both Kazakh and Turkmen natural gas, beginning a gas pipeline from Kazakhstan in 2008 that is part of the greater Trans-Caspian Gas Pipeline linking China with Turkmenistan, Uzbekistan, and Kazakhstan and is scheduled for completion in 2013.[38] In addition, a gas pipeline from the Tarim Basin gas fields in Xinjiang to Shanghai was completed in 2004, with half the US$5.2 billion cost paid by an international consortium led by the Shell Corporation.[39] It is this pipeline with which the Turkmenistan-China gas pipeline will connect. The Turkmenistan-China pipeline also provides Turkmenistan with a good alternative customer to Russia, as, like Kazakhstan, Turkmenistan has had disputes with Russia over gas shipments in the past. These disputes included a Russian freeze in 1997 on all shipments of Turkmen gas, which severely impacted Turkmenistan's economy.[40]

This international competition for energy resources and the politics it entails have been christened by some as the New Great Game, in reference to the nineteenth-century Anglo-Russian territorial competition in Central Asia known as the Great Game. China, Russia, and the United States are generally considered to be the major players in this latest iteration, with smaller powers such as India, Iran, and Turkey operating at a lower level, while Japan has also recently begun to initiate dialogue with the CARs. The CARs are attractive not just for their resources but also for their strategic position; for China and other countries with interests in the region, they provide a gateway to the Middle East through Iran and to Europe through Turkey and Russia.[41]

China is also interested in consolidating its political influence in the region in order to deal with what it perceives as the Uighur separatist issue in Xinjiang[42]—particularly as many Uyghur separatists have fled China to the CARs, mostly Kazakhstan and Kyrgyzstan—and to counter American hegemony.[43] Its leadership of the SCO can be seen as a means of achieving this, as the original "Shanghai Five" organization developed from security treaties signed between China and the CARs with the aim of clearly demarcating borders and controlling separatism.[44]

After the Soviet Union collapsed in December 1991, China was particularly quick to establish diplomatic relations with the new CARs. Relations were formalized with Uzbekistan (January 2, 1992), Kazakhstan (January 3, 1992), Tajikistan (January 4, 1992), Kyrgyzstan (January 5, 1992), and Turkmenistan (January 6, 1992). It was a triumph of proactive diplomacy. China saw the opportunity and capitalized swiftly on it, whereas India took a long time to decide how, why, and when it wanted to engage with the region. The immediate aftermath of the Soviet Union's demise provided extensive opportunities for the surrounding countries to engage in infrastructure projects because the CARs suddenly found themselves newly independent but with all their major Soviet infrastructure projects, funding, and personnel withdrawn to Russia. China was extremely proactive in laying the groundwork for good relations with the CARs. Twenty years later, this is starting to pay dividends in the form of pipeline projects and political groupings such as the SCO, which developed as a consequence of China's involvement in the region and evolved as a vehicle through which it could consolidate its influence.

The SCO is currently the only multilateral organization that includes the CARs and is focused on the region. It now comprises six member states (China, Kazakhstan, Kyrgyzstan, Russia, Tajikistan, and Uzbekistan; Turkmenistan declined to be involved as it pursues a policy of neutrality) and four observer states (India, Iran, Mongolia, and Pakistan).[45] China and Russia are the main drivers of the organization, and it is generally accepted that the SCO is a major part of Chinese foreign policy in the region, both in terms of building a new type of multilateralism and as a means of enhancing bilateral relations with Russia and the CARs.[46]

In the West, and particularly the United States, there have been competing views about how exactly to characterize or respond to the SCO, which in turn depend on whether it is perceived as part of a narrow exchange strategy of engagement designed to fulfill discrete interests or part of a wider catalytic strategy of shifting Central Asian states toward policies better and more permanently aligned with China. It has been called an "Asian NATO" at various points, mostly by the media, but this is now generally dismissed as inaccurate because although the SCO undertakes combined joint military and counterterrorism exercises, including the annual Peace Mission exercises, it is not a mutual assistance treaty in the same way that NATO is.[47] Indeed, the complex ethnic, tribal, and territorial issues in Central Asia mean that the SCO would not easily be able to intervene in a regional conflict—for example, Afghanistan after the US withdrawal.

At this point, the SCO is primarily an economic organization, although this is not without significant hiccups. The huge disparity in development between the SCO's richest members (China and Russia) and its poorest (Kyrgyzstan and Tajikistan) has meant that most trade between members is bilateral rather than multilateral. For its part, China has offered US$10 billion in soft/preferential loans to SCO member states.[48]

The question of membership expansion is another major issue presently confronting the SCO. The four observer states have been pushing for full membership, and although this looked unlikely when a freeze on all new memberships was announced, at the 2010 and 2011 meetings of the SCO the possibility that new members might be admitted began to be explored.[49] In the case of India and Pakistan, the question is highly political. China would happily extend full membership to its staunch ally Pakistan, but in return Russia would insist on membership for India, most likely as part of a hedging strategy aimed at preventing Chinese control of the SCO—and by extension its influence in Central Asia—from becoming too marked.

The issue of SCO membership is part of a larger debate on the impact that Chinese influence may have on the region. Russia sees China as encroaching on its traditional strategic backyard—although not to the extent that Russia is unprepared to work with China in the SCO—and the United States worries about extensive Chinese influence in the region and its relationship with Iran.[50] There is also the potential, however, for China to have a positive effect on the politics of the CARs, particularly in relation to staunching the seepage of radical Islam from Afghanistan and Pakistan into Central Asia and China. China's extensive investments in an Afghan copper mine, for example, mean that it now has "skin in the game"—an interest in keeping Islamic extremism away from its investments and ensuring stability.[51] Coupled with the fact that China has suffered a spate of kidnappings and killings of its citizens in Pakistan in recent years, it is possible that it may begin to pressure Pakistan—behind the scenes, at least—to crack down on extremism and help to stabilize the region.

In spite of the enormous advantages brought to Central Asia by Chinese involvement in the region, there are also some concerns about how extensive this involvement might become. These concerns are most notable in Kazakhstan, which, as well as bearing the bulk of Chinese investment, shares a sizeable border with China. The dispute over this border was resolved in 1998–99 and led to Kazakhstan retaining 57 percent of the disputed territory and China 43 percent, although the agreement still provoked criticism in Kazakhstan.[52] In spite of the resolution of the border dispute, however, there are still concerns in Kazakhstan about the growing influx of Chinese workers. These concerns were illustrated at the beginning of 2010 by protests in Kazakhstan claiming that China was flooding the Kazakh market with Chinese labor and Chinese products and was taking resources away from Kazakhstan and the other CARs, thus making them dependent on China. A Chinese rebuttal, however, argues that it adheres firmly to Kazakh labor laws, that there are very few illegal Chinese workers in the country, and that in addition to developing the resource sector, it is also helping to develop the agricultural and manufacturing sectors. Discontent remains, however, adding to the political instability that continues to plague the CARs.

In addition to these bilateral issues with the CARs, the other major powers operating in the region (the United States and Russia) are also concerned about growing Chinese influence. As well as being involved in the conflict in Afghanistan, the United States has several strategic assets in the region, such as the controversial air base at Manas in Kyrgyzstan, near Bishkek. Now known as the Transit Centre at Manas, it was opened in 2001 as a transit point for troops going to and from Afghanistan. After the Kyrgyz parliament voted to close it in 2009 due to its disagreement with the US government about rent, the contract was renegotiated for US$60 million, three times the previous amount. Unsettled about the impact of a major US presence in their spheres of influence, China and Russia have been pushing for several years for the base to be closed. In February 2009, when negotiations were taking place between the US and Kyrgyz governments, the Chinese allegedly offered the Kyrgyz government a US$3 billion financial package to close the base at Manas, and US$2 billion worth of Russian assistance to Kyrgyzstan around the same time was also probably linked to its closure.[53] China is worried about stability in the region, particularly in relation to Kyrgyzstan; there is a fear that the United States will promote "color revolutions" of the type that occurred throughout Eastern Europe in the early 2000s, including Kyrgyzstan's "Tulip Revolution" in 2005. The 2010 riots that overthrew the Tulip Revolution government in Kyrgyzstan were also viewed with apprehension by the Chinese, who worried that the instability might spill over into the other CARs.

This example illustrates the complex Chinese-Russian-US strategic triangle that is operating in the region, with Russia using China to balance US influence there but at the same time becoming concerned about the growing Chinese footprint.[54] This means that new and smaller players such as India must not only negotiate their own commercial interests in the region but also tread delicately through this finely balanced web of politics, complicated by their own bilateral relations with China, Russia, and the United States.

For those countries prepared to delve into the complex geopolitics of Central Asia, the region provides both a wealth of opportunities and a host of potential problems, as China is discovering. On the one hand, China can access hydrocarbon resources, which enables it to diversify its energy sources and helps to reduce its dependence on the Malacca Strait. The CARs, in turn, benefit from extensive Chinese investment in the region, not just in the oil and gas industries but also in infrastructure such as roads, railways, hospitals, and sporting facilities. However, this construction often uses imported Chinese workers rather than local labor, which inflames unrest, particularly in Kazakhstan. As well as encountering local anxiety about growing Chinese influence, China must also combat larger geopolitical concerns from the United States, Russia, and other major players in Central Asia, as well as juggle multilateral politics through the SCO. Achieving a balance between commercial imperatives and maintaining good bilateral and multilateral relationships, as well as managing regional unrest, particularly in the context of Afghanistan, will be the major challenge for China in Central Asia.

Sino-Indian Rivalry and Cooperation in Central Asia: Incidental or Grand Strategy?

The narrative of India and China as the two "rising powers" of Asia who must therefore be in some sort of competition or cooperation is a pervasive but erroneous one. A study of the two countries' policies in Central Asia, for example, shows that not only are there marked differences between India's and China's approaches but that the way in which they interact cannot be broken down simply into competition or cooperation. The two countries are actually pursuing parallel agendas in Central Asia, with incidental elements of competition or cooperation but nothing of significance. This observation emphasizes not only the importance of context—geographic, political, economic, and historical—in determining a country's policies but also that competition and cooperation are not mutually exclusive and in fact can (and do) occur simultaneously.

Although the nature of pipeline politics encourages competition, China and India have quickly discovered that in certain areas, cooperation is more mutually beneficial. This was precipitated by a string of deals in which competition increased the eventual contract price considerably, most notably in relation to the PetroKazakhstan takeover in 2005. In June of that year, investors in the Canadian-owned, Kazakhstan-based oil company watched the company's share price skyrocket on rumors of a takeover. PetroKazakhstan's control of the Kumkol oil fields made it attractive, and, according to the rumors, the main player was India's OVL. If the OVL bid had been successful, the deal would have been a watershed in terms of India's entry into the Central Asian hydrocarbon market. On October 26, 2005, however, the China National Petroleum Corporation pipped OVL at the post, finalizing its takeover of PetroKazakhstan for US$4.2 billion, making it the largest overseas acquisition ever undertaken by a Chinese company. The sale was an echo of the race for energy resources taking place in Africa—particularly Angola and Nigeria—which has seen India trumped by China in similar deals.

This sort of economic rivalry, whether between China and India or other players in the region, is of little benefit to anyone (except of course the likes of PetroKazakhstan); it only serves to increase prices beyond their real value. However, although cooperation is the best option for both parties in circumstances such as these, it is still relatively rare.

One interesting, albeit unlikely, plan for Sino-Indian cooperation has been mooted by retired Indian diplomat and author Rajiv Sikri, who proposed a parallel oil and gas pipeline from Central Asia through Xinjiang in China to India via the disputed (but Chinese-administered) Aksai Chin territory in Kashmir. The logic behind such a proposal is to create mutual dependence between the two countries, with India receiving Central Asian and Russian gas while sending oil from the Persian Gulf to China.[55] Sikri argues that both China and India would gain by cooperating on such a project by securing Eurasian hydrocarbons for Asia and this pipeline would provide a more secure alternative than the other pipeline routes being proposed, such as the Turkmenistan-Afghanistan-Pakistan-India pipeline.

Sikri's proposal for Sino-Indian mutual energy dependence has merit in terms of both securing the two countries' energy needs and promoting bilateral cooperation. He acknowledges, however, that there are considerable obstacles, not least the ongoing dispute over control of the Aksai Chin area.[56] As well as raising political considerations, including the vulnerability of such a pipeline through Xinjiang and Kashmir due to instability and insurgency in those regions, the actual construction of pipelines along this route would be an enormous technical challenge. These pipelines would have to cross both the Karakoram and Himalayan mountain ranges at altitudes of over five thousand meters, with all the resultant issues in both initial construction and ongoing transportation of oil and gas that working at such heights entails. It is for these reasons that an Aksai Chin pipeline is barely on the radar of most analysts, in both China and India.

Nevertheless, the underlying idea of greater Sino-Indian cooperation is strong, as there have been and will continue to be situations where both countries' interests are better served by cooperation rather than rivalry. The real question is whether the political animosity over the border issue and Pakistan can be put aside in the interest of mutually beneficial cooperation.[57] Increased cooperation also depends naturally on an overlapping of interests, which is the main reason it has yet to occur on a major scale in Central Asia. At this stage, China's interests are best served by developing strong bilateral relations with the CARs, and, except in the case of deals like PetroKazakhstan where competition becomes detrimental, China at present has little interest in cooperating with India. Thus, while cooperating with China in certain sectors might, in theory, provide India with many advantages, until it also serves Chinese interests to enter into joint enterprises, cooperation will be limited. It cannot be ruled out entirely, however, and significant cooperation between China and India would change the dynamics of the region substantially.

One of the major difficulties with the discussion of Sino-Indian rivalry (or lack of it) in Central Asia is differentiating between standard commercial competition and political rivalry. The former is most apparent in the energy sector, where Indian national oil companies have consistently been outbid by their Chinese counterparts on various hydrocarbon deals in the CARs. Because the major Indian and Chinese players in this field are state-owned companies, there is a tendency to link the outcomes of these oil and gas deals with greater geopolitical implications. Yet while the politics of a country or region naturally impacts on the way business is done there, at present the Chinese hydrocarbon companies' successes in Central Asia at the expense of India are fundamentally the result of commercial considerations rather than overt displays of political game-playing.

There is, of course, geopolitical rivalry in Central Asia in regard to oil and gas and the development of broader political influence, but it is not occurring between China and India as such, at least at present. Due to various circumstances, including geography and domestic government stability and regulation, the playing field on which China and India are operating is strongly skewed in favor of the former. China's influence in Central Asia strongly outweighs India's, meaning that the main competition taking place in the region is between China and the other great powers—the United States and Russia. India's current counterparts in terms of influence are Iran, Pakistan, and Turkey, all of which are essentially minor players in the region for now.

The volatility of Central Asia and its geopolitical significance as a playing field for great powers, however, is what makes it an interesting case study. If the rumors of anti-Chinese feelings in places such as Kazakhstan continue to grow, and if India manages to successfully mitigate its access problem and finds a way to capitalize on the goodwill it holds in the region, then the situation could change. As noted above, both countries have significant interests in the region and not just in the context of oil and gas. At the moment, China and India are operating on separate tracks, but if and when the power balance changes and the two countries' interests begin to intersect more, the prospect of rivalry may become an issue.

Phunchok Stobdan, an expert on Central Asia with the Institute of Defence Studies and Analyses in New Delhi, argues that China and India are neither competing nor cooperating in any meaningful way because both countries have advantages and disadvantages that are essentially complementary at this stage. For example, China's direct borders with the region allow it to easily supply Central Asia's needs by building infrastructure (as well as tapping into the region's resources) in a way that India is unable to, but China also faces a significant threat perception in Central Asia that does not afflict India.[58] Stobdan also argues that China is constrained by the export-oriented nature of its economy, which may prove to be disadvantageous in the long term, as antipathy grows in Central Asia due to the destruction of indigenous industries under the weight of Chinese imports.[59]

Conclusion: Alternative Strategies in a New Regional Playground

The problems in Central Asia highlight specific features of Chinese and Indian foreign policy. China has been pursuing a policy of active engagement with the region, mainly using economic exchange strategies, since the early 1990s, and this is now beginning to bear fruit in the form of lucrative energy and infrastructure contracts. India, on the other hand, failed to capitalize on the opportunities thrust at it by the CARs in the wake of the Soviet Union's downfall and is only now beginning to claw its way back. Even so, there is considerable debate as to whether India should be expending resources in Central Asia. In terms of hydrocarbon resources, the lack of a land border makes it extremely difficult for India to access Central Asia's oil and gas, as opposed to its major source from the Persian Gulf, which is easily shipped across the Arabian Sea. As India's population continues to grow, however, and demand for energy continues to outstrip supply, there may soon be a more pressing need for the country to diversify its energy resources.

China and India also do business in Central Asia in markedly different ways. India seems content to simply dip its toes in the water of Central Asian energy commerce through strategic partnerships and memorandums of understanding, while China jumps right in with a strategy that is undoubtedly higher-risk but also produces higher returns. There are several reasons for this, and they go some way to explaining why Sino-Indian competition is presently insignificant in Central Asia.

The first issue is financial. China is significantly further along the development track than India and is able to divert more funds for overseas investments. It also has greater economic influence beyond its borders. In addition, China's state-owned energy companies have considerably more autonomy than their Indian counterparts and are not subject to the same degree of red tape and overregulation that have seen Indian overseas investment deals collapse in the past.

The second reason is access. Capitalizing on Central Asian resources is infinitely easier for China than for India due to its direct borders with Kazakhstan, Kyrgyzstan, and Tajikistan. This enables the construction of pipelines and other infrastructure, as well as the easy export of Chinese labor, in a way that is not possible for India. It is up to India, however, to decide whether to view the access issue as an insurmountable problem or as a challenge and opportunity. Presently there is a tendency toward the former, although attempts to cultivate a better relationship with Iran in order to gain access to Central Asia may indicate a change in attitude toward this problem. If India can overcome its access problem, it will be in a far better position to develop its presence in Central Asia, although unlike China it will always be beholden to third and possibly even fourth countries to transit resources, which puts it at a disadvantage.

The third issue is that India has yet to work out how to capitalize fully on its strengths in the region. Notwithstanding its financial and access limitations, India has the advantage of being seen as a benign power in the region, a friend to Central Asia with ties that continued even through Soviet times and with no expansionist designs on the CARs. This is in direct contrast to China, which is beginning to encounter political and social problems because of its massive injection of Chinese labor into the area. India must decide how best to capitalize on this goodwill in order to smooth the way for investment opportunities in the future. Although there has been some attempt at this with infrastructure projects, some military cooperation in Tajikistan, and educational scholarships, there is no concerted plan. China too has been attempting to wield its soft power through limited use of catalytic engagement strategies, especially in education and particularly of young Kazakhs and the establishment of Confucius Institutes in Kazakhstan, Kyrgyzstan, Tajikistan, and Uzbekistan.[60]

China and India are essentially pursuing separate agendas in Central Asia, with small elements of cooperation or rivalry but little of significance in either aspect. In some ways their operations in the region can be seen to be a microcosm of the two countries' places in wider global affairs: China has a strong economy and is a source of cheap goods but at the same time has a poor national image, which leads to concerns about excessive Chinese influence. India, on the other hand, lags behind economically but possesses a sense of trust and goodwill, which means it is not seen as a threat in the same way. If India continues to become more influential economically and China fails to find an effective way to counter the threat perception, then the playing field will be considerably more even, and the potential for both cooperation and competition will increase. So while the idea of Sino-Indian rivalry in Central Asia is a flawed dichotomy propagated mostly by Western analysts, it cannot be discounted as a possibility for the future.

What is clear from an examination of Chinese and Indian behavior in Central Asia is that the two countries' policy formations are still very much in the early stages. With the major Chinese leadership change that occurred in late 2012 and Indian general elections to be held in 2014, it is difficult to predict how the two countries' policies will evolve over the next five years. The most likely outcome, however, is not a concerted policy of either rivalry or cooperation but rather the opportunistic pursuit of both in accordance with their national interests, utilizing simple exchange strategies of engagement. China will likely continue to be an active power in the region, while India is still coming to terms with its role, aims, and how it wishes to assert itself. With the two countries' policies in Central Asia in many ways reflecting their attitudes toward wider international relations, how China and India approach the region in the coming years may well have far-reaching implications.

Notes

1. ONGC Videsh Ltd. is the overseas arm of state-run Indian oil company Oil and Natural Gas Corporation (ONGC). ONGC engages in the exploration and development of domestic oil and gas fields, while OVL handles international exploration and development. See www.ongcindia.com (ONGC) and www.ongcvidesh.com (OVL).

2. "Sarl," from the French *société à résponsabilité limitée,* means "limited liability company." Mittal Investments Sarl is the parent company of Mittal Steel.

3. "ONGC Mittal Energy Limited (OMEL) and KazMuaniGas [sic] (KMG) Signed a HOA on January 24, 2009," Oil and Natural Gas Corporation Limited, January 24, 2009, www.ongcvidesh.com/NewsContent.aspx?ID = 161&AspxAutoDetectCookie Support = 1, (accessed February 13, 2009).

4. "Turkmenistan, India Sign Landmark MoU for Oil and Gas Cooperation," *News Central Asia*, April 5, 2008, www.newscentralasia.net/moreNews.php?nID = 155 (accessed February 13, 2009).

5. M. K. Bhadrakumar, "India Follows China's Central Asian Steps," *Asia Times Online*, November 9, 2004, www.atimes.com/atimes/South_Asia/FK09Df04.html (accessed February 2, 2009).

6. Author interviews with Ranjit Gupta, New Delhi, December 2009, with M. K. Bhadrakumar, New Delhi, December 2009, and with Shivshankar Menon, New Delhi, December 2009.

7. Ibid.

8. Author interview with Bhadrakumar, December 2009.

9. Ibid.

10. Ibid.

11. Ibid.

12. Sachin Parashar, "India Embarks on Connect Central Asia Policy," *Times of India*, June 13, 2012.

13. Author interview with Indranil Banerjie, SAPRA India Foundation, New Delhi, March 2010.

14. Author interview with Wang Dehua, Institute of South and Central Asian Studies, Shanghai Academy of Social Sciences, Shanghai, June 2010.

15. "Pak Perception of Indian Role in Afghan a Matter of Concern: US," *Indian Express*, November 24, 2010.

16. William Wan, "Defense Secretary Leon Panetta Urges India to Take Larger Role in Afghanistan," *Washington Post*, June 6, 2012.

17. Author interview with Phunchok Stobdan, Institute of Defence Studies and Analyses, New Delhi, March 2010.

18. Indrani Bagchi, "India Votes against Iran at IAEA," *Times of India*, November 28, 2009, and author interview with Nirmala Joshi, India-Central Asia Foundation, New Delhi, March 2010.

19. Sandeep Dikshit, "India, Iran Plan Talks to Bypass Western Sanctions on Tehran," *The Hindu*, May 31, 2012.

20. Author interview with Joshi, March 2010.

21. Angira Sen Sarma, *India and Central Asia: Redefining Energy and Trade Links* (New Delhi: Pentagon Press, 2010), 97.

22. Ibid., 98.

23. Ibid., 113; author interview with Swaran Singh, Jawaharlal Nehru University and Fudan University, Shanghai, June 2010; and author interview with Joshi, March 2010.

24. Author interview with Joshi, March 2010.

25. Author interview with Meena Singh Roy, Institute of Defence Studies and Analyses, New Delhi, March 2010.

26. For a thorough examination of India's relations with Tajikistan and the development of the Ayni air base, see Sudha Ramachandran, "India's Foray into Central Asia," *Asia Times Online*, August 12, 2006, www.atimes.com/atimes/South_Asia/HH12Df01.html (accessed January 18, 2011).

27. Author interview with Roy, March 2010, and author interview with Banerjie, March 2010.

28. Joshua Kucera, "Why Is Tajikistan's Ayni Air Base Idle?" *Eurasianet.org*, July 9, 2010, www.eurasianet.org/node/61503 (accessed January 18, 2011).

29. Ibid.

30. Author interview with Roy, March 2010.

31. Author interview with Gupta, December 2009.

32. Author interview with Bhadrakumar, December 2009.

33. Sean R. Roberts, "A 'Land of Borderlands': Implications of Xinjiang's Trans-border Interactions," in *Xinjiang: China's Muslim Borderland*, ed. S. Frederick Starr (Armonk, NY: M. E. Sharpe, 2004), 221.

34. Jennifer DeLay, "The Caspian Oil Pipeline Tangle: A Steel Web of Confusion," in *Oil and Geopolitics in the Caspian Sea Region*, ed. Michael P. Croissant and Bülent Aras (Westport, CT: Praeger, 1999), 57.

35. Ibid., 59.

36. Lutz Kleveman, *The New Great Game: Blood and Oil in Central Asia* (London: Atlantic Books, 2003), 113.

37. Chengxin Pan, "Is the South China Sea a New 'Dangerous Ground' for US-China Rivalry?" *East Asia Forum*, May 24, 2011, www.eastasiaforum.org/2011/05/24/is-the-south -china-sea-a-new-dan gerous-ground -for-us-china-rivalry/ (accessed May 30, 2011).

38. Olzhas Auyezov, "Kazakhstan Starts Building Gas Pipeline to China," *Reuters*, July 9, 2008, http://uk.reuters.com/article/2008/07/09/kazakhstan-china-pipeline-idUKL0939802620080709 (accessed May 26, 2011).

39. "West-East Gas Pipeline Wrapped Up," *China Daily*, August 4, 2004, and Kleveman, *New Great Game*, 113.

40. DeLay, "Caspian Oil Pipeline Tangle," 69.

41. Author interview with Joshi, March 2010.

42. The western Chinese province of Xinjiang, which borders the CARs and is home to the majority of China's oil and gas resources, has long had separatist issues with its major non-Han population, the Uighurs, who are a Muslim Turkic people closely related to various Central Asian ethnic groups. They have been campaigning for an East Turkestan state since the beginning of the twentieth century, although tensions particularly began to flare up again in the 1980s and 1990s. At times they have resorted to terrorist acts, such as placing bombs on buses, but the overall death toll has remained relatively low. In 2009, there was a major crackdown by the Chinese government following riots in the provincial capital, Urumqi. Concerned that Uighur separatists are receiving training and assistance from supporters in Afghanistan and the CARs, the Xinjiang issue is one of the major reasons why China is so invested in the region. For more information, see Starr, *Xinjiang*, and Yitzhak Schicor, "China's Central Asian Strategy and the Xinjiang Connection: Predicaments and Medicaments in a Contemporary Perspective," *China and Eurasia Forum Quarterly* 6, no. 2 (2008): 55–73.

43. According to Indian China-watcher Srikanth Kondapalli, Chinese involvement in Central Asia over the Xinjiang issue has a long history. The region was heavily destabilized after the Soviet invasion of Afghanistan in 1979, and China countered the Soviet Union by supporting the mujahideen in Afghanistan, who are now, in the "blowback" characteristic of

Central Asian politics, supporting the Uighurs in their fight for secession. Kondapalli claims that Chinese general Xiong Guangkai trained five thousand mujahideen from 1979 to 1989 and also supplied Red Arrow missiles that are now being used against the Chinese. The United States also had an intelligence-sharing operation with China during the latter part of the Cold War, including two Soviet Union–facing signals intelligence facilities at Qitai and Korla in Xinjiang. Mujahideen training programs in Pakistan were also conducted jointly by the Central Intelligence Agency and the People's Liberation Army's International Liaison Department (a counterespionage outfit publicly known as the China Association for International Friendly Contacts), as were counter-Soviet operations in Afghanistan, Angola, and Cambodia. Author interview with Srikanth Kondapalli, Jawaharlal Nehru University, New Delhi, March 2010. See also Jeffrey T. Richelson, *The US Intelligence Community*, 2nd ed. (Cambridge, MA: Ballinger, 1989), 280.

44. Roberts, "'Land of Borderlands,'" 233.

45. Michael Clarke, "China and the Shanghai Cooperation Organization: The Dynamics of 'New Regionalism,' 'Vassalization,' and Geopolitics in Central Asia," in *The New Central Asia: The Regional Impact of International Actors*, ed. Emilian Kavalski (Singapore: World Scientific Publishing, 2010), 117.

46. Author interview with Hu Shisheng, China Institute of Contemporary International Relations, Beijing, May 2010. For a detailed analysis of Chinese involvement with the SCO, see Clarke, "China and the Shanghai Cooperation Organization."

47. Zachary Fillingham, "SCO Reality Check," *Geopolitical Monitor*, June 5, 2009, www.geopoliticalmonitor.com/sco-reality-check/ (accessed May 27, 2011).

48. "China to Provide 10-Billion-Dollar Loan to SCO Members," *Xinhua News*, June 16, 2009, http://news.xinhuanet.com/English/2009–06/16/content_11552439.htm (accessed September 18, 2013).

49. Jiao Wu and Xiaokun Li, "SCO Agrees Deal to Admit New Members," *China Daily*, June 12, 2010, and Guangjin Cheng, "Hopeful Members Knocking on SCO's Door," *China Daily*, June 16, 2011.

50. Bhadrakumar, "India Follows China's Central Asian Steps"; Nirmala Joshi, "India-Russia Relations and the Strategic Environment in Eurasia," in *Eager Eyes Fixed on Eurasia, Volume 1: Russia and Its Neighbors in Crisis*, ed. Akihiro Iwashita (Sapporo: Slavic Research Center, Hokkaido University, 2007): 195–210; and Matthew Brummer, "The Shanghai Cooperation Organization and Iran: A Power-Full Union," *Journal of International Affairs* 60, no. 2 (2007): 185–98.

51. Author interview with Banerjie, March 2010.

52. Jyotsna Bakshi, "Russia-China Boundary Agreement: Relevance for India," *Strategic Analysis* 24, no. 10 (2001): 1852.

53. Chris Good, "Flustered Chinese Ambassador Warned of 'Revolution,'" *The Atlantic*, November 29, 2010, www.theatlantic.com/international/archive/2010/11/flustered-chinese-ambassador-warned-of-revolution/67114/ (accessed July 1, 2012), and Joshua Kucera, "'Bakiyev Can Be Bought': US Embassy Tied Rent for Kyrgyz Air Base to President's Reelection," *Eurasianet.org*, January 5, 2012, www.eurasianet.org/node/64797 (accessed July 1, 2012).

54. Author interview with Liu Fenghua, Institute of Russian, Eastern European and Central Asian Studies, Chinese Academy of Social Sciences, Beijing, May 2010.

55. Sikri in Sarma, *India and Central Asia*, 100.

56. Ibid., 101.

57. In some small aspects this has begun to occur, for example, with the first-ever joint naval exercises in 2003 held off the Shanghai coast and joint antiterrorism exercises held in Karnataka in India in 2008. Author interview with Zhao Gancheng (Shanghai Institute of International Studies, Shanghai Academy of Social Sciences, and Fudan University), June 2010, and Islamic Republic News Agency, "Indo-China Joint Army Exercise Begins Saturday in Karnataka," *GlobalSecurity.org*, December 6, 2008, www.globalsecurity.org/military/library/news/2008/12/mil-081206-i rna01.htm (accessed September 21, 2009). Hotlines in the border areas and between the Indian prime minister and Chinese president have also been established (author interview with Zhao, June 2010). Although these are important confidence-building measures, they are still a long way from full cooperation.

58. Author interview with Phunchok Stobdan, Institute of Defence Studies and Analyses, New Delhi, March 2010.

59. Ibid.

60. Author interview with Pan Guang, Shanghai Academy of Social Sciences, Shanghai, June 2010.

CHAPTER 6

CHINA'S HALF-HEARTED ENGAGEMENT AND INDIA'S PROACTIVE BALANCING

Harsh V. Pant

IN ENGAGING NEW DELHI over the last two decades, China has primarily relied on an exchange strategy of economic engagement and a partial conformity with India in its views on global issues. But this strategy has failed to produce any breakthrough in Sino-Indian relations. In the absence of a serious diplomatic engagement that tackles some of the thorniest issues dogging Sino-Indian relations for years, there is little likelihood of an improvement in Sino-Indian ties. Despite growing economic linkages, there is a rising suspicion among Indian elites that China does not take India seriously and, worse, is working actively to stymie India's rise. As a consequence, the engagement strategy employed by China has had limited success.

Where China seeks to engage India as a regional South Asian power, India seeks engagement from China as an equal, rising global power. This has led to a serious asymmetry in perceptions between the two. There is also a growing perception in New Delhi that among the major powers, China is the only one that does not accept India as a rising global player that should be accommodated in the global political order. The dichotomy between China's and India's global convergence and their growing bilateral divergence has allowed India to collude with China as a power bloc against Western positions at the global level, even as at the bilateral level New Delhi is not averse to leveraging its relationship with Washington in order to constrain China. This has resulted in Sino-Indian cooperation at the multilateral level and the emergence of such groupings as BRICS (Brazil, Russia, India, China, and South Africa) without any substantive improvement at the bilateral level.

For some time, the Sino-Indian economic engagement and their joint opposition to US unipolarity seemed to suggest that China's strategy of primarily relying on economic engagement might work. But structural constraints have become more powerful in redefining Indian priorities. China's rapid economic and military rise has generated apprehensions about China's intentions, and China's inability to assuage Indian concerns about key security issues has reinforced suspicions about China. This chapter first delineates the evolution in Sino-Indian engagement over the last two decades. Subsequently, it highlights the convergence of Sino-Indian interests in their engagement at the global level by focusing on global trade, environment, and energy security. Finally, the inability of the two nations to transcend their bilateral differences by using global convergence is discussed.

Sino-Indian Engagement after 1998

Bilateral relations between India and China have indeed come a long way since their nadir in the immediate aftermath of India's nuclear tests in May 1998. China had been singled out as the "number one" security threat to India by its defense minister just before the nuclear tests.[1] After the tests, Indian prime minister Atal Bihari Vajpayee wrote to US president Bill Clinton justifying Indian nuclear tests as a response to the threat posed by China.[2] Not surprisingly, China reacted strongly, and diplomatic relations between the two countries plummeted to an all-time low.

However, some twelve years later, relations between India and China, at least on the surface, seemed to be on a much firmer footing, as they have tried to reduce the prospect for rivalry and expand areas of cooperation. The visit of the Indian external affairs minister to China in 1999 marked the resumption of high-level dialogue, and the two sides declared that they were not threats to each other. A bilateral security dialogue was also initiated that helped the two countries in openly expressing and sharing their security concerns with each other. Both China and India continue to emphasize that neither side should let differences act as an impediment to the growth of functional cooperation between the two states. India and China also decided to expedite the process of demarcation of the Line of Actual Control (LAC), and the Joint Working Group (JWG) on the boundary question, set up in 1988, has been meeting regularly. As a first step in this direction, the two countries exchanged border maps on the least controversial middle sector of the LAC. Both nations have finalized a set of political "guiding principles" that will govern the parameters of the dispute settlement. China has expressed its desire to seek a "fair" resolution to the vexed boundary issue on the basis of "mutual accommodation, respect for history and accommodation of reality."[3]

The visit by Indian prime minister Vajpayee in June 2003 was the first by an Indian premier in a decade. The joint declaration signed during this visit expressed the view that China was not a threat to India.[4] The two states appointed special representatives in order to impart momentum to border negotiations that have lasted now for more than twenty years, with the prime minister's principal secretary becoming India's political-level negotiator, replacing the India-China JWG. India and China also decided to hold their first joint naval and air exercises. More significantly, India acknowledged China's sovereignty over Tibet and pledged not to allow "anti-China" political activities in India. On its part, China has acknowledged India's 1975 annexation of the former monarchy of Sikkim by agreeing to open a trading post along the border with the former kingdom and later by rectifying its official maps to include Sikkim as part of India.[5] After being closed for sixty years, the century-old trading post at Nathu La, a mountain pass between Tibet and Sikkim, was reopened in 2006. High-level political interactions have continued unabated since then. The two states have set up institutionalized defense consultation mechanisms to reduce suspicions and identify areas of cooperation on security issues.

Soon after assuming office in 2004, the Manmohan Singh government also made it clear that it was in favor of closer ties with China and would continue to work toward improving relations. When Singh visited China in 2008, the two states signed the "shared visions for the 21st century" declaration "to promote the building of a harmonious world of durable peace and common prosperity through developing the Strategic and Cooperative Partnership for Peace and Prosperity between the two countries," while also reiterating support for the 2005 boundary settlement agreement.[6] The two sides have decided to elevate the boundary negotiations to the level of a strategic dialogue, with plans for a hotline between the Indian prime minister and the Chinese premier as a means for preventing misunderstanding and reducing tensions at the earliest. Their public vision suggested that this relationship would have "a positive influence on the future of the international system."[7]

This has been happening at a time when economic relations between the two have burgeoned, with China emerging as India's largest trading partner. Sino-Indian trade is on course to achieve a trade volume of US$100 billion by 2015, providing a basis for long-term engagement.

Global Engagement

The Structural Imperative

It is at the international level that India and China have found some real convergence of interests. Both share similar concerns about the international dominance of the United States, the threat of fundamentalist religious and ethnic movements in the form of terrorism, and the need to accord primacy to economic development. India and China have both expressed concern about the American use of military power around the world, and both were publicly opposed to the war in Iraq. This was merely a continuation of the desire of both states to oppose the US hyperpower ever since the end of the Cold War.

Both China and India, much like other major powers in the international system, favor a multipolar world order where US unipolarity remains constrained by the other "poles" in the system. China and India zealously guard their national sovereignty and have been wary of US attempts to interfere in what they see as domestic affairs of other states, be they Serbia, Kosovo, Iraq, Libya, or Syria. Both took strong exception to the US air strikes on Iraq in 1998, the United States–led air campaign against Yugoslavia in 1999, and the US campaign against Saddam Hussein, arguing that these violated the sovereignty of both countries and undermined the authority of the United Nations (UN) system.[8] China and India share an interest in resisting interventionist foreign policy doctrines emanating from the West, particularly the United States, and display "conservative attitudes on the prerogatives of sovereignty."[9]

China and India have coordinated their efforts on issues as wide-ranging as climate change, trade negotiations, energy security, and the global financial crisis. Both nations favor more democratic international economic regimes. Sino-Indian coordination on climate change and global trade negotiations, as well as in demanding a restructuring of financial institutions in view of the world economy's shifting center of gravity, has had a significant impact on the course of international politics over the last few years. It is being argued that the forces of globalization have led to a certain convergence of Sino-Indian interests in the economic realm as the two nations become even more deeply engaged in the international trading economy and more integrated into global financial networks.[10] The two have strongly resisted efforts by the United States and other developed nations to link global trade to labor and environmental standards, realizing clearly that this would put them at a huge disadvantage in relation to the developed world, thereby hampering their drive toward economic development, the number-one priority for both countries. Both have committed themselves to crafting joint Sino-Indian positions in the World Trade Organization (WTO) and global trade negotiations in the hope that this might provide them greater negotiating leverage over other developed states. They would like to see further liberalization of agricultural trade in the developed countries, tightening of the rules on antidumping measures and ensuring that non–trade-related issues such as labor and environment are not allowed to come to the WTO. Both have fought carbon emission caps proposed by the industrialized world and have resisted Western pressure to open their agricultural markets.

Global Trade Dynamic

World trade is in grave danger of shrinking over the next few years because of the ongoing global financial crisis that is showing no signs of abating. Given this bleak outlook, a revival of the Doha round of trade talks can send the right kind of signals to various stakeholders in the global economy. The West as well as China and India have hinted that they are also ready to relaunch efforts to reach a new global trade deal under the Doha negotiations. The talks had collapsed in 2008 after coming very close to an agreement primarily because of differences between Washington and emerging economies, led by India, over proposals to help farmers in poor nations. China teamed up with India to scuttle the Doha round. Because of their much greater economic power (compared to the past), states such as China and India now have much greater bargaining clout. The West has serious differences with the developing countries on the level of protection that can be given to farmers if the global market for farm products is opened up.

The United States has suggested that developing nations such as India need to provide greater market access for the talks to advance. India and China argue that they cannot compromise on food security and livelihood concerns even as the United States and the European Union remain resistant to scaling down their own agricultural subsidies for fear of offending their domestic farm lobbies. China and India have made it clear that they would be able to make unpopular concessions at home only if the developed world provides reciprocal concessions by phasing out its own agricultural subsidies, something that is highly unlikely in the present climate of economic turmoil in the developed world.

Officially neither the United States nor India nor China has provided any specific details about its plans to break the impasse over the agricultural sector that has been a bone of contention. Although the dismal state of the global economy and the need to revive global trade might be prompting the United States as well as China and India to rethink their earlier strategies, the domestic political constraints remain as strong as ever, with New Delhi and Beijing converging in their shared opposition to Western demands.

Climate-Change Policies

This convergence is also reflected in the postures China and India have adopted on issues related to climate change. As the date neared for the UN climate treaty to be negotiated in Copenhagen in December 2009, the West, led by the United States, and emerging powers such as China and India tried to bridge their differences on how to reduce greenhouse gas emissions. The United States wanted developing countries such as India and China to agree to control the emissions produced by their rapidly growing economies, setting time-bound targets to this effect. China and India argued that this would hurt their economic growth and wanted the industrialized world to curb its pollution as well as fund new technologies in the developing world, underlining that they had low emissions per capita. Beijing and New Delhi had no appetite for conceding on this issue, with both finding it politically difficult to agree on binding targets.

For the Barack Obama administration, on the other hand, it was important that India and China take some meaningful steps to reduce emissions if it was to have any hope of persuading the skeptics in Congress of its own domestic climate-change agenda. Therefore, carbon reductions by China and India were a "core part of these negotiations" for the United States.[11] Even as the West, China, and India settled on the need for an agreement at Copenhagen, the two emerging economies made it clear that they could not accept legally binding limits on carbon emissions. Although around 80 percent of world growth in carbon emissions is coming from rapidly growing economies such as India's and China's, their governments argue that even if these economies continue to grow at current levels for the next decade or two, their per capita emissions would still be below those of the developed countries.

China and India together blocked such a protocol that called for a more ambitious climate target and mandatory greenhouse gas emissions cuts from both industrialized and major emerging economies. China and India joined Brazil and South Africa and drew up a basic draft for negotiating reductions in greenhouse gas emissions on the principle of differentiated responsibility.[12] As a result, the West found it difficult to get its way at Copenhagen.

India has followed China in devising its own domestic climate-change policies. Toward this end, the two have been conducting regular dialogues to exchange views on their respective action plans. China has declared that it is pursuing its National Climate Change Program, which includes mandatory targets for reducing energy intensity and discharge of major pollutants, as well as increasing forest coverage and its share of renewable energy during the period 2005–10. India followed suit by committing itself to a mandatory fuel efficiency cap in 2011 and a change in its energy matrix whereby renewable sources will account for 20 percent of India's power usage by 2020, as well as announcing an ambitious solar energy plan.

The Energy Matrix

It is against an increasingly complex strategic background that states such as China and India are trying to shape their own energy policies. Their approach toward their energy predicament remains rather traditional insofar as it is largely state-centric, supply-side biased, mainly reliant on oil, and tending to privilege self-sufficiency.[13] It is toward an aggressive pursuit of energy resources (particularly oil) across the globe that China and India seem to have focused their diplomatic energies in recent years, with some far-reaching implications.

For some time now, there has been a debate about the consequences for the international system of the global pursuit of energy resources by emerging powers such as China and India. This debate has largely focused on China, with some claiming that its hunger for energy will force it to pursue policies that could be destabilizing, while others argue that China's energy needs will integrate it even more into the international system.[14] India's pursuit of energy security also brings some of the same issues to the fore, and as both China and India try to gear their foreign policies to meet this challenge, the dynamic between these two Asian neighbors is bound to have consequences.

India's greatest challenge is to ensure successful diversification of sources for oil procurement to minimize possibilities of disruption in supplies. It is toward this end that India has devoted its diplomatic energies in recent times as it encourages its public-sector companies to acquire stakes in oil and gas fields abroad. India, like China, is reshaping its diplomacy to serve energy needs because its booming economy also needs new supplies of oil to ensure its continued growth. The one reality that Indian diplomacy has to confront in its search for the nation's energy security is the presence of China almost everywhere and its relative success in achieving desirable outcomes.

Both China and India are feeling the pressure of diminishing oil discoveries and flat-lined oil production at a time when expansion of their domestic economies is rapidly increasing demand for energy. They have made energy the focal point of their diplomatic overtures to states far and wide. More significantly, faced with a market in which politics has an equal, if not greater, influence on price as economics, the two have also coordinated their efforts to secure energy resources overseas. In essence, China and India plan to work together to secure energy resources without unnecessarily bidding up the price of those resources, thereby agreeing to a consumer's cartel representing 2.3 billion potential consumers. Together their combined markets and purchasing power offers an extremely attractive partner to energy-producing states, especially those that face Western pressure over their human rights records or the nature of their political institutions.

It may be that cooperation between China and India on energy issues is the only way ahead if both states want to gain economies of scale and negotiation muscle. In many ways, both states face similar constraints in achieving energy security, and a coordinated approach would benefit them both. Competition only ends up driving up the costs of acquisition, thereby diminishing future returns. And there has been recognition of this at the highest levels of the government in both states.

China and India have signed a range of memorandums on energy cooperation that cover a full scope of areas, including upstream exploration and production, the refining and marketing of petroleum products and petrochemicals, the laying of national and transnational oil and gas pipelines, frontier and cutting-edge research and development, and the promotion of environment-friendly fuels.[15]

The two states have agreed to strengthen the exchange of information when bidding for oil resources in a third-party country in order to realize mutual benefit. China has pledged to promote cooperation with India in civil nuclear energy and to view this cooperation in the context of climate change and increasing nonpolluting sources in the energy mix. Former Indian petroleum minister Mani Shankar Aiyar made it clear that he thought that India and China joining hands to bid jointly for oil and gas assets under a "monopsonistic" arrangement was much better than the two states competing in their quest for energy resources.[16] He even floated the idea of an Asian energy grid that might follow the trajectory of the European Coal and Steel Community, which grew into the European Union. According to Aiyar, "India and China don't have to go through fratricide in order to arrive at the conclusion that it is better to cooperate on energy security."[17]

Two of the most talked-about ventures exemplifying Sino-Indian cooperation in this area have been investments by them in the exploration of hydrocarbon fields in Iran and Sudan. China and India hold a 50 percent and 20 percent stake, respectively, in the development and exploration of the Yadavaran field in Iran, while China's share is 40 percent and India's 25 percent in Sudan's Greater Nile Oil Pipeline project. The proposal for a single transportation route for natural gas imports from Iran has also been discussed, with the promise of extending the India-Iran gas pipeline via Pakistan to China. In a first alliance of its kind between the Chinese and Indian state energy companies, a successful joint offer was made to buy Petro Canada's 38 percent stake in the Al Furat Production Company, Syria's largest oil producer, which is operated and majority-owned by Royal Dutch Shell. This was followed by India's largest gas distributor, Gas Authority of India, setting up a joint venture with the Beijing Gas Group Company to distribute compressed natural gas in Beijing. It has also signed a memorandum of understanding with the China National Offshore Oil Corporation to develop offshore oil and gas projects in Indonesia and Australia. India and China had also jointly bid for stakes in oil ventures in Colombia and Kazakhstan. China has sought close cooperation with India in its offshore and deep-sea oil exploration projects.

From Global to Bilateral without Much Success

In recent years, China has attempted to build its bilateral relationship with India on the basis of their larger worldview of international politics. As New Delhi and Beijing discovered a distinct convergence of interests on the world stage, they have used this to strengthen their bilateral relations, mainly through simple exchange strategies of diplomatic and economic engagement. They have established and maintained regular, reciprocal high-level visits between political leaders. There has been a serious attempt to improve trade relations, and China has sought to compartmentalize intractable issues with India that make it difficult for their bilateral relationship to move forward.

India and China have strengthened their bilateral relationship in areas as distinct as cultural and educational exchanges, military exchanges, and science and technology cooperation. The two nations are working toward strengthening the bilateral relationship by creating larger stakes in each other's economic future. Bilateral trade has grown rapidly, and the two states are evaluating the possibility of signing a comprehensive economic cooperation agreement and a free-trade agreement, thereby building on strong complementarities between the two. Given the complementary nature of their economies and the size of their markets (nearly 2.3 billion people in total), this nascent Sino-Indian cooperation holds the potential to dramatically alter the world trade balance. There is general recognition of a division of labor within the information-technology sector, with China manufacturing chips and electronic components and India excelling at writing the software. Indian software companies are increasingly opening businesses in China, sensing great opportunities in one of the largest, fastest-growing economies in the world. Former Chinese premier Zhu Rongji has suggested that the combination of Chinese hardware and Indian software would be irresistible to the global market. In addition to information-technology trade and interaction, India facilitates China's economic development by exporting raw materials and semifinished goods, as well as shipping Chinese cargo overseas. Chinese companies have begun to tap India's ever-expanding consumer market by exporting electrical machinery, home appliances, consumer electronics, and mechanical goods. Both nations are increasingly looking beyond the existing trade and trying to identify new milestones that can intensify the growing economic ties between the two, including greater exchange in scientific research and technology.

Both states are also taking steps to upgrade their military-related cooperation, leading to greater understanding on the bilateral military front, something that would have been unthinkable just a few years ago.[18] As a first step in this direction, the Chinese and Indian navies carried out joint search-and-rescue operations off the Shanghai coast in November 2003. The two militaries conducted joint antiterrorism exercises in 2007, the first time that Indian soldiers had set foot on Chinese soil since the Sino-Indian War of 1962. Since then, joint naval and army exercises have become a regular feature. High-level delegations from India have been visiting China and vice versa, including officials in charge of army deployment along the India-China border. Both states have also sought cooperation on the nuclear front, with China importing heavy water from India to be utilized in the pressurized heavy-water reactors near Shanghai.[19]

Growing Frictions

Despite these changing atmospherics, bilateral ties between China and India nosedived so dramatically in 2009 that Indian strategists were even predicting "the year of the Chinese attack on India"; it was suggested that China would attack India by 2012 primarily to divert attention from its growing domestic troubles.[20] This suggestion received widespread coverage in the Indian media, which seemed more interested in sensationalizing the issue than questioning the claims.[21]

Meanwhile, the official Chinese media picked up the story and gave it another spin. It argued that while a Chinese attack on India was highly unlikely, a conflict between the two neighbors could occur in one scenario: an aggressive Indian policy toward China about their border dispute, forcing China to take military action. The Chinese media speculated that the "China will attack India" line might just be a pretext for India to deploy more troops to the border areas.[22]

This curious exchange merely reflects an uneasiness that exists between the two Asian giants as they continue their ascent in the global interstate hierarchy. Even as they sign loftily worded documents year after year, the distrust between the two is actually growing at an alarming rate. True, economic cooperation and bilateral political, as well as sociocultural, exchanges are at an all-time high, and China is India's largest trading partner. But this cooperation has done little to assuage each country's concerns about the other's intentions. The two sides are locked in a classic security dilemma, where any action taken by one is immediately interpreted by the other as a threat to its interests.

At the global level, the rhetoric is all about cooperation. Indeed, as discussed earlier, the two sides have worked together on climate-change and global trade negotiations and have demanded a restructuring of global financial institutions in view of the global economy's shifting center of gravity. At the bilateral level, however, mounting tensions reached an impasse in 2009 when China took its territorial dispute with India to the Asian Development Bank. There China blocked India's application for a loan that included money for development projects in the Indian state of Arunachal Pradesh, which China continues to claim as part of its territory.[23] China's efforts to block the US-Indian civilian nuclear energy cooperation pact in the Nuclear Suppliers Group and its obstructionist stance on bringing to justice the masterminds of the November 2008 terrorist attacks in Mumbai seem to have further confirmed Indian suspicions about China's lack of sensitivity to India's security interests and its failure to recognize India as a global power. This perception was only reinforced by China's suggestion to the US Pacific Fleet commander in 2009 that the Indian Ocean be recognized as part of a Chinese sphere of influence.[24]

Sino-Indian frictions are growing, and the potential for conflict remains high. Alarm is rising in India because of frequent and strident Chinese claims about the LAC in Arunachal Pradesh and Sikkim, where Indians complain of a dramatic rise in Chinese intrusions into Indian territory over the last few years, most along the border in Arunachal Pradesh, which China refers to as "Southern Tibet." China has also upped the ante on the border issue. It has regularly protested against the Indian prime minister's visit to Arunachal Pradesh, asserting its claims over the territory.[25] What has caught most observers of Sino-Indian ties by surprise, however, is the vehemence with which Beijing has contested recent Indian administrative and political actions in the state, even denying visas to Indian citizens of Arunachal Pradesh. The recent rounds of boundary negotiations have been a disappointing failure, with a growing perception in India that China is less willing to adhere to earlier political understandings about how to address the boundary dispute.

Pakistan, of course, has always been a crucial foreign policy asset for China, but with India's rise and US-Indian rapprochement, its role in China's grand strategy is bound to grow even further. Not surprisingly, China's shift away from its more cautious approach on Jammu and Kashmir, its growing military presence in Pakistan, its planned infrastructure linking Xinjiang and Gwadar, its issuing of stapled visas to residents of Jammu and Kashmir, and its supplying of nuclear reactors to Pakistan all confirm a new intensity behind China's old strategy of using Pakistan to secure its interests in the region.[26]

Strained Economic Ties

Even the much-vaunted economic ties have come under strain as the economic disparities between China and India have increased. Although India has achieved some remarkable growth rates in the last few years—indeed enjoying average annual rates of real income growth of 6 percent in the last two decades of the twentieth century—it still lags far behind China and will need many more years to match China's impressive economic performance. China has outperformed India in terms of levels of growth, of education, health, and living standards of its population, and of integrating its economy into the global economy. In sectors where India and China compete with each other for export markets, such as textiles, China is far ahead even as Sino-Indian competition for third markets is bound to further intensify. China's gross domestic product is four times that of India's. India accounts for less than 1 percent of world trade in goods and services and has been unable to market itself as attractive a destination for foreign direct investment as China. Meanwhile, investments by China account for merely 0.01 percent of total foreign investment in India. China's annual trade with India is only a fraction of its trade with Europe, Japan, and the United States. Indian exports to China are primarily dominated by raw materials and iron ore. India's challenge is to match Chinese exports to India and diversify India's export basket.[27] A rising trade deficit that is in favor of China is problematic for India, as is the Indian failure to use its core competencies to enter the Chinese market.

Sino-Indian trade tensions have also increased, especially as the economic downturn that started in 2008 began to make its effect palpable in China and India. Economic nationalism is on the rise in China, and the business environment is deteriorating, with China's attempt to force foreign companies to hand over their intellectual property and other trademarks if they want to keep selling their goods in China. As the two states compete across the globe for export markets, energy assets, and investment projects, some amount of competition is inevitable. This economic rivalry has intensified as both intrude into each other's strong areas, with China shifting its economy toward services and high-technology industries and India trying to rapidly expand its manufacturing base. India remains concerned about the Chinese imports flooding Indian markets and has accused Chinese companies of swamping its markets with low-quality products, even banning, albeit briefly and for safety reasons, Chinese-made toys in early 2009, and is the largest initiator of antidumping investigations against China under the WTO.[28] In the words of the Indian commerce secretary, "cooperation [between China and India] hasn't really worked."[29]

India remains reluctant to open up those domestic industries that have not faced foreign competition and ambivalent about allowing Chinese firms a "level playing field." The Indian security establishment views Chinese firms suspiciously as potential security hazards, given that the People's Liberation Army holds a stake in a number of Chinese companies. China has complained that its investments are subjected to rigorous security reviews and work visas for its executives are not swiftly processed. China has been vocal about its concerns about the investment climate in India as it relates to the Chinese firms, although most of the foreign direct-investment proposals from Chinese companies have managed to receive clearance from the Indian government in recent years.[30] There has been talk of a Sino-Indian free trade agreement for some time, but it is not readily evident that it would be a good idea. Given China's manipulation of its currency exchange rate, some see a "yuan trap" in the free-trade agreement.[31] Although India's long-term economic prospects may be much better than China's, and Chinese policymakers, under pressure from the United States to revalue their currency, are increasingly worried about India's competitive advantage, China remains the undisputed economic powerhouse driving the Asian and global economy, with India lagging somewhere behind.

Energy Competition

China is working aggressively to satisfy its energy requirements in the future. Recent Indian attempts notwithstanding, China has left India far behind insofar as its international diplomacy in the energy realm is concerned. Despite all the talk of Sino-Indian cooperation on energy security, the two sides are actually competing aggressively as their energy demands surge. While there have indeed been some attempts at cooperation, engendering a lot of enthusiasm in some quarters, these developments form a small part of a much broader Chinese-Indian energy relationship, which remains largely competitive, if not conflictual.

Indian concerns about rising Chinese influence across the globe are derived from the Indian perception that it is losing out to China in the energy race. The Chinese have an upper hand over India in bidding because they can clinch a deal at any cost, while Indian public-sector companies need to ensure that the investment provides at least a 12 percent rate of return. Chinese companies not only enjoy a head start over their Indian rivals but also have deeper pockets. India is a recent entrant into the global bidding process because the Indian government only deregulated the domestic oil sector in 2002. Buying foreign oil and gas fields for energy security has become a central mission for China, and the Chinese government has allowed its oil majors unprecedented freedom to achieve that goal. China realizes that its energy interests lie in geopolitical relations and thus focuses intensely on them to address its security needs. In that pursuit, Chinese oil companies have used all sorts of government aid to lure energy-rich states, including nonoil commitments, transfer of missile technologies, the veto of UN sanctions against countries where China has oil interests, and even education and development aid. The results are evident.

While India and China may collaborate in some overseas bids for foreign energy projects to avoid cut-throat competition, a lasting cooperative arrangement is highly unlikely. China is ahead of India in this process, and while it may try to assuage some Indian concerns by partnering with it on some projects, it is unlikely to gain much from the collaboration. It is India that needs to cooperate with China, rather than the other way around, because it is difficult for India to win over China when they bid for assets. Given that the Chinese are much larger participants in the global oil market, it is not clear what advantages they would derive from cooperation. In the long term, Chinese companies may see more gains in forming ventures with such experienced majors as BP, Royal Dutch Shell, and Exxon Mobil Corporation than in teaming with their Indian counterparts.

As a consequence, Sino-Indian relations have reached a stage where tensions are visible in almost all aspects of their bilateral relationship. The Chinese engagement policy of relying on economics and a selective convergence on global issues has reached a dead end. While India has not yet achieved the regional and global economic and political profile that China enjoys, it is increasingly bracketed with China as a rising or emerging power or even a global superpower. Indian elites who have been obsessed with Pakistan for more than sixty years have suddenly found a new object of fascination. India's main security concern now is not the increasingly decrepit state of Pakistan but an ever more assertive China, a shift that is widely viewed inside India as one that can facilitate better strategic planning. China is viewed by a large section of the Indian policy elite as a growing, aggressive nationalistic power whose ambitions are likely to reshape the contours of the regional and global balance of power, with deleterious consequences for Indian interests.

India Balances a Rising China

China's recent hardening toward India might well be a function of its internal vulnerabilities, but that is hardly a consolation to Indian policymakers who have to respond to an Indian public that increasingly wants the country to assert itself in the region and beyond. New Delhi has responded to the challenge posed by a rising China by adopting a more hardnosed policy vis-à-vis Beijing.

While there have always been and continue to be a range of opinions in India on how best to deal with China, a consensus seems to be evolving among the highest echelons of military planners and policymakers.[32] For a long time, Indian defense officials have been warning their government in rather blunt terms about the growing disparity between the two Asian powers. But the political leadership in India continued to act on the assumption that Beijing is not a short-term threat to India but rather needs to be watched over the long term. However, that assessment seems to be changing. After trying to ignore significant differences with China, Indian decision makers are finally acknowledging that the relationship between the countries is becoming increasingly contentious. Prime Minister Singh has suggested that "China would like to have a foothold in South Asia and we have to reflect on this reality. . . . It's important to be prepared."[33] The Indian defense minister has argued that China's increasing assertiveness is a "serious threat."[34] And a former national security adviser and special envoy to China, M. K. Narayanan, has openly accused Chinese hackers of attacking his website, as well as those of other government departments.[35]

An elite consensus is evolving in India that China's rise is posing problems for the country. "We are friends, not rivals," said the Chinese premier in India.[36]

But a growing number of Indians now see China as a competitor, if not a rival. Pew Research Center polls in 2011 and 2012 suggested that only 25 and 23 percent of Indians held a favorable view of China, with many viewing their neighbor as a "very serious threat."[37] More damaging is the perception gaining ground in India that China is the only major power that does not accept India as a rising global player that must be accommodated. The discord between the two countries thus remains entrenched, and their increasing economic strength and geopolitical standing has only underlined their rapidly growing ambitions. Although it is not entirely clear if China has well-defined policy objectives vis-à-vis India, Beijing's economic and military means to pursue its goals are greater than at any time in the recent past. In response, a process of military consolidation and buildup of key external partnerships is under way in India.

With a new robustness in its dealings with Beijing, New Delhi is signaling that there are limits to what is negotiable in Sino-Indian ties. In particular, it has adopted a harder line on Tibet by making it clear that it expects China to reciprocate on Jammu and Kashmir just as India has respected Chinese sensitivities on Tibet and Taiwan. Overriding Chinese objections, for example, the Indian government allowed one of its central universities, the Indira Gandhi National Open University, to confer an honorary doctorate on the Dalai Lama.[38] This is the same government that just a few years ago sent a note to all its ministers advising them not to attend a function organized by the Gandhi Peace Foundation to honor the Dalai Lama so as not to offend China.[39]

Ignoring pressures from Beijing, India also took part in the Nobel Peace Prize ceremony for Chinese dissident Liu Xiaobo in Oslo in November 2010. Beijing had asked several countries, including India, to boycott the ceremony or face its displeasure, describing the prize as open support for criminal activities in China. India was among the forty-four states that decided to participate, even as Iran, Iraq, Pakistan, Russia, and Saudi Arabia were among the nations that did not. There were suggestions that the Chinese premier might cancel his India trip in response, but this did not happen. Likewise, after Beijing began issuing stapled visas to the residents of Jammu and Kashmir and then denied a visa to the head of the Indian Army's northern command, New Delhi reacted forcefully and hinted that it was ready to review its long-standing Tibet and Taiwan policies. India also declined to endorse the "one China" policy during Wen's visit to India, a departure from past statements.[40] These developments are further evidence that India is reassessing its policy toward China as the latter's faster-than-expected rise has challenged the fundamentals of New Delhi's traditional approach to Beijing. India's robust partnership with the United States, its burgeoning ties with East and Southeast Asian nations as part of its Look East policy, and its military modernization are all aimed at managing China's dramatic rise.

Conclusion

India is gearing up to respond to China's rise with its own diplomatic and military overtures to the region, setting the stage for Sino-Indian strategic rivalry. The Indian policy trajectory toward China is evolving as India pursues a more forceful policy of internal and external balancing in an attempt to protect its core interests. The government is trying to fashion an effective response to the rise of China at a time of great regional and global turbulence. Although it is not entirely clear if there is a larger strategic framework shaping India's China policy, India's approach toward China is indeed undergoing a transformation, the full consequences of which will only be visible a few years down the line.

Both India and China have a vested interest in stabilizing their relationship by seeking out issues where their interests converge, but pursuing mutually desirable interests does not inevitably produce satisfactory solutions to strategic problems. A troubled history, coupled with structural uncertainties engendered by their simultaneous rise, is propelling the two Asian giants into a trajectory that they might find rather difficult to navigate in the coming years. For India, symbolism matters, especially in the context of acknowledging its rise as a major global power. That symbolism has not yet come from China. Sino-Indian ties have entered turbulent times, and they are likely to remain so for the foreseeable future.

India's economic engagement with China has merely produced a misperception that things are going well in Sino-Indian ties. However, the level of distrust has never been higher. Even in the economic realm, there are now questions about the lopsided nature of the relationship. China's belief that economic engagement with India will convince Indian elites to compromise on other, more contentious issues has not come to fruition. Unless Beijing is able to demonstrate that it is serious about addressing India's core security concerns, there is little likelihood of Sino-Indian relations getting back on an even keel. The Chinese exchange strategy of primarily relying on economic engagement seems to be failing, and an immediate reorientation is needed.

Notes

1. "China Is Threat No.1, Says Fernandes," *Hindustan Times*, May 3, 1998.
2. "Nuclear Anxiety: Indian's Letter to Clinton on the Nuclear Testing," *New York Times*, May 13, 1998.
3. Anil K. Joseph, "Wen to Seek Resolution of Border Dispute," *Indian Express*, March 15, 2005.
4. "Declaration on Principles for Relations and Comprehensive Cooperation between the People's Republic of China and the Republic of India," Ministry of Foreign Affairs of the

People's Republic of China, June 23, 2003, www.fmprc.gov.cn/eng/wjdt/2649/t22852.htm (accessed September 27, 2012).

5. Amit Baruah, "China Keeps Its Word on Sikkim," *The Hindu*, May 7, 2004.

6. "A Shared Vision for the 21st Century of the People's Republic of China and the Republic of India," Ministry of Foreign Affairs of the People's Republic of China, January 14, 2008, www.fmprc.gov.cn/eng/wjdt/2649/t399545.htm (accessed September 27, 2012).

7. Ibid. The declaration included a statement of particular interest to India: "The Indian side reiterates its aspirations for permanent membership of the UN Security Council. The Chinese side attaches great importance to India's position as a major developing country in international affairs. The Chinese side understands and supports India's aspirations to play a greater role in the United Nations, including in the Security Council."

8. "India-Russia-China Axis Hinted at after Kosovo Strikes," *Associated Foreign Press*, March 28, 1999. See also "Russia, China, India Pile Up Pressure on West over Kosovo," *Indian Express*, March 26, 1999.

9. James Clad, "Convergent Chinese and Indian Perspectives on the Global Order," in *The India-China Relationship: What the United States Needs to Know*, ed. Francine R. Frankel and Harry Harding (New York: Columbia University Press, 2004), 285.

10. Ibid.

11. Juliet Eilperin, "US Pushes for Emissions Cuts from China, Developing Nations," *Washington Post*, December 19, 2009.

12. K. G. Narendranath, "Jairam Has a Copenhagen Axis: India, China, Brazil, South Africa," *Indian Express*, December 8, 2009.

13. Edward R. Fried and Philip H. Trezise, *Oil Security: Retrospect and Prospect* (Washington, DC: Brookings Institution Press, 1993), 1.

14. Erica Downs, "The Chinese Energy Security Debate," *China Quarterly* 177, March (2004): 21–22.

15. Siddhartha Varadarajan, "India, China Primed for Energy Cooperation," *The Hindu*, January 13, 2006.

16. Pranab Dhal Samanta, "N-Energy, UN: China and India Signal Friendship, Not Rivalry," *Indian Express*, January 15, 2008.

17. Siddharth Srivastava, "The Foundations for an Asian Oil and Gas Grid," *Asia Times Online*, December 1, 2005, www.atimes.com/atimes/South_Asia/GL01Df02.html (accessed October 10, 2013).

18. Yan Zhang, "India-China Relations in One of the Best Periods in History," *The Hindu*, April 9, 2009.

19. S. Laxman, "China Seeks Nuclear Input from India," *Times of India*, December 13, 2003.

20. "Nervous China May Attack India by 2012: Defence Expert," *Indian Express*, July 12, 2009.

21. See, for example, "China Could Attack India by 2012, Claims Analyst," *Press Trust of India*, July 12, 2009.

22. Li Hongmei, "Veiled Threat or Good Neighbor?," *People's Daily Online*, June 19, 2009, http://english.peopledaily.com.cn/90002/96417/6682302.html (accessed September 27, 2012).

23. "China Blocked India's ADB Plan over Arunachal, Confirms Krishna," *Indian Express*, July 10, 2009.

24. Yuriko Koike, "The Struggle for Mastery of the Pacific," Project Syndicate, May 12, 2010, www.project-syndicate.org/commentary/koike5/English (accessed September 27, 2012).

25. "China 'Strongly' Protests over PM's Visit to Arunachal Pradesh," *Daily News and Analysis*, October 13, 2009.

26. On the China-Pakistan-India triangle, see Harsh V. Pant, "The Pakistan Thorn in China-India-US Relations," *Washington Quarterly* 35, no. 1 (2012): 83–95.

27. Amit Mitra, "An Unequal Relationship," *Times of India*, January 12, 2008.

28. Peter Wonacott, "Downturn Heightens China-India Tension on Trade," *Wall Street Journal*, March 20, 2009.

29. Ibid.

30. Shishir Gupta, "Contrary to What Left Says, 87% of FDI Proposals from Chinese Firms Cleared," *Indian Express*, November 13, 2006.

31. Swaminathan S. Anklesaria Aiyar, "Free Trade Area or Yuan Trap?" *Times of India*, November 26, 2006.

32. For a good typology of India's China debate, see Mohan Malik, "Eyeing the Dragon: India's China Debate," Special Assessment (Honolulu: Asia-Pacific Center for Security Studies, December 2003), www.apcss.org/Publications/SAS/ChinaDebate/ChinaDebate_Malik.pdf (accessed September 27, 2012).

33. "PM Warns on China's S Asia Foothold," *Indian Express*, September 7, 2010.

34. Rajat Pandit, "Assertive China a Worry, Says Antony," *Times of India*, September 14, 2010.

35. "Chinese Hacked PMO Computers, says Narayanan," *Indian Express*, January 19, 2010.

36. Jim Yardley, "In India, Chinese Leader Pushes Trade," *New York Times*, December 16, 2010.

37. The details of these polls are available at "Opinion of China: Do You Have a Favorable or Unfavorable View of China? Percent Responding Favorable, All Years Measured," Pew Global Attitudes Project, Key Indicators Database, http://pewglobal.org/database/?indicator=24&survey=12&response=Favorable&mode=table (accessed September 27, 2012).

38. Anubhuti Vishnoi, "MEA Gives Nod to IGNOU for Doctorate to Dalai Lama," *Indian Express*, April 24, 2011.

39. "Pleasing Beijing, Govt Tells Its Ministers Don't Attend Dalai Lama Honour Function," *Indian Express*, November 4, 2007.

40. Pramit Pal Chaudhuri, "China's Flip-Flop on Kashmir," *Hindustan Times*, April 15, 2011.

CHAPTER 7

AUSTRALIA'S FITFUL ENGAGEMENTS OF INDIA

Ian Hall

INDIA HAS BEEN CALLED Australia's "neglected neighbor," and many observers complain that it has long lacked the level of official and public interest it deserves.[1] Yet for more than forty years, successive Australian governments have sought—periodically but quite sincerely—to engage India and to build stronger bilateral ties, especially in trade and regional security. These attempts at engagement have, admittedly, been fitful, and they have not always borne fruit. Sometimes they have not succeeded for simple reasons: a lack of mutual interests, understanding, or investment; a change of government; or a foreign policy misstep. But the history of these engagements also shows a much bigger challenge for Australian policymakers and those of other middling to small states. Australia's intermittent engagements of India, this chapter argues, demonstrate above all the problems faced by states beyond India's immediate region in gaining diplomatic traction in New Delhi. For states like Australia—a "middle power" with limited global influence—engaging states like India is much harder than some observers are willing to acknowledge.[2]

This chapter examines Australia's strategies for engaging India over the past forty years, with emphasis on the period since 1991. The first part looks back at what estranged postimperial Australia and postcolonial India in the postwar era. The second examines the attempts to engage India using catalytic strategies, through public diplomacy and then trade, in the 1970s and 1980s. The third looks at the critical period after 1991 in which India emerged in both academic and policy circles as a putative and actual priority for Canberra and in which public and commercial engagement was intensified, only to come to a halt in 1998 after India's nuclear tests and Australia's harsh response. The fourth section explores attempts to reengage India after the Pokhran II nuclear tests, efforts that shifted focus away from public and economic strategies toward traditional and nontraditional security issues. The penultimate part assesses the various reasons why Australia's engagements of India have failed to gain traction with India. The conclusion looks at the prospects for improved relations in the coming decade.

Estrangement

Australia and India soon became estranged during the early Cold War period, despite early goodwill, the establishment of diplomatic missions in New Delhi in 1944 and Canberra in 1945, and Jawaharlal Nehru's invitation to Australia to observe the Asian Relations Conference in 1947. Difficult personal relations between Nehru (prime minister from 1947 to 1964) and Robert Menzies (prime minister from 1949 to 1965) and tensions over the "White Australia Policy," as well as contrasting imperial and superpower loyalties, pushed Australia and India apart during the 1950s and 1960s. Whether or not Menzies was indifferent to Asia—a topic much debated by historians—it was the case that he and Nehru had contrasting political ideologies and style.[3] They clashed repeatedly over the future of the Commonwealth, about nonalignment, and by extension about the best means to ensure regional security. Menzies denounced Nehru as a neutralist; Nehru denounced Menzies as a cold warrior.[4] Indian policymakers and journalists complained about Australia's immigration policies and about its refusal to condemn apartheid in South Africa, sometimes implying racism was the reason for both.[5] The two governments disagreed about the threat posed by communism and about the status of the People's Republic of China. Although Menzies went three times to New Delhi and posted a series of leading diplomats to the Australian mission, Nehru never deigned to visit Australia and—perhaps in recognition of the latter's national obsession but perhaps also to indicate his view of Australia's geopolitical importance—dispatched a series of sportsmen rather than professional diplomats as high commissioners, including former Test cricketer Kumar Shri Duleepsinhji.[6]

These clashes of personalities and principles were matched by contrasting economic and security interests. Under Nehru, India moved toward economic self-reliance. Australia, by contrast, was and remains a trading state, albeit one with deeply entrenched protectionist tendencies in the labor market and in certain manufacturing industries. Australia succeeded in exporting certain goods to India during the Cold War, primarily wool, vegetables (mainly pulses), coal, and some metals (especially lead and zinc) but never more than 1 or 2 percent of its exports.[7] Australia also sent India a great deal of aid, both as part of the Colombo Plan for regional development in the Asia-Pacific and as part of other schemes; as Meg Gurry notes, until 1972, Australia gave more aid to India than to any other state bar one.[8] This aid was only a fraction, however, of that contributed by others (Gurry estimates Australia's aid at about one-thirteenth that given by Canada), and Australia balanced its donations to India with those it gave to Pakistan, earning little credit as a consequence from either.[9]

Even greater divergences of interest existed in the realm of security. Australia was—and again remains—an enthusiast for alliances and multilateral institutions, remaining tightly tied to the United States by the Australia, New Zealand, United States (ANZUS) Security Treaty throughout and after the Cold War.[10] Under Menzies, it was a cheerleader for the Southeast Asia Treaty Organization, founded in 1954 with Pakistan as a member, and which India perceived as a possible source of trouble.[11] India's commitments to nonalignment, then to different conceptions of "strategic autonomy,"[12] and then after 1971 to the Soviet Union[13] placed it starkly at odds with Australia's favored approach to regional security challenges. Moreover, its core security interests—maintaining domestic stability and the stability of its immediate region, while managing possible threats from Pakistan and China—did not lend themselves to wider concerns or entanglements in alliances and institutions. Mounting suspicion of American motives in particular, and Western motives in general, during the latter half of the Cold War made it even more difficult for Indian policymakers to conceive of their interests as convergent or congruent with Australia's.

Edging Away from Estrangement

Although Indira Gandhi visited Australia in 1968, no Australian prime minister traveled in the opposite direction for more than a decade after Menzies's last trip in 1959. This lack of personal contact between prime ministers symbolized the distance between the two states: Divided over America's role in the region, Commonwealth issues, and communism, they also had few interests in common. Yet despite these challenges, Australia made a series of attempts to engage India from the early 1970s onward, seeking to move beyond more than two decades of estrangement during which the volume of bilateral trade declined and diplomatic relations became attenuated. In part, this shift was part of a long-running debate among Australian policymakers and strategists about the Asia-Pacific region and Australia's place within it.[14] In part too, the shift was a function of the change of government in 1972 that brought the Australian Labor Party (ALP) back to power for the first time in twenty-three years, with the mercurial Gough Whitlam as prime minister.[15] Whitlam soon embarked on a busy schedule of visits to regional capitals, as he had done—sometimes controversially, as in the case of his 1971 trip to Beijing—while in Opposition.

Whitlam's attempted engagement of India concentrated, in the main, on public diplomacy, employing a catalytic strategy to try to shift the attitudes of policymakers and the Indian populace about Australia. He dispatched a new high commissioner to New Delhi, Bruce Grant, with a mandate to improve cultural ties and mutual public understanding.[16] And he provided Grant with a good story to tell, pronouncing that Australia would henceforth pursue a more "independent" line in its foreign policy and dismantle the last vestiges of the White Australia Policy, opening Australia to migrants from Asia as well as Europe.[17] Whitlam showed himself both tolerant of India's closeness to the Soviet Union after 1971 and even of India's nuclear test in 1974 and Indira Gandhi's declaration of the Emergency the following year, tempering official criticism of both. In the main, however, Whitlam's engagement of India remained at this level of gesture politics, even to those sympathetic to him. Despite Australia's newfound "independence" and despite suggestions that Whitlam or his representatives might attend summits of the Non-Aligned Movement, to take but two examples, Australia remained staunchly committed to the ANZUS Treaty and to the United States.[18] And Whitlam dragged his feet when it came to the substantive issues, notably India's proposal for an Indian Ocean zone of peace, which would have excluded the Americans from the region and ran counter to Australian strategic orthodoxy. His and successive governments paid lip service to the proposal but did little to advance it.[19]

The more substantive breakthroughs came under Whitlam's conservative successor, Malcolm Fraser. In 1976, Australia and India finally concluded a bilateral trade agreement, although not hoped-for tariff reductions, leading to a significant, if not dramatic, increase in the value of Australian exports during the latter half of the 1970s and into the 1980s.[20] Gurry argues that Fraser also made good use of the Commonwealth to engage a number of states, including India, winning favor in New Delhi and elsewhere by criticizing South Africa for its policy of apartheid and creating new working parties within the organization to examine a number of transnational challenges faced by member states, from trade to terrorism.[21] Nor was Fraser shy of gesture politics, making in 1979 the longest trip to India of any prime minister then or since and taking his immediate family with him. An apparently appreciative Indian government made him the guest of honor at that year's Republic Day parade.

These slow, incremental improvements to some aspects of the relationship continued under the ALP government of Bob Hawke (1983–91), but other elements either failed to improve or slowly deteriorated. An Australia-India Business Council was set up in 1986 to promote trade and investment. Although Australia's exports to India grew—albeit unevenly—from A$220 million in 1982–83 to A$555 million in 1988–89, Indian exports to Australia grew more slowly, from A$171 million in 1985–86 to A$247 million in 1988–89.[22] At an official level, a flurry of meetings and forums were arranged from 1987 onward, with a joint ministerial commission in 1989 and defense and disarmament talks being held a year later. But elsewhere there were signs of Australian neglect of the relationship. Sandy Gordon observes that by 1988, Australia was providing more foreign aid to Mauritius, Nepal, and Sri Lanka than the mere A$2.8 million it gave to India in that year. The impression that Australia was less than wholly committed to India was compounded by the fact that while Canberra claimed that it could not provide more on a tight budget, it still found the means to give A$35 million to China.[23] Australia's priorities were also evident in the respective budgets for cultural diplomacy in New Delhi: A paltry A$30,000 was allocated for the high commission during most of the 1980s, compared to A$1 million for the embassy in Beijing.[24]

At the close of the Cold War, Australia and India remained, if not worlds apart as some studies might have it, certainly at some distance.[25] The relationship still had tensions, and it was not free of outright suspicion. Toward the end of the 1980s, India's decision to begin to modernize and expand its navy, together with Australia's move to a two-ocean strategy, involving relocating naval assets to Western Australia, generated concern about possible clashes of interests.[26] Journalists and Opposition politicians in Canberra openly discussed the possibility that India's navy might threaten Australian assets in the Indian Ocean, while the defense minister, Kim Beazley, from Western Australia, called its modernization "intriguing."[27] A 1990 Senate report expanded on such doubts, observing that "India does not represent a threat to Australia or the countries of South East Asia" but also cautioning that "India has a responsibility . . . not to raise concerns among its neighbours that Indian military capability might be used against them without direct provocation."[28] Moreover, it noted "grounds for concern about India's views of its role as a regional policeman and the degree to which coercion enters into its calculations of enforcement," as well as worries about a possible drive toward acquiring a nuclear weapon.[29] These suspicions were balanced by the belief, expressed most clearly by the Department of Defence, that India's naval buildup was more about status than power projection, but such reservations about India's military power and strategic intentions were not wholly forgotten in Canberra until well into the 1990s.[30]

Catalysis and Condemnation

The early 1990s saw a significant push from both within and outside the Australian government for a new attempt at engaging India. This change was brought about by the perception that India was beginning to emerge as a significant economic force in the region after the economic reforms of the Rajiv Gandhi government and the more dramatic changes under the leadership of P. V. Narasimha Rao in 1991 and 1992. But there was also a concerted effort made by academics and other commentators to highlight Australia's apparent "neglect" of India and a call for a different, broader approach to engagement that went beyond official meetings and bilateral trade.

These concerns and proposals were set out most frankly in a report of the Senate Committee on Foreign Affairs, Defence and Trade, *Australia-India Relations: Trade and Security*, a prosaically titled document of remarkable candidness. The report complained about a "weak institutional memory and little empathy with Indian culture" in Canberra and, in response to a series of submissions from academics in the field, lamented the lack of sustained support for scholarly and policy-relevant work on South Asia.[31] It noted that only one Australian media outlet, the government-funded Australian Broadcasting Corporation, had a correspondent in New Delhi and that there was a "high state of ignorance or neglect of India in Australia."[32] The contrast with the efforts displayed in seeking to understand China was stark, and the report called for a similar "strategic change of direction" in Australian policy to that undertaken with regard to China in the mid to late 1970s.[33]

The Senate report made recommendations in four areas, consistent with a catalytic strategy of public diplomatic, educational, and economic engagement. First, it urged new initiatives in education, including the creation of a new Indian Studies Centre that could conduct scholarly research and help train experts for the foreign affairs, defense, and intelligence communities, as well as provide information to Australian businesses. Alongside it, the report recommended the founding of an Australia-India Council with funds to support cultural linkages and people-to-people connections.[34] Second, the report called for a new "information policy" with regard to India, generating a "whole of government" approach to gathering and sharing political and economic intelligence to aid policymaking.[35] Third, it recommended investment in government support for trade and the development of a new strategy for supporting Australian businesses in India. And last, it urged a new diplomatic approach that concentrated on better explaining Australia's views on core interests and on encouraging India to further liberalize and open up its economy, in parallel to similar work done by the Americans and other Western states.[36]

The Senate report led to significant new attempts at engagement in the areas it identified. A National Centre for South Asian Studies—although not "Indian Studies"—was created in 1992, with initial funds from the Commonwealth Department of Education and eight Australian universities, and was based in Melbourne at Monash University. One of its early tasks, apart from consolidating a network of Australian scholars in the field, was to produce a package of India-related teaching materials for Australian secondary schools. An Australia-India Council was also founded by the Department of Foreign Affairs and Trade (DFAT) at the same time—albeit fourteen years after its counterpart for China—and was followed by an India-Australia Council in New Delhi three years later. Efforts were also made to improve official knowledge of India and to encourage information sharing across government, not least with the publication in 1994 of a major study, *India's Economy at the Midnight Hour*, produced (tellingly) by DFAT's East Asia Analytical Unit and intended to underpin Australia's economic engagement of India. The report dwelled on the emergence of a new Indian middle class and the opportunities it might have for Australian businesses.[37] Funds were also located in both New Delhi and Canberra to provide for a series of high-profile public and economic diplomacy initiatives. In 1994, the "India Today" exhibition toured Australian cities; in 1996, the "Australia-India New Horizons" program took place in six cities in India.[38]

These various initiatives paid some dividends. Bilateral trade grew quite strongly from 1989–90 to 1994–95, with Australian exports up from A$590 million to A$975 million and Indian exports up from A$278 million to A$532 million.[39] Political interactions increased in intensity, despite the fact that, as the first foreign affairs white paper of John Howard's prime ministership (1996–2007) declared, India was not a state that "most substantially engage[d] Australia's interests."[40] Although there were no prime ministerial trips in either direction during the 1990s, there were a number of official dialogues at lower levels and the start of track 1.5 and track 2 dialogues on the Indian Ocean, some under the auspices of a new Indian Ocean Centre at Curtin University in Perth, Western Australia.[41]

This gradual improvement in relations ended with India's nuclear tests in 1998 and Australia's highly critical response to them. Australia's reaction to the Pokhran II tests was, as one observer has called it, "extreme": Although Australia did not go so far as to impose economic sanctions, it suspended all official visits and aid (except humanitarian programs), recalled its defense attaché from New Delhi, and loudly declaimed India's actions, as well as Pakistan's.[42] In the media, policymakers, scholars, and commentators were equally harsh in their criticism, and their "tone," one Indian expert has observed, "was seen by India as rude, offensive and on occasions abusive."[43] Both the official and the media responses were also perceived in New Delhi to be hypocritical—with some justification, since Australia's national security is guaranteed, at least in part, by American nuclear weapons through extended nuclear deterrence and since Australia remained willing to sell uranium to France, which had recently tested weapons of its own in the South Pacific.[44]

Although defense ties were restored in mid-2000 following a Senate report on the Indian and Pakistani tests and prior to Howard's visit to New Delhi, Canberra's exaggerated response to the nuclear tests caused lasting damage to Indian perceptions of Australia and a significant setback in Australia's attempts at engaging India. It was not until the mid-2000s that momentum was restored to those efforts.

Reengaging

Australia began to reengage India, as America did, after the events of September 11, 2001, changed the regional security dynamics of South Asia.[45] Although it continued to develop economic ties and the diplomatic infrastructure needed to support Australian businesses in India, this new round of engagement especially emphasized security issues rather than education or public diplomacy. Government support for the latter declined. To take just one high-profile initiative as an example, the National Centre for South Asian Studies, less than ten years old, was downsized and merged into the Monash Asia Institute in 2001 as government and other funds dried up. Other kinds of formal and informal public engagement emerged but did not completely take the place of these efforts. An Australia-India Strategic Research Fund was set up in 2006 to support work in science and technology, especially biotechnology, and facilitate the movement of scholars between Australia and India. The Australia India Institute was founded by the University of Melbourne in 2008 with funds from the Commonwealth Department of Education, Employment, and Workplace Relations, as well as the University of New South Wales and La Trobe University.[46] And while South Asian studies as a field arguably languished at Australian universities, South Asian students, many of them from India, began to study other subjects in those institutions in large numbers. Back in 1993, there were barely seven hundred Indian students at Australian universities, but by the peak year of 2007–8, there were almost thirty-five thousand.[47] This influx of students, as we shall see, generated new challenges in the bilateral relationship, although they made a significant contribution to the Australian economy.

The wider economic relationship improved during the 2000s but then stalled after the global financial crisis of 2007–8 slowed growth in both states. Two-way trade increased from A$3.3 billion in 2000 to A$20.9 billion in 2009, and investment flowed in both directions, although more from India to Australia, mainly into the mining sector, than in the opposite direction.[48] Thereafter, however, the growth leveled off, with bilateral trade remaining at or slightly below A$20 billion per annum. Today India accounts for about 3 percent of Australia's trade, compared to about 20 percent for China but up from the 0.5–1.5 percent of the 1970s and 1980s.[49] This trade remains, as it has for decades, heavily weighted in Australia's favor, with A$14.5 billion worth of exports going to India in 2009, and it also remains dominated by a narrow range of goods and services. The biggest growth area, as the 1990s Senate and DFAT reports predicted, was in energy resources, especially coal, but natural gas and uranium are emerging as new commodities for trade with India.[50] In these areas, Australia has seen significant business and investment from Indian firms, especially in liquefied natural gas.[51] Australian government support for its businesses in India has also expanded significantly since the late 1990s. By 2013, Austrade had opened as many offices in India as they had in China—eleven in total, from Ahmedabad to Pune and Kolkata to Kochi—and Australia is seeking a comprehensive economic cooperation agreement to eliminate tariffs and other barriers to trade.[52]

In parallel DFAT has expanded its footprint in India, upgrading its mission in Chennai to a consulate general in 2007, doubling its staff at the consulate in Mumbai, and adding further diplomats to the high commission in New Delhi.[53] These diplomatic initiatives were reinforced with a series of ministerial-level interactions. There are now annual dialogues between Australian and Indian foreign and education ministers, as well as a joint ministerial commission that involves trade ministers in its discussions.

Security was the issue, however, that dominated Australia's reengagement of India after 2001, under both the Howard coalition government and the Kevin Rudd–Julia Gillard ALP-led administrations. This area, once one of some tension in the bilateral relationship, was opened up by mutual concerns about terrorism and—sotto voce—about the rise of China.[54] But they also emerged from a period of far more intense, high-level political and official engagement than had occurred at any time before. Howard (in 2000 and 2006), Rudd (2009), and Gillard (2012) each traveled to India, as did a number of prominent ministers and politicians. Rupakjyoti Borah notes more than half a dozen visits to India by Australian politicians in 2000 alone, including those by Foreign Minister Alexander Downer, his ALP counterpart, Opposition Leader Beazley, and Trade Minister Mark Vaile.[55] In late August 2001, the first India-Australia Strategic Dialogue was held in New Delhi. These various meetings and others bore fruit in a series of bilateral deals on security issues during the remainder of the 2000s.

In 2003, the two states concluded a Memorandum of Understanding on Cooperation in Combating International Terrorism, mandating greater intelligence-sharing and interagency collaboration in counterterrorism.[56] This was followed by the 2006 India-Australia Memorandum of Understanding on Defence Cooperation, signed during Howard's final visit to India as prime minister. Three years later they agreed the 2009 India-Australia Joint Declaration on Security Cooperation, noting shared concerns in regional institutions, maritime security, terrorism, and organized crime, as well as disarmament and nonproliferation, and pledged to generate a "comprehensive framework" to address these issues.[57] This framework was to involve visits and talks from the foreign-minister level downward, including service-to-service exchanges, training, and joint exercises.

Having inveigled India into becoming a "strategic partner," Canberra then set about attempting to cajole New Delhi into the kind of regional security multilateralism Australians have long preferred. This marked a partial reversal of earlier approaches to India's involvement in East Asian affairs. When prime minister in the late 1980s, Paul Keating had snubbed India when it sought support to join the Asia-Pacific Economic Cooperation (APEC) forum. By the mid-2000s, however, Australia had determined to bring India into the multilateral fold. Rudd envisaged India as an integral part of his mooted "Asia Pacific Community" put forward in 2008, prompting a mildly enthusiastic response from Pranab Mukherjee, then India's external affairs minister.[58] While this idea did not survive Rudd's sacking as prime minister in 2010, Australia has persisted with the multilateral approach, most clearly in the joint Australian-Indian scheme to revitalize the Indian Ocean Rim Association for Regional Cooperation (created in 1997) and the Indian Ocean Naval Symposium (created in 2008). Canberra sees both organizations as means by which to involve India in multilateral modes of tackling regional security challenges, from piracy and other nontraditional threats to the security of the northern Indian Ocean sea lanes of communication (SLOCs).[59]

In sum, whereas in 1990 Australia had worried about India becoming a destabilizing force in its own region and in the wider Indo-Pacific, by the mid-2000s it had come to regard India as a trustworthy partner and security provider.[60] It was in this context that the ALP-led government of Gillard (2010–13) was able to reverse its long-standing policy of opposing the export of uranium to India in late 2011—one of the few examples of Australia utilizing a simple exchange strategy of engagement. The uranium issue had long rankled both Indian governments and the Indian population more broadly, both noting that Australia was willing to sell the resource to China, with its somewhat checkered proliferation history, but not to democratic India.[61] The Howard government had signaled in 2006 that, in the aftermath of the US-Indian Civil Nuclear Agreement, it would be willing to consider uranium sales, only to have this policy overturned after the election of Rudd in 2007. Gillard's decision was followed by the commencement of talks for an Australian-Indian civil nuclear agreement, the outcome of which is still pending.

Neglected Neighbor?

Since the 1970s, Australia has engaged India repeatedly, as we have seen, although fitfully.[62] There have been periods of outright neglect—deliberate and unintentional—but equally there have been periods of sincere effort. In the main, Australia has employed catalytic strategies: using public diplomacy in the early 1970s and again in the early 1990s, letting trade and investment take the lead in the 1980s, and concentrating on building ties to India's diplomatic, defense, and intelligence communities during the 2000s and afterward, with a focus on mutual security concerns. Personal diplomacy by individual leaders and high-ranking politicians and officials has also been used, from Menzies's early trips to New Delhi through to the flurry of interactions in 2008.[63] Only very rarely, as with the uranium decision in 2011, have exchange strategies been utilized.

The payoffs from these bouts of engagement may have been modest, but it is unclear whether "neglect" per se is to blame. As we have seen, Australian prime ministers have shown themselves far more willing to visit India than their Indian counterparts have been keen to make the trip to Australia, making eleven visits between 1951 and 2013, compared to an Indian total of four. Australia has, moreover, dispatched a series of its best diplomats to India, from Sir Walter Crocker and Sir Arthur Tange in the 1950s and 1960s to, more recently, John McCarthy (high commissioner to India 2004–09) and Peter Varghese, former director of the peak intelligence assessment body, the Office of National Assessments, then high commissioner to India (2009–12), and now secretary of DFAT. Australian public investment in the study of India has been modest but is nonetheless significant, and Australia has hosted a series of internationally prominent experts on that country, from A. L. Basham to Robin Jeffrey, as well as research centers.[64]

Australia has also long faced a chronic problem in dealing with India: the sheer challenge of attracting and holding the attention of its tiny political and bureaucratic elite, faced as it is with multiple domestic and international issues. This problem is especially acute in foreign affairs. The Indian Foreign Service (IFS) is minuscule by international standards, especially for an aspiring great power, with barely seven hundred officers, and remains hidebound by out-of-date selection, promotion, and career development processes, as well as inadequate support from think tanks and universities.[65] It has very limited resources deployed for dealing with middling to small states such as Australia—perhaps only a couple of IFS officers are able to spare their attention for a few hours a week. These challenges are compounded by the residual belief of some in New Delhi that Australia is a far-away country of little consequence to its core concerns or an American satrap with little will or capacity for an independent foreign or strategic policy.[66]

Concentrating on "neglect" also distracts attention from a number of avoidable missteps made by Australia in its dealings with India that have nothing to do with intentional or accidental inattention. Australian support for the exclusion of India from APEC is one such mistake.[67] The decision to sell surplus-to-requirements Mirage IIIs to Pakistan in 1990 is another classic example: Despite apparent reluctance on the part of DFAT, this sale went ahead at a time of significant tension between the South Asian neighbors and seemingly without adequate warning to the Indian government.[68] Further problems have arisen in terms of the treatment of Indian citizens in Australia and the management of the Indian media. The detention and deportation of Dr. Mohamed Haneef on entirely spurious grounds of involvement in terrorism in 2007,[69] followed by the lackluster official response to attacks on Indian students in Melbourne in 2009, significantly damaged Australia's reputation as a welcoming destination for Indian migrants and students.[70] But the biggest self-generated obstacle of all was Australia's stance on nuclear nonproliferation and uranium sales, albeit modified in 2011, which rankled Indian policymakers and public opinion alike.

None of this is to deny that Australia was too slow to recognize India's potential and slow to devise strategies for engagement, especially when its approach is compared to its policies toward China. With the latter, Australian officials and businesspeople began exploring economic opportunities—initially for the export of raw materials, especially coal and wool—very early, in the late 1970s, as Deng Xiaoping took his first steps toward liberalization. Moreover, Australia was able to offer China something that it could not get elsewhere at that time: cheap and accessible raw materials for industry and infrastructure and a chance to get to know Western business practices in a relatively benign political environment. Because it took another decade at least before Australia began to explore its opportunities in India, other players were able to establish themselves and provide India's economy, in particular, with similar goods and services to those Australia had to offer. Public and economic engagement during the latter part of the 1980s and 1990s admittedly produced some rewards, especially in trade. And Australia has arguably done well to forge a strategic partnership with India since 1998, especially given its unusually harsh criticism of Pokhran II. Whether Australia and India can build on the foundations and achieve a closer working relationship on Indian Ocean security and other issues, however, remains to be seen.

Conclusion: From Engagement to Enmeshment?

Australia has struggled to engage India, with neither exchange nor catalytic strategies working as well as might have been expected. The Australian government is often blamed for what failures there have been, from diplomatic missteps to short-term, impatient attitudes that may well be ill-suited to the particular challenge of engaging India. But Australian officialdom is not wholly at fault. In large part, Australia has struggled to engage India because it is too marginal a regional player, to Indian minds, and because it has tried to get New Delhi's attention at much the same time as many other, bigger, louder, richer, and more powerful suitors. Since 1991 and especially since 2001, America, China, various

European countries, and many other Asian states have sought to grab and hold India's attention. And the capacity of India's government to cope with the entreaties of multiple would-be engagers, especially in terms of its tiny Ministry of External Affairs, remains extremely limited.

Two factors, however, may reshape Australia-India relations in the coming decade. The first is what David Brewster has called "strategic convergence"—the alignment of strategic policies driven by common challenges, especially concerning China and the security of the northern Indian Ocean SLOCs.[71] For some analysts, this convergence of interests between Australia and India heralds a new era of strategic engagement between them.[72] But as Brewster warns, India's strategists have paid very little attention to what Australia might offer beyond resources and to whether Australia is capable of action independent of the United States. As a consequence, he writes, "there is little perceived imperative to engage with Australia or any real sense that India should take Australia's opinions into consideration, particularly when making judgments about China or the Indian Ocean."[73] The US "pivot" to the Asia-Pacific may change these dynamics, helping to bridge the divide, but it is equally possible that, despite common interests, Australia is left on the sidelines, watching as naval rivalry between China, on the one side, and India and the United States, on the other, develops off its western coast.

The second factor may have more positive effects. Australia itself is changing, shifting understandings of India and relationships with Indians. Permanent migration from India is growing. In 1982, barely 1,600 Indians migrated to Australia to live and work. That number increased to around 5,500 by 1991, but it was not until the 2000s that Indian migrants really began to flow into Australia.[74] By 2011–12, their numbers had grown so much that India overtook China and the United Kingdom as the source of the largest number of permanent migrants—28,310 in that year alone.[75] Alongside them came temporary entrants—students and workers on short-term visas. On July 1, 2011, there were 343,070 Indian-born people in Australia, a number 90 percent higher than the corresponding figure for June 30, 2006.[76] To put this in perspective, the number of Indian-born Australian residents is now almost as large as the number of Chinese-born Australian residents (391,060 in June 2011), with only the United Kingdom (1,180,160) and New Zealand (564,920) supplying more foreign-born residents.[77] This influx is transforming Australian society, bringing not just new skills but also new cuisine, dress, popular culture, and ideas. And while the Indian diaspora in Australia has not yet begun to exercise political influence as it has, for example, in Canada, the United States, or the United Kingdom, it is reasonable to think that it will begin to do so soon. Australia's fitful engagements of India may become less fitful once that influence is felt.

Notes

1. See Meg Gurry, *India: Australia's Neglected Neighbour? 1947–1996* (Brisbane: Centre for the Study of Australia-Asia Relations, Griffith University, 1996), or Peter Mayer and Purnendra Jain, "Beyond Cricket: Australia-India Evolving Relations," *Australian Journal of Political Science* 45, no. 1 (2010): 133–48.

2. On Australia as a "middle power," see inter alia Mark Beeson, "Can Australia Save the World? The Limits and Possibilities of Middle Power Diplomacy," *Australian Journal of International Affairs* 65, no. 5 (2011): 563–77.

3. For a critical view of Menzies, Asia in general, and India in particular, see Gurry, *Neglected Neighbour?*, 15–17, 27–30. For a revisionist view, see David Martin Jones and Mike Lawrence Smith, "Misreading Menzies and Whitlam: Reassessing the Ideological Construction of Australian Foreign Policy," *The Round Table* 89, no. 355 (2000): 387–406.

4. See especially Meg Gurry, "Leadership and Bilateral Relations: Menzies and Nehru, Australia and India, 1949–1964," *Pacific Affairs* 65, no. 4 (1992/1993): 510–26.

5. Gurry, *Neglected Neighbour?*, 17–18.

6. Ramachandra Guha, foreword to Walter Crocker, *Nehru: A Contemporary's Estimate*, new ed. (Noida: Random House India, 2008), vii. Australia took a more serious approach to its diplomatic appointments. Among those posted to New Delhi by Menzies and his Liberal Party successors were Sir Walter Crocker (1952–54, 1958–62), Sir Peter Heydon (1955–58), Sir James Plimsoll (1962–65), and the former secretary of the Department of External Affairs, Sir Arthur Tange (1965–70).

7. Senate Standing Committee on Foreign Affairs, Defence and Trade, *Australia-India Relations: Trade and Security* (Canberra: Australian Government Publishing Service, 1990), 23.

8. Gurry, *Neglected Neighbour?*, 40.

9. Ibid., 19.

10. The ANZUS Treaty was signed on September 1, 1951, and, despite New Zealand's departure from the arrangement in 1984, it still constitutes a formal alliance between Australia and the United States.

11. Y. Yagama Reddy, "India-Australia Relations: Pattern of Alternation between Convergences and Divergences," in *India-Australia Relations: Convergences and Divergences*, ed. D. Gopal (Delhi: Shipra, 2008), 162–64.

12. On this concept and its centrality to Indian foreign policy after Nehru, see Guillem Monsonis, "India's Strategic Autonomy and Rapprochement with the US," *Strategic Analysis* 34, no. 4 (2010).

13. The Indo-Soviet Treaty of Peace, Friendship, and Cooperation was concluded on August 9, 1971, marking a move away from nonalignment.

14. For a flavor of this debate, see the essays in Hedley Bull, ed., *Asia and the Western Pacific: Towards a New International Order* (Sydney: Nelson, 1975).

15. Auriol Weigold, "Engagement versus Neglect: Australia in the Indian Ocean, 1960–2000," *Journal of the Indian Ocean Region* 7, no. 1 (2011): 37.

16. Grant recounts aspects of this mission in his memoir, *Gods and Politicians: Politics as Culture; An Australian View of India* (Melbourne: Penguin, 1984).

17. Matthew Jordan, "The Reappraisal of the White Australia Policy against the Background of a Changing Asia, 1945–67," *Australian Journal of Politics and History* 52, no. 2 (2006): 224–43.

18. Gurry, *Neglected Neighbour?*, 53–59.

19. Sandy Gordon, *The Search for Substance: Australia-India Relations into the Nineties and Beyond* (Canberra: Department of International Relations, Australian National University, 1993), 15.

20. Weigold, "Engagement versus Neglect," 39. Gurry notes that exports to India doubled between the fiscal periods 1975–76 and 1983–84 but declined as a percentage of Australia's total exports. See Gurry, *Neglected Neighbour?*, 66.

21. Gurry, *Neglected Neighbour?*, 62–64.

22. Senate Standing Committee on Foreign Affairs, Defence and Trade, *Australia-India Relations*, 23, 34.

23. Gordon, *Search for Substance*, 22–23.

24. Ibid., 23.

25. See, for example, Brian Stoddart and Auriol Weigold, eds., *India and Australia: Bridging Different Worlds* (New Delhi: Readworthy, 2011).

26. See especially the Australian government's defense white paper, Australian Department of Defence, *The Defence of Australia 1987* (Canberra: Department of Defence, 1987).

27. Quoted in Gurry, *Neglected Neighbour?*, 79.

28. Senate Standing Committee on Foreign Affairs, Defence and Trade, *Australia-India Relations*, 71.

29. Ibid., 93.

30. See the quoted submissions from the Department of Defence to Senate Standing Committee on Foreign Affairs, Defence and Trade, *Australia-India Relations*, 68–71.

31. Ibid., 16.

32. Ibid., 9, 10.

33. Ibid., 16.

34. Ibid., 100–105.

35. Ibid., 105–7.

36. Ibid., 107–10.

37. Australian Department of Foreign Affairs and Trade, East Asia Analytical Unit, *India's Economy at the Midnight Hour: Australia's India Strategy* (Canberra: Australian Government Publishing Service, 1994).

38. Rupakjyoti Borah, "Australia-India Relations during the Howard Era," in Gopal, *India-Australia Relations*, 174–75.

39. Gurry, *Neglected Neighbour?*, 83.

40. Quoted in Kaushik Kapisthalam, "Australia and Asia's Rise," *Australian Journal of International Affairs* 60, no. 3 (2006): 370.

41. Weigold, "Engagement versus Neglect," 45–46.

42. Marika Vicziany, "Australia-India Security Dialogues: Academic Leadership in the Diplomatic Vacuum," *South Asia: Journal of South Asian Studies* 23, special issue (2000): 160–61.

43. Borah, "Australia-India Relations during the Howard Era," 177.

44. Ibid.

45. Meg Gurry, "India, the New Centre of Gravity: Australia-India Relations under the Howard Government," *South Asia: Journal of South Asian Studies* 35, no. 2 (2012): 288–90.

46. The institute's website is www.aii.unimelb.edu.au/.

47. Marika Vicziany, quoted in *Roundtable Discussion on Australia-India Relations,* arranged by the Australian High Commission, New Delhi, and the Nehru Memorial Museum and Library on behalf of the Australia India Council, February 14, 1995 (New Delhi: Australian High Commission, 1995), 16, and Benjamin Preiss, "Indian Student Numbers Falling," *Sydney Morning Herald,* December 14, 2012. It should be noted that by 2011–12, the latter number had declined back to just under ten thousand.

48. Sally Percival Wood and Michael Leach, "'Rediscovery', 'Reinvigoration' and 'Redefinition' in Perpetuity: Australian Engagement with India 1983–2011," *Australian Journal of Politics and History* 57, no. 4 (2011): 539.

49. See the figures for 2011 in Australian Department of Foreign Affairs and Trade, "Trade at a Glance 2012," www.dfat.gov.au/publications/trade/trade-at-a-glance-2012.html (accessed October 2, 2013).

50. Rahul Mishra, "India-Australia Energy Cooperation: The Road Ahead," *Strategic Analysis* 34, no. 6 (2010): 826–32.

51. Jenelle Bonnor, "Australia-India: An Important Partnership," *South Asian Survey* 15, no. 1 (2008): 166–68.

52. Australian Department of Foreign Affairs and Trade, *India Country Strategy: Australia in the Asian Century; Towards 2025* (Canberra: Department of Foreign Affairs and Trade, 2013), 5.

53. DFAT claims that its official representation in India has increased by 85 percent since 2009. See Australian Department of Foreign Affairs and Trade, *India Country Strategy,* 20.

54. Rory Medcalf, *Problems to Partnership: A Plan for Australia-India Strategic Ties* (Sydney: Lowy Institute for International Policy, 2009), 5.

55. Borah, "Australia-India Relations during the Howard Era," 179.

56. Alexander Downer, "Australia and India Sign Counter-Terrorism MOU," Media Release FA107, August 28, 2003, www.foreignminister.gov.au/releases/2003/fa107_03.html (accessed October 2, 2013).

57. Australian High Commission India, "India-Australia Joint Declaration on Security Cooperation," November 12, 2009, www.india.embassy.gov.au/ndli/pa5009jsb.html (accessed October 2, 2013).

58. Gary Smith, "Australia and the Rise of India," *Australian Journal of International Affairs* 64, no. 5 (2010).

59. Australia, Department of Foreign Affairs and Trade, *India Country Strategy,* 25. See also Andrew Phillips, "Australia and the Challenges of Order-Building in the Indian Ocean Region," *Australian Journal of International Affairs* 67, no. 2 (2013): 136–38.

60. Arvind Gupta, "Australia in the Asian Century: Australian Government's White Paper, Strong and Secure: A Strategy for Australia's National Security," *Strategic Analysis* 37, no. 4 (2013): 505–9.

61. On the Australian debates over this issue, see Michael Clarke, "Australia, India and the Uranium Question," *Australian Journal of Political Science* 46, no. 3 (2011).

62. Wood and Leach, "'Rediscovery', 'Reinvigoration' and 'Redefinition' in Perpetuity."

63. DFAT records twenty-six high-level Indian visits to Australia in that year and thirty-nine from Australia to India. See Australian Department of Foreign Affairs and Trade, "India Country Brief," www.dfat.gov.au/geo/india/india_brief.html (accessed October 2, 2013).

64. Within the Commonwealth of Nations, of which Australia and India are part, ambassadors are designated "high commissioners." See also A. L. Basham, *The Wonder That Was India: A Survey of the History and Culture of the Indian Sub-Continent before the Coming of the Muslims* (New Delhi: Picador, 2004 [1954]), and, among other works, Robin Jeffrey, ed., *People, Princes, and Paramount Power: Society and Politics in the Indian Princely States* (Oxford: Oxford University Press, 1978), and Robin Jeffrey, *What's Happening to India? Punjab, Ethnic Conflict, Mrs. Gandhi's Death, and the Test for Federalism* (Basingstoke, UK: Macmillan, 1986). The South Asian Studies Association of Australia dates back to 1969 and has published a journal, *South Asia*, since 1971.

65. Daniel Markey, "Developing India's Foreign Policy 'Software,'" *Asia Policy* 8, July (2009): 73–96.

66. Sadly, this attitude is sometimes mirrored in Canberra and elsewhere in Australia, where some officials and scholars see South Asia as a "strategic and economic backwater" compared to the fast-paced, dynamic international relations of East Asia. See Gordon, *Search for Substance*, 3.

67. Purnendra Jain, "Australia Plays Catch-Up in India," *East Asia Forum*, October 23, 2012, www.eastasiaforum.org/2012/10/23/australia-plays-catch-up-in-india/ (accessed October 2, 2013).

68. Gordon, *Search for Substance*, 25–26.

69. For an analysis of this case, see Sharon Pickering and Jude McCulloch, "The Haneef Case and Counter-Terrorism Policing in Australia," *Policing and Society* 20, no. 1 (2010): 21–38.

70. The India-Australia Poll 2013, conducted by the Lowy Institute for International Policy and the Australia India Institute, found that 62 percent of respondents thought that "Australia is currently a dangerous place for Indian students," and 61 percent thought that "attacks on Indian students . . . were mostly caused by racism." See Rory Medcalf, "India-Australia Poll 2013: Partners, Problems and Prospects: Indian Attitudes to Australia" (Sydney and Melbourne: Lowy Institute for International Policy and Australia India Institute, 2013), 6. An earlier Australian Institute of Criminology report found that most attacks were not racially motivated; see Jacqueline Joudo Larsen, Jason Payne, and Adam Tomison, *Crimes against International Students in Australia: 2005–09* (Canberra: Australian Institute of Criminology, 2011).

71. David Brewster, "Australia and India: The Indian Ocean and the Limits of Strategic Convergence," *Australian Journal of International Affairs* 64, no. 5 (2010): 549–65.

72. See, for example, Vibhanshu Shekhar, "India and Australia in the Twenty-First Century: Emerging Parameters of Strategic Engagement," *India Quarterly* 66, no. 4 (2010): 397–412.

73. Brewster, "Australia and India," 553.

74. Gordon, *Search for Substance*, 98.

75. Australian Department of Immigration and Citizenship, *Australian Migration Trends 2011–12* (Canberra: Commonwealth of Australia, 2013), 4.

76. Ibid., 115.

77. Ibid., 116.

CHAPTER 8

INDIA'S ENGAGEMENTS WITH SOUTHEAST ASIA

Singapore, Vietnam, and Indonesia

David Brewster

OVER THE LAST TWO DECADES, India has assumed an increasingly important economic, political, and strategic role in Southeast Asia. Its regional engagements are primarily economic but also have important political and strategic elements. This chapter provides an overview of the development of India's relationship with Southeast Asia and considers how the region has engaged with India, focusing on three key regional partners: Singapore, Vietnam, and Indonesia.

India's engagement with Southeast Asia can be understood in different ways. While India has not clearly articulated any "grand strategy" in relation to Southeast Asia, several themes can be discerned. Deeper economic engagement is India's most immediate regional goal, pursued by simple exchange strategies, and this is the primary form of Indian engagement with the region as a whole. The integration of India's economy with the dynamic Asia-Pacific economies, particularly in Southeast Asia, is becoming an important factor in India's economic development. Balancing against China's growing economic, political, and military power in Southeast Asia is also a major factor, and the desire to hedge against China is a driving force for many Indian relationships in the region. In geopolitical terms, one can also see India's engagement with Southeast Asia as reflecting the "natural" expansion of India's strategic space. However, one must view India's regional engagements with a degree of caution. Although India has several imperatives to play a greater role in Southeast Asia, its lack of economic and military strength compared with other major powers, particularly China, means it must remain flexible and discreet in its engagement with the region in the hope that its relative power will grow in coming decades. India still needs to prove itself as a dependable and even an indispensable partner to the region if it is to catalyze broader changes in regional attitudes toward it.

India's Relationship with the Region

India has long been seen as having a potentially important role to play in Southeast Asia. But it is still addressing the consequences of years of relative disengagement from the region. For decades following independence, India's economic, political, and security relationship with the region was somewhat distant. India is still overcoming this period of indifference and lost opportunities as it seeks to build its role in the region.

India's cultural and religious links with Southeast Asia are profound. The region's main religious influences—Buddhism, Sufi Islam, and Hinduism—were received from or largely derived through India. For centuries Indianized kingdoms ruled large parts of modern-day Indochina and Indonesia, as those names attest. India's strong cultural influence is still reflected in Southeast Asian art, language, and mythology. India also played an influential role in the region during colonial times. The British often used India as an intermediary in dealing with its possessions in Southeast Asia. India was the source of local administrators, merchants, and workers, as well as troops, to enforce Pax Britannica. Singapore was founded as a way-station for trade between British India and China and was directly administered from India for many years. Many colonial-era legacies, including Indian communities and institutions, live on in the region.

During the 1930s and 1940s, many Indian scholars wrote about a Greater India to describe what they saw as India's "commanding" cultural influence over South and Southeast Asia. Indian strategists such as K. M. Panikkar, known as the father of Indian maritime strategy, also had a clear understanding of the strategic significance of Southeast Asia to India. Among other things, he proposed that India and Indonesia should take joint responsibility for the security of Singapore and argued that India should develop a close strategic relationship with Vietnam.[1]

However, India's inward turn in the years following independence led to a relatively distant relationship between India and the region until the early 1990s. Engagement with countries in the region often took place more on a rhetorical than a practical level. India adopted an autarkic economic system that effectively discouraged investment and trade between India and Southeast Asia. It also largely failed to utilize the large Indian merchant communities in countries such as Singapore and Malaysia that could have formed the basis of close economic relationships. Nehruvian strategic doctrine, which was the guiding light of Indian strategic thinking in the decades following independence, eschewed a direct security role for India outside of South Asia. Instead, New Delhi saw its strategic interests in Southeast Asia as limited to ineffective rhetorical efforts to minimize the "intrusion" of other major powers into the region. Jawaharlal Nehru had particular contempt for Western-leaning governments of Southeast Asia, and he discouraged attempts to engage with them over their political or security concerns.[2] However, he was not willing to counter the growing US strategic and cultural influence in Southeast Asia through developing India's own presence in the region.

During the 1960s, there were several proposals from inside and outside the region for India to join in collective defense arrangements to counter Chinese-sponsored subversion and fill a "power vacuum" that was feared would arise following the British withdrawal from east of Suez. Many in Southeast Asia saw India as a natural strategic partner and security guarantor. But consistent with its principles of nonalignment, India refused to participate in any regional security arrangements in Southeast Asia throughout the Cold War. Many Southeast Asian states also saw India as potentially playing an important economic role in the region. Some Southeast Asian states, such as Singapore, reportedly tried to encourage India to join the Association of Southeast Asian Nations (ASEAN) upon its formation in 1967. This was motivated not only by a desire to increase India's stake in the region but also, perhaps, with a view to helping balance Indonesia's role within that grouping. India, apparently uninterested in developing economic links in the region and suspicious of a possible security dimension to ASEAN, declined any tentative approaches regarding its participation.[3]

India's apparent disinterest in the region and its persistent downplaying of regional security concerns may have seemed "callous, incredible and unrealistic" to Southeast Asians.[4] However, during this period the Indians saw themselves as hardly capable of providing for their own security, let alone acting as a regional security provider. As the junior Indian foreign minister B. R. Bhagat argued in the Indian parliament in April 1968: "If there was a defence agreement [with Southeast Asia] it would only mean India committing her manpower to the defence of areas which is beyond our capacity at present. . . . If we dispersed our efforts and took on responsibilities that we are not capable of shouldering, it would not only weaken our own defence but would create a false sense of security and might even provoke a greater tension in the area."[5] India's estrangement from much of Southeast Asia was reinforced by India's move toward a closer economic, political, and security relationship with the Soviet Union in the late 1960s. From that point until the end of the Cold War, many ASEAN members were highly suspicious of India's links with the Soviet Union and its communist allies, such as North Vietnam.

It is only in the last two decades that India has really sought to comprehensively engage with Southeast Asia. In the depths of India's post–Cold War economic and political crisis in 1992, the P. V. Narasimha Rao government launched the Look East policy, which was designed to expand economic, political, and security ties with Southeast Asia. India also saw its inclusion in various Southeast Asian groupings as an important way to avoid the marginalization of India in the post–Cold War international landscape.

The immediate motivation of the Look East policy was the need to expand trade and investment links with Southeast Asia in the face of a major economic crisis. India sought to engage with several Southeast Asian states, although much of the initial focus was on Singapore. Although there was a great deal of enthusiasm in Southeast Asia for building economic relationships with India, the economic engagement has developed much more slowly than was initially hoped. Many Southeast Asian states found India's bureaucracy and protectionist ways too difficult to deal with. India's legacy of Nehruvian economic policies meant that it took a decade or more for substantive economic engagement between Southeast Asia and India.

Despite the rhetoric of the Look East policy, in practice India has been relatively slow to reduce protectionist barriers to trade with Southeast Asia, reflecting fears that Indian markets would be swamped with cheap products. It took until 2009, after six years of negotiations, to conclude a multilateral ASEAN-India Free Trade Agreement. This reduced tariffs on most manufactured items, with the exception of important sectors such as textiles, chemicals, automobiles, and steel. The deal is largely confined to manufactured goods, allowing India to continue to protect agriculture, while ASEAN members would continue to protect their services sectors. Multilateral agreements on trade in services and investment are still being negotiated. India has finalized comprehensive bilateral free-trade arrangements only with Singapore and Malaysia, although several bilateral trade agreements with ASEAN members are under negotiation that would go further than the multilateral arrangement with ASEAN. In negotiating trade arrangements, New Delhi has often allowed domestic political considerations, particularly in the agricultural sector, to trump longer-term strategic and economic considerations. India's nonstrategic approach in this respect contrasts sharply with the more generous approach shown by China in negotiating trade agreements, which has facilitated the growth of China's political and economic influence in Southeast Asia.

The economic relationship currently represents only a fraction of its potential. Volume of trade and investment flows between ASEAN and India are still relatively low compared with ASEAN's other main economic partners, although it is growing quickly. Bilateral trade between India and ASEAN members grew from US$49.91 billion in 2009–10 to around US$79 billion in 2011–12. There is considerable potential for further growth in trade. In 2011, India was ASEAN's sixth largest trading partner, representing around 2.9 percent of ASEAN's total trade.[6] For India, ASEAN represents around 10 percent of total trade. Investment flows are also well below their potential. Between 2008 and 2010, India was the seventh largest source of foreign direct investment (FDI) in ASEAN, responsible for some 2.4 percent of total FDI in ASEAN. There have been significant increases in Indian investment in ASEAN over the last couple of years, led by Indian power companies' investment in the Indonesian coal sector. FDI from ASEAN members to India aggregated US$16.91 billion between April 2000 and December 2011. FDI from ASEAN accounted for 10.08 percent of India's total FDI inflow in 2011.[7]

While India's post–Cold War engagement with Southeast Asia was initially focused on economic links, India also sought a closer security engagement with ASEAN. As Indian Prime Minister Rao declared in 1994, "India would like to be a part of the evolving security framework in the region to assuage doubts arising from its potential military might as well as to contribute to the security edifice that was being crafted by the Asia-Pacific powers."[8] The majority of ASEAN members have, to a greater or lesser degree, welcomed an increased regional role for India, particularly in maritime security. India is generally seen as a benign security presence and a potentially important regional counterweight to China. As discussed below, the Indian Navy has taken a leading role in developing security relationships in the region through politically astute naval diplomacy and promoting itself as a benign provider of maritime security.

India's political engagement with the region has had a strong focus on the development of multilateral links and participation in ASEAN-based organizations. This has been facilitated by key partners such as Singapore. India became a full dialogue partner to ASEAN in 1995. India also joined the ASEAN Regional Forum in 1996 following considerable diplomatic efforts by Singapore to overcome fears that India's membership would import the India-Pakistan dispute into the forum. When India was refused membership in the ASEAN + 3 grouping (China, Japan, and South Korea) in 2000 (reportedly at the instigation of China), Singapore successfully lobbied for a separate India-ASEAN summit, which was first held in November 2002.[9] In 2005, Singapore, along with Indonesia, supported the inclusion of India in the first East Asia Summit. India also participated in the first meeting in 2010 of the ADMM + 8, which comprises the ASEAN Defence Ministers Meeting (ADMM) plus the defense ministers or secretaries of Australia, China, India, Japan, New Zealand, Russia, South Korea, and the United States.

Despite these developments, India remains somewhat of an outsider in regional multilateral institutions. It continues to be excluded from membership of groupings such as the Asia-Pacific Economic Cooperation and ASEAN + 3. In some institutions to which India has been admitted, such as the East Asia Summit, there may still be a perception in some quarters that India has not even been granted full membership, let alone recognition as a principal power. China has not always welcomed India's presence in East Asian institutions, and there may be lingering questions among some other East Asian states (such as Malaysia) as to how the presence of India might affect the "East Asian" identity of such institutions. Despite India's claims to the contrary, gaining a major role in these institutions is an important objective for New Delhi. India's reliance on ASEAN in extending its influence into the broader Asia-Pacific region also means that India is likely to be an important supporter of ASEAN's continued role as the organizational focus of Asia-Pacific political, economic, and security arrangements.

India has also sponsored the establishment of new subregional multilateral organizations. India, together with Thailand, sponsored the establishment of the Bay of Bengal Initiative for Multi-Sectoral Technical and Economic Cooperation (BIMSTEC) grouping in 1997 to promote technical and economic cooperation among states in the northeast Indian Ocean region (including Bangladesh, Myanmar, Sri Lanka, and Thailand). In 2000, India, again with Thailand, founded the Mekong-Ganga Cooperation grouping to promote greater east-west transport connectivity between South Asia and Indochina (through Thailand). Both organizations are symbolically significant in joining several Southeast Asian states with India—without the participation of China. However, neither of these groupings has yet played a significant role in promoting intraregional trade or in extending India's strategic influence.

Alongside multilateral engagement with the region, India has also engaged on a bilateral basis with key states in the region. There are considerable differences in these relationships. India's most successful engagement in the region has been with Singapore, with which it has developed a comprehensive relationship in the economic, political, and security dimensions. India has, with mixed results, also sought to expand its long-standing political engagement with Vietnam into a security partnership. India has also identified Indonesia as a key regional partner. Although its engagement with Indonesia in the political and security dimensions remains aspirational in many respects, over the last several years the economic relationship, particularly relating to resources, has developed very quickly.

India's Comprehensive Relationship with Singapore

Over the last two decades, India has developed a comprehensive economic, political, and security relationship with Singapore.[10] The relationship dates from the founding of Singapore by the British East India Company in 1819 as a trading post for its China trade. For years after gaining independence in 1965, Singapore's leader Lee Kwan Yew unsuccessfully lobbied New Delhi to involve itself in Singapore's security, with the idea that India would in some way take over Britain's role as a "protecting" power. When India announced its Look East policy in 1992, Singapore responded with enthusiasm and quickly positioned itself as India's de facto regional sponsor and became central to India's engagement with Southeast Asia. As Indian defense minister Pranab Mukherjee commented in 2006, Singapore has become the "hub for India's expanding economic, political and security ties with East Asia."[11] Singapore is now India's foremost regional advocate, its economic and political gateway into Southeast Asia, and its most enthusiastic security partner.

Singapore has aggressively pursued economic ties with India since the early 1990s and benefits from its role as an economic gateway between China and Southeast Asia. However, India could present an even greater opportunity for Singapore given that its direct economic ties with the region are much less established than China's. As well as acting as India's gateway to Southeast Asia, the Singaporeans also hope to become trade and financial intermediaries between India and China.[12] In June 2005, India and Singapore signed a broad-ranging comprehensive economic cooperation agreement (CECA), the first such arrangement India has entered into with a developed country. This CECA is unusually comprehensive, covering not just trade in goods but also services, investment, and taxes. The agreement potentially gives Singapore a gateway role with respect to India—particularly in relation to financial services and investment—that it could never realistically hope to achieve with China.

Singapore is now India's largest trade and investment partner in ASEAN. Economic and commercial ties have expanded significantly in recent years, with bilateral trade reaching US$21.34 billion in 2012–13. The composition of imports and exports is relatively diversified. More than half of Singapore's exports to India are basically "re-exports"—items that had been imported from India and subject to further processing. Just as important as trade are investment flows. According to one report, Singapore has also become India's largest inward foreign direct investor, accounting for 17 percent (US$9 billion) of cumulative post-2000 inflows up to 2010, and is challenging Mauritius as the primary gateway of global FDI into India.[13] Singapore has also encouraged Indian companies to establish themselves in Singapore. As a result, it has become the preferred center of operations for Indian companies active in the Asia-Pacific region and is used as a logistics and financial hub for many major Indian companies.

Closer security links have developed in parallel with the economic relationship. Under Lee, Singapore recognized India as having a "natural" strategic role in Southeast Asia. As K. Kesavapany, a former senior Singaporean diplomat, put it, "India has *de facto* inherited the British security role" stretching from Aden to Singapore.[14] In 2003, India and Singapore entered into a comprehensive defense cooperation agreement, which has facilitated annual defense policy dialogues, joint exercises, intelligence sharing, and cooperation in defense technology. Over the last decade or so, the Indian and Singapore armed forces have developed a close relationship. The army and air forces have conducted annual exercises since 2004. The Singaporean air force was given long-term use of India's Kalaikunda air base, and India has agreed to the stationing of Singaporean army personnel and equipment at its Babina and Deololli firing ranges. While such arrangements are of obvious benefit to Singapore, which possesses few training areas of its own, India also benefits from being able to conduct extended training with Singaporean forces. The use of Indian territory by foreign defense forces represents a major policy shift for India, which, since independence, fiercely opposed any foreign military bases anywhere in Asia.

However, maritime security is at the core of the security relationship, particularly given the position of Singapore at the head of the Malacca Strait. The Singaporean and Indian navies have exercised together frequently since 1993, making Singapore India's longest-running naval exercise partner in Asia and India's only regular bilateral exercise partner in the region. While most of their joint maritime exercises have been held in the Bay of Bengal, several exercises have been held in the South China Sea. It has been reported that an arrangement allowing for "frequent" visits of Indian naval vessels to Changi Naval Base is already in place, and the development of a semipermanent Indian logistical presence seems not beyond the realm of possibility.[15]

From India's perspective, Singapore, in terms of its size, economic role, and geographic position, makes it an almost ideal partner for extending its influence in Southeast Asia. Singapore's role as a trading and services hub gives India an expeditious way of expanding its economic presence in the region. Singapore's clear-sighted approach to its own needs and those of the region allows the relationship with India to develop without the historical or ideological baggage that could be a factor in some of India's other relationships. In strategic terms, access to Singapore's port and air facilities, in combination with India's bases in the Andaman Islands, places India in an excellent position to project power into the Malacca Strait and potentially the South China Sea.

There are, however, some important limitations to the relationship. The very ease and convenience for India of the Singapore relationship may to some extent have delayed India's imperatives to develop its own close bilateral security relationships with other countries in the region. Indeed India faces the risk of Singapore shaping its agenda for the entire region, especially in light of India's very limited diplomatic resources. In the longer run, Singapore can only be a stepping-stone for India to develop stronger bilateral relationships with larger states if India wishes to have a major role in the region.

India's Political Partnership with Vietnam

Over the last decade, India has been seeking—with only limited success—to develop the nature of its engagement with Vietnam. Indeed, the relationship exemplifies many of India's limitations as a strategic partner.[16]

New Delhi and Hanoi have had a close political relationship dating from the 1960s. However, the engagement largely remained at a political and diplomatic level and lacked substance in economic or security terms. India provided considerable rhetorical and political support to North Vietnam during the Vietnam War. Not only did they share opposition to US hegemony, but Indira Gandhi also saw Vietnam as a bulwark against Chinese domination of Southeast Asia. According to Gandhi, a strong, anti-Chinese Indochina, led by Vietnam, would guard the flank of India's "sphere of influence" in South Asia.[17]

The relationship was reinforced by their common connection with the Soviet Union. During the 1970s and 1980s, there were also influential calls in New Delhi to create an India-Vietnam axis to contain China, in the nature of the "all-weather friendship" between China and Pakistan, although these came to little. India renewed its support for Hanoi in the face of China's invasion of Vietnam in 1979, which was in retaliation for Vietnam's occupation of Kampuchea. China's actions evoked bitter memories of India's defeat by China in 1962. India provided rhetorical and diplomatic support for Vietnam over Kampuchea at some cost to its relationships elsewhere in the region. In the face of considerable ASEAN hostility to Vietnam, India canceled discussions over its planned elevation as a full ASEAN dialogue partner and officially recognized the Vietnam-installed Kampuchean government (becoming the first noncommunist state to do so). Through much of the 1980s, India's support for Vietnam was widely interpreted in Southeast Asia as proof of it toeing the Moscow-Hanoi line.

At the turn of this century, India took its first steps toward a substantive security engagement with Vietnam. During a visit by Vietnamese prime minister Phan Van Khai to New Delhi in 2000, Indian defense minister George Fernandes called for a renewed political relationship with a strong security focus, describing Vietnam as India's "most trusted friend and ally."[18] Fernandes proposed the development of a naval presence at the Cam Ranh Bay naval base, joint defense training, and the supply of advanced weapons to Vietnam. The Indians and Vietnamese formalized a wide-ranging defense cooperation agreement providing for exchange of intelligence, training, repair of Vietnamese aircraft, and Indian assistance on small and medium arms production. Fernandes also declared that India could supply Vietnam with warships and antiship and air-defense missiles.[19] The Joint Declaration on the Comprehensive Cooperation Framework was announced in 2003, which included commitments to regular high-level meetings, close cooperation in international forums, and gradual steps to expand cooperation in security and defense. In 2007, India and Vietnam agreed to hold annual security dialogues.

However, a substantive security engagement has in fact developed slowly, more often than not due to India's disjointed political and bureaucratic decision-making processes. India has turned out to be a less than reliable weapon supplier to Vietnam, proving itself often uncompetitive, bureaucratic, and politically hesitant. The Indians found themselves undercut by cheap suppliers of equipment from Belarus, Ukraine, and Russia. Other deals have been lost through payment-related problems and Indian bureaucratic bottlenecks. One Indian observer complained of excessive bureaucracy coupled with highly complex and uncoordinated procedures that were required to export military goods.[20] There was also a significant element of political caution on the part of India, particularly in relation to the supply of advanced missile technology. The supply of BrahMos missiles to Vietnam was blocked by India's Russian partners. Although the Indians reportedly agreed "in principle" to the sale of Prithvi missiles, they have since stalled.[21]

India's attempts to engage with Vietnam have been motivated by a desire to balance against China and to develop a strategic role for India in the South China Sea. Indian strategists have long recognized the potential role of Vietnam in controlling the South China Sea and blocking Chinese naval penetration of the Indian Ocean.[22] In the early 1990s, there had reportedly been preliminary talks between Indian and Vietnamese officers about the use of Cam Ranh Bay by Indian warships and reconnaissance aircraft.[23] In 2000, Fernandes proffered India's capabilities not only in policing sea lanes of communication in the South China Sea but, significantly, also India's capability in "containing" regional conflicts. In referring to the South China Sea, he stated, "A strong India, economically and militarily well endowed, will be a very solid agent to see that the sea lanes are not disturbed and that conflict situations are contained."[24]

But it was always unlikely that Vietnam would meet India's ambitions to establish a permanent presence at Cam Ranh Bay. Since the late 1980s, Vietnam has sought to use Cam Ranh Bay in a subtle game of balancing relations with China and as leverage in its relations with the United States, Japan, and others in order to increase its strategic options. China's assertive position over the South China Sea over the last few years has significantly altered the security dynamics in the region. While not wishing to internationalize the dispute, Vietnam certainly wants to garner as much explicit and implicit support from as many major powers as possible, including the United States, Russia, Japan, and India. In 2011, the Indian navy announced that it intended to establish what it called a "sustainable presence" at the small port of Nha Trang, located close to Cam Ranh Bay. The first Indian visit under this new arrangement led to some controversy after the INS *Airavat* was supposedly challenged off the coast of Nha Trang by a radio caller who claimed that the ship was in Chinese waters. Whether the radio call was from a Chinese official source or was merely a prank is unclear. However, while both New Delhi and Beijing hosed down the controversy with suitable denials, the incident (or nonincident) may have given India pause for thought about its presence in Vietnam. As the former chief of Indian naval staff, Adm. Arun Prakash, commented soon afterward, "even if India is about to take a, long overdue, stand on principles, or to adopt an assertive posture *vis-à-vis* China, a distant location like the South China Sea is hardly an ideal setting to demonstrate India's maritime or other strengths."[25]

New Delhi understands that China would regard a significant Indian naval presence in Southeast Asia as a major strategic challenge that could affect the whole framework of India-China relations. Provided that China does not develop a significant naval presence in the Indian Ocean, there seems little need for India to push too hard for a direct security role in the Malacca Strait, to establish anything more than a discreet naval presence in Singapore, or to venture into the South China Sea more than on an occasional basis. As Adm. Nirmal Verma, the retiring Indian naval chief of staff, commented in July 2012, "at this point of time, Pacific and South China Sea are of concern to the global community, but in terms of any active deployment from our side, it is not on the cards."[26] For the present, in building its relationships in Southeast Asia, India will focus on its capabilities in maritime policing and disaster relief functions.

Over the last decade, the bilateral engagement between India and Vietnam has increasingly emphasized economic aspects of the relationship. Vietnam has considerable concerns about Chinese economic dominance and sees greater economic engagement with India as potentially helping to provide some balance. As one senior Vietnamese foreign ministry official commented, "the dragon is scratching away and the elephant must move fast."[27] While Vietnam has experienced high economic growth in recent years, it remains relatively poor and many years behind India in economic development. As a result, Vietnam looks to India as a potential investor and provider of technology and manufactured goods.

Indian-Vietnamese bilateral trade is growing strongly (although from a low base) from a nominal US$72 million in 1995 to US$3.9 billion in 2011, with an agreed target of US$7 billion by 2015.[28] In the reverse of India's normal trading position in Asia, the Indian-Vietnamese balance of trade is in favor of India. The Vietnamese are impatient to gain greater access to the Indian market through a reduction of tariff barriers over agricultural and manufactured goods. In July 2007, the Vietnamese proposed negotiations on a bilateral free trade agreement, but the Indians, as beneficiaries of the trade imbalance, have stalled.

Some might see the failure of India to open its markets to Vietnam and actively pursue an economic partnership as being short-sighted in view of India's broader strategic ambitions for the relationship. Indian FDI in Vietnam is growing slowly. Some large investments have been announced, including a proposed US$5 billion steel plant to be built by Tata Steel (which may not be realized). Although an Indian state-owned oil company, ONGC Videsh Ltd (OVL), acquired exploration rights to offshore oil and gas blocks (in waters claimed by China), in 2012 it unsuccessfully tried to hand these rights back. It was rumored that the Indian government pressured OVL to keep its offshore stake in the South China Sea.

An important objective in India's engagement with Vietnam—whether it be in the political, economic, or security dimension—has been to strengthen Vietnam as a partial balance to China. Many Indian strategists see strong parallels between China's strategic relationship with Pakistan and India's relationship with Vietnam. Bharat Karnad, a noted Indian nuclear strategist, claims that "by cultivating a resolute Vietnam as a close regional ally and security partner in the manner China has done Pakistan, India can pay Beijing back in the same coin."[29] Hanoi also sees China as a key factor in its relationship with India, although it will likely carefully calibrate the relationship depending on China's assertiveness. As C. Raja Mohan commented, "an acute sensitivity to the changing balance of power in Asia guides the current Vietnamese strategy of befriending the US and Japan, and intensifying security cooperation with India without antagonising China."[30]

It seems likely in the long term that the relationship will grow in significance—if nothing else as a result of India's closer engagement with the region as a whole. Their shared concerns about China are derived from their past experience of Chinese military aggression and fears of future economic domination. However, the failure of India to develop a comprehensive security relationship with Vietnam over the last decade also highlights some of the limitations of New Delhi as a regional security partner, including its reliability as an arms supplier, its limited ability to project power beyond its immediate neighborhood, and its failure to fully understand the security dynamics of East Asia.

India's Growing Relationship with Indonesia

Although India's relationship with Indonesia is somewhat undeveloped, it may be key to an expanded role for India in Southeast Asia. There are indications that India now sees Indonesia as an essential partner in expanding its strategic influence there.[31] Indonesia is important to India's regional engagement in several ways. It is by far the largest state in Southeast Asia and is regarded as primus inter pares in ASEAN. Indonesia represents a big market for Indian exports and a major supplier of resources, particularly coal. A close relationship with Indonesia would significantly enhance India's role in the region, and help India develop its other relationships across Southeast Asia. Indonesia's historical concern about China also makes it a potentially important partner in balancing China's economic, political, and strategic influence in East Asia.

India also has a considerable stake in the continued stability of Indonesia, the world's largest Muslim majority nation, as a secular and democratic state. The advent of an Islamist and nonsecular Indonesia could have major ramifications for India's relationships in Asia and the Middle East, as well as India's internal stability. The modern Indian and Indonesian states share secular traditions, and Indonesia's relatively tolerant (or syncretic) Islamic tradition has many links with the Islamic Sufi traditions practiced in India. For decades, Indonesia has generally tried to downplay the Islamic factor in its relationship with India, including its refusal to support Pakistan's stance on Kashmir. However, the Islamic factor continues to act as a brake on Jakarta's willingness to be seen as moving too close to New Delhi.

Nevertheless, Indonesia has given considerable support to India's engagement with the region. According to Lee Kuan Yew, in the 1990s Indonesian president Suharto came to the conclusion that the region would be dominated by China or Japan after the Americans eventually left, so he decided to help bring India into the region.[32] Although ideological differences between Indonesia and China have been reduced, the growth of China's power in the region has increased Indonesia's need for partners such as India. A relationship with India may also fit well with Jakarta's aspirations to extend its reach beyond ASEAN toward other major powers and, ultimately, to sit alongside India at the top table in a multipolar regional order.

Over the last decade or so, much of the emphasis, particularly from the Indonesian side, has been on the development of the economic relationship with India. For Indonesia, India represents a potential source of capital and an enormous market for Indonesian resources (particularly coal) and agricultural products. In the last several years there has been an explosion of trade and investment links. Bilateral trade has grown from some US$7 billion in 2006–7 to US$20 billion in 2010–11 and is targeted by Indonesia to reach US$45 billion by 2015.[33] This will likely make Indonesia India's largest bilateral trading partner in Southeast Asia. While Indian exports to Indonesia are relatively diversified, Indonesian exports to India are highly concentrated in coal: Indonesia is India's major source of noncoking coal. Much of the projected expansion in trade will come from Indonesian coal exports to India, and the balance of trade is likely to favor Indonesia by a considerable margin. The investment relationship is similarly unbalanced. Many investments have involved acquisitions in the coal sector by major Indian power companies for the purpose of securing supplies. In October 2011, the Indian government claimed that investments of some US$25 billion by Indian companies were "in the pipeline." A bilateral CECA has stalled since 2005, largely on issues of access to Indian markets for Indonesian palm oil and other key agricultural products, although the two sides have now agreed to fast-track negotiations.

Engagement in the security dimension has been more symbolic than substantive. India and Indonesia signed a defense-cooperation agreement in 2001, which, due to the vagaries of the Indonesian political process, was not ratified by the Indonesian parliament until 2006. The agreement nominally provides for the supply by India of training and defense equipment and the development of the Indonesian defense industry, but it is seen in both Jakarta and New Delhi in broader symbolic terms. Indian assistance in defense technology and training could, at least in theory, be of particular value to Indonesia in light of India's capabilities in producing and supporting Russian-designed equipment and Indonesia's goal of diversifying its defense supply arrangements. However, there has been little real progress in this area. Indonesia has unsuccessfully sought to acquire Indian radar systems, BrahMos cruise missiles, and training for its Russian-built Su-30 aircraft, and there have been indications of interest in Indian advanced light helicopters and communication and networking technology.[34] It is understood that the Indian shipbuilder Pipavav has signed a memorandum of understanding to build corvettes in Surabaya, Indonesia. However, the prospect of India becoming a significant supplier of defense technology and services to Indonesia is severely constrained both by the small size of Indonesia's defense acquisition budget and India's limitations.

India has also provided assistance to Indonesia in countering domestic threats from Islamic jihadists. At the turn of this century, New Delhi's concerns about possible links between Pakistan and the secessionist Free Aceh Movement (Gerakan Aceh Merdeka) and the use of isolated islands in the Nicobar Islands for gunrunning to Aceh led to a cooperative maritime security arrangement called the India-Indonesia Coordinated Patrol. Under this agreement, the Indian and Indonesian navies have, since 2002, undertaken biannual coordinated naval patrols in the Andaman Sea, in the Six-Degree Channel at the northern entrance to the Malacca Strait, through which most of the strait's traffic passes. Although token in practical terms, such joint military action, particularly at that part of the Malacca Strait, has significant symbolic value. Many believe that in the long term India may be a useful partner in developing Indonesia's naval capabilities.

Arguably Indonesia's leading role in Southeast Asia, together with its geographical position as gatekeeper between the Indian and Pacific Oceans, makes it an indispensable regional partner for India. A broad-based strategic partnership between India and Indonesia could transform India's role in Southeast Asia.

However, one should treat developments in the relationship with caution. While bilateral trade is growing very quickly, both India and Indonesia are subject to significant internal constraints that make any political or security engagement slow and hesitant. A close relationship with Indonesia would involve a much greater level of commitment by India compared to its commitment to, say, Singapore. The asymmetry in size between India and Singapore has made their relationship relatively easy from New Delhi's standpoint, as have the economic complementarities and Singapore's clear-sighted and proactive approach to foreign policy. The development of a broad-based relationship with Indonesia would require a major political, economic, and security commitment by New Delhi that has so far not been forthcoming and could even be beyond its current economic and military capabilities. As Mohan has commented about the relationship, "while India might have a set of complementary interests with Indonesia, both countries are notorious for their inability to turn words into practical deeds."[35]

Understanding India's Engagement with Southeast Asia

There is no single template for understanding India's engagement with Southeast Asia. Since the end of the Cold War, India has been feeling its way forward in developing a role in the region. India has not clearly articulated any "grand strategy" and seems unlikely to do so in the near future. Nevertheless, it is possible to understand India's engagement with the region in several different ways.[36]

Economic Factors in Regional Engagement with India

Economic engagement is India's most immediate regional goal and the primary form of India's engagement with the region as a whole. The integration of India's economy with the dynamic Asia-Pacific economies, particularly in Southeast Asia, is now a key factor in India's economic development. Access to Southeast Asian capital, technology, and markets will be important in driving India's future economic growth and in transforming India's economy into an outward-looking, trade-oriented economy comparable with other major powers. ASEAN members have been particularly keen to encourage India's economic integration with the region. They are attracted to the huge Indian market and, for relatively less developed ASEAN members, the prospect of investment from India.

Wealthier ASEAN members such as Singapore (and to a lesser extent Malaysia) see significant economic benefit in positioning themselves as trading, services, and financial intermediaries between the huge economies of India and

China. Prime Minister Goh Chok Tong explained in 2004: "We see Singapore as being lifted by these two economies. I visualize ASEAN as a fuselage of a jumbo plane with China as one wing, and India the other wing. If both wings take off, ASEAN as the fuselage will also be lifted."[37] The CECA between India and Singapore has also allowed Singapore to successfully position itself as India's economic gateway into Southeast Asia and as the gateway for Southeast Asian investment into India. As Singaporean minister of trade and industry George Yeo commented, "Singapore will be to India what Hong Kong is to China."[38]

India's economic engagement with Indonesia has grown at an incredible rate over the last few years, largely driven by India's surging demand for coal to fuel its power plants. Indonesia is likely to become India's largest bilateral trading partner in the region, although it may take time to broaden the trading relationship. In contrast, India's economic engagement with Vietnam has grown more slowly. It seems that India may be at a disadvantage in competing with China in Vietnam in terms of trade and investment, and India has also been slow to open its own markets to Vietnamese products.

The China Factor in India's Regional Engagement

Balancing against China's growing economic, political, and military power in Southeast Asia has also been a major factor in India's engagement with the region. From New Delhi's perspective, an imbalance of power in China's favor raises the prospect of a bipolar regional order in which power is shared between the United States and China or even the prospect of Chinese predominance in the event of US withdrawal from the region. Either result would be seen as inimical to India's interests.

Nevertheless, while India is seeking to develop partnerships with key states in the region, it should not necessarily be understood as involving a regional coalition against China. Certainly, most Southeast Asian states studiously avoid any suggestion of a coalition with India *against* China; rather, they seek a balanced *distribution* of power through developing a balanced role for several extra-regional powers with interests in the region. This would involve encouraging the United States to continue its stabilizing role in the region, while accommodating or facilitating the regional roles of China, Japan, and India.

Singapore has been the most enthusiastic and articulate sponsor of India's increased role in the region. It has consistently welcomed and encouraged greater regional engagement by India on the basis that competition between major regional powers "must be squarely confronted and cannot be wished away."[39] Singapore's conception of a balance of power involves a multipolar balance that provides freedom to smaller states. As Singapore's first and long-serving foreign minister S. Rajaratnam explained, "where there is a multiplicity of suns, the gravitational pull of each is not only weakened but also by a judicious use of the pulls and counter-pulls of gravitational forces, the minor planets have a greater freedom of navigation."[40] Similarly, as Prime Minister Lee Hsien Loong argued when he was deputy prime minister, Singapore's concept of a balance of power "depends on the competing interests of several big powers in the region, rather than on linking the nation's fortunes to one overbearing power. The big powers can keep one another in check, and will prevent any one of them from dominating the entire region, and so allow small states to survive in the interstices between them."[41] Indonesia also sees India as potentially playing an important balancing role with China. However, consistent with its long-standing views on extraregional powers, it would also see any direct security role for India in the region in more limited terms than does Singapore.

Vietnam has a slightly different perspective due to its history and proximity to China. Since the turn of this century, Vietnam has been engaging with the United States as well as Japan, Russia, and India in an effort to draw them into the region, while also periodically showing a calculated level of deference toward China. Some in New Delhi hope that India can cultivate a de facto alliance with Vietnam aimed at China in the nature of China's relationships with Pakistan or Myanmar in South Asia, which are seen as being aimed at India. However, it seems unlikely that Vietnam would risk entering into any alliance with India that would provoke China and add little to Vietnam's capabilities. If Vietnam requires a balancing partner against China, it would almost certainly turn to the United States, not India.

India and the Intraregional Balance of Power

Another factor in the Southeast Asian strategic calculus, and one that is rarely discussed, is India's potential impact on the intraregional balance of power in Southeast Asia. Although India largely eschewed any security role in Southeast Asia during the Cold War, intentionally or not it played a role in the intraregional balance of power. This included India's diplomatic support for Malaya/Malaysia against Indonesia during the Konfrontasi period, India's refusal to support the newly independent Singapore against a potentially revanchist Malaysia in the late 1960s and early 1970s, and India's perceived support for Vietnam's bid to dominate Indochina during the 1980s. With India's increased engagement with Southeast Asia, its potential role in the intraregional balance of power will increase even as India tries to avoid involvement in intraregional disputes. Singapore benefits from its "special relationship" with India through improving its power and political bargaining position vis-à-vis its large Muslim neighbors, Malaysia and Indonesia. The extent to which Singapore is able to make itself indispensable to India's regional ambitions will help leverage Singapore's bargaining position throughout the region. The relatively warm state of India's relations with Indonesia also contrasts with India's somewhat cooler relations with Indonesia's main regional rival, Malaysia (although this relationship has itself developed in recent years). While largely inchoate, this dimension could become more prominent if ASEAN is unable to mitigate long-standing rivalries or if regional rivalries (for example, in Indochina) otherwise become enmeshed in broader Sino-Indian rivalry.

Geopolitical Factors in India's Regional Engagement

A further way of seeing India's engagement with Southeast Asia is that it reflects the "natural" expansion of India's strategic space. The expansion of strategic space is a common—if not universal—feature of aspiring great powers, and one would expect India to have similar ambitions as its economic and military power grows.[42]

Since the end of the Cold War there has been an increasing view of a "natural" sphere of Indian influence extending well beyond the subcontinent. India's "strategic footprint," at least in maritime terms, is seen as extending from Southern Africa to the Persian Gulf and the Malacca Strait and beyond into the South China Sea. Anxieties over China's increased influence in the Indian Ocean also undoubtedly serve to heighten New Delhi's defensive imperatives to secure the Malacca Strait and expand its strategic space into the South China Sea.

Conclusion

Although India sees a number of imperatives to playing a greater role in Southeast Asia, India's lack of economic and military strength compared with other major powers, particularly China, means it must remain flexible and discreet in its engagement with the region. Some have argued that India's approach in Southeast Asia can be compared with Deng Xiaoping's advice about China "keeping a low profile and never taking the lead."[43] This is only partly true. While India has shown a degree of political sensitivity in its dealings in the region, it has been far from passive in pursuing a security role in Southeast Asia and has been much more active than, say, China in developing security relationships in the region. India has been successful in recent years in expanding its influence in Southeast Asia in a cooperative and relatively benign manner, using simple exchange strategies. In coming years it will continue trying to prove itself as a dependable and even indispensable partner to the region.

Notes

1. K. M. Panikkar, *The Future of South-East Asia: An Indian View* (New York: Macmillan, 1943), 100–101, and K. M. Panikkar, *India and the Indian Ocean: An Essay on the Influence of Sea Power on Indian History* (London: George Allen & Unwin, 1945), 85.

2. J. N. Dixit, *Makers of India's Foreign Policy: Raja Ram Mohun Roy to Yashwant Sinha* (New Delhi: HarperCollins, 2004), 12.

3. Kripa Sridharan, *The ASEAN Region in India's Foreign Policy* (Aldershot, UK: Dartmouth, 1996), 49.

4. Kripa Sridharan, "Regional Perceptions of India," in *India and ASEAN: The Politics of India's Look East Policy*, ed. Frederick Grare and Amitabh Mattoo (New Delhi: Manohar in association with Centre de Sciences Humaines, 2001), 74.

5. *Foreign Affairs Record* (New Delhi) 14 (April 1968): 97.

6. ASEAN Secretariat, *ASEAN Community in Figures (ACIF) 2012* (Jakarta: ASEAN Secretariat, March 2013), www.asean.org/resources/2012-02-10-08-47-55/statistical-publica tions (accessed August 16, 2013).

7. ASEAN, "Macroeconomic Indicators," ASEANstats, www.aseansec.org/macroeco nomic/yearbook.htm (accessed November 14, 2012).

8. Sridharan, *ASEAN Region in India's Foreign Policy*, 178.

9. Malaysia, Thailand, and the Philippines reportedly opposed it despite Singapore's energetic advocacy. Kripa Sridharan, "Transcending the Region: Singapore's India Policy," in *Emerging Asia: Challenges for India and Singapore*, ed. N. N. Vohra (New Delhi: Manohar, 2003), 28–29.

10. See generally David Brewster, "India's Security Partnership with Singapore," *Pacific Review* 22, no. 5 (2009): 597–618.

11. Pranab Mukherjee, "India: A Rising Global Player," address to the Fifth IISS (International Institute for Strategic Studies) Asian Security Summit, the Shangri-La Dialogue, Singapore, June 3, 2006.

12. George Yeo, address to the Global Leadership Forum, Kuala Lumpur, September 6, 2005.

13. See Premila Nazareth Satyanand and Pramila Raghavendran, "Inward FDI in India and Its Policy Context," Vale Columbia Center on Sustainable International Investment, March 12, 2010, www.vcc.columbia.edu/files/vale/documents/India_IFDI_2010_-_FINAL .pdf (accessed September 27, 2012).

14. K. Kesavapany, *India's Tryst with Asia* (New Delhi: Asian Institute of Transport Development, 2006), 48.

15. C. Raja Mohan, "India's Geopolitics and Southeast Asian Security," in *Southeast Asian Affairs 2008*, ed. Daljit Singh and Tin Maung Than (Singapore: Institute of Southeast Asian Studies, 2008), 43–60.

16. See generally David Brewster, "India's Strategic Partnership with Vietnam: The Search for a Diamond on the South China Sea?" *Asian Security* 5, no. 1 (2009): 24–44.

17. John W. Garver, "Chinese-Indian Rivalry in Indochina," *Asian Survey* 27, no. 11 (1987): 1207–8.

18. "India Must Not Ignore SE Asia: Fernandes," *The Hindu*, March 28, 2000.

19. Micool Brooke, "India Courts Vietnam with Arms and Nuclear Technology," Asia-Pacific Defence Reporter 25, August/September (2000).

20. Rahul Bedi, "Despite India's Protests, Vietnam Buys Arms from Pakistan," *India News*, August 17, 2007.

21. Rahul Bedi, "Strategic Realignments," *Frontline* 20, no. 13 (June 21–July 4, 2003), www.frontline.in/static/html/fl2013/stories/20030704002104700.htm (accessed November 14, 2012).

22. Panikkar, *India and the Indian Ocean*, 85.

23. Annuar Kassim, "New Delhi Wants Use of Hanoi Naval Facilities," *Asian Defence Journal* 9, September (1990): 108, and H. Jenkins, "Dwindling Support Throws *Status Quo* into Sea of Change," *Insight*, January 14, 1991, 29.

24. Nayan Chanda, "After the Bomb," *Far Eastern Economic Review*, April 13, 2000, 20.

25. Arun Prakash, "India Must Pause before Venturing into Choppy Waters," Rediff News, September 26, 2011, www.rediff.com/news/column/column-india-must-pause-beforejy-venturing-into-choppy-waters/20110926.htm (accessed October 10, 2012).

26. "India against Direct Intervention in South China Sea Disputes Despite Having Stakes in the Region," *India Today*, August 8, 2012.

27. Press Trust of India, "Vietnam for Greater Economic Engagement with India," *Times of India*, June 20, 2007.

28. "India-Vietnam Trade to Touch $7 Billion by 2015," *Economic Times* (India), November 1, 2012.

29. Bharat Karnad, "China Uses Pak, Vietnam Open to India," *Express India*, October 3, 2005.

30. C. Raja Mohan, "The Importance of Being Vietnam," *Indian Express*, July 9, 2007.

31. See David Brewster, "The Relationship between India and Indonesia," *Asian Survey* 51, no. 2 (2011): 221–44.

32. Sunanda K. Datta-Ray, *Looking East to Look West: Lee Kuan Yew's Mission India* (Singapore: Institute of Southeast Asian Studies, 2009), 289.

33. "India–Indonesia Bilateral Trade Target Revised to $45 Billion," *Times of India*, April 22, 2012.

34. Frontier India News Network, "Indonesia and Malaysia Keen on Buying Brahmos," *Frontier India*, April 13, 2007, http://frontierindia.net/indianesia-and-malasia-keen-on-buying-brahmos (accessed June 5, 2012), and Amitav Ranjan, "India Says Not Yet to Indonesian Plea," *India Express*, April 21, 2004.

35. C. Raja Mohan, "Is India an East Asian Power? Explaining New Delhi's Security Politics in the Western Pacific," ISAS Working Paper No. 81 (Singapore: Institute of South Asian Studies, National University of Singapore, August 11, 2009), 13.

36. See generally David Brewster, *India as an Asia Pacific Power* (London: Routledge, 2012), chapter 10.

37. Asad-ul Iqbal Latif, *Between Rising Powers: China, Singapore and India* (Singapore: Institute of Southeast Asian Studies, 2007), 274.

38. George Yeo, speech at the Confederation of Indian Industry meeting on "India-Singapore: A Strategic and Economic Partnership," New Delhi, February 18, 2004.

39. Goh Chok Tong, "Constructing East Asia," speech to Asia Society, Fifteenth Asian Corporate Conference, Bangkok, June 9, 2005.

40. Quoted in Chong Guan Kwa, ed., *S. Rajaratnam on Singapore: From Ideas to Reality* (Hackensack, NJ: World Scientific, 2006), 7.

41. Lee Hsien Loong, "Security Options for Small States," speech to the Singapore Institute of International Affairs, Shangri-La Hotel, Singapore, October 16, 1984, reprinted in *Straits Times*, November 6, 1984, 20.

42. Manjeet Singh Pardesi, "Deducing India's Grand Strategy of Regional Hegemony from Historical and Conceptual Perspectives," RSIS Working Paper No. 76 (Singapore: Institute of Defence and Strategic Studies, April 2005).

43. C. Raja Mohan, "India in the Emerging Asian Architecture: Prospects for Security Cooperation with ASEAN and Australia," in *ASEAN India Australia: Towards Closer Engagement in a New Asia*, ed. William T. Tow and Chin Kin Wah (Singapore: Institute of Southeast Asian Studies, 2009), 50.

CHAPTER 9

PARADIGM SHIFT

India during and after the Cold War

Rajesh Basrur

ALTHOUGH THE RISING profile of India in international politics has produced a burgeoning literature, much of this has lacked a theoretical foundation and a systematic understanding of critical aspects of this rise.[1] There is a general consensus that Indian foreign policy has undergone a dramatic change, with the period around 1990–91 as a watershed—a time when India abandoned its central guiding principles: autarky and nonalignment. Ideology, it is said, no longer drives India's relationship with the external world; rather, it has become a "pragmatic" power that today barely gives a passing nod to nonalignment, the foreign policy cornerstone of yesteryear.[2] What kind of a power in the making is India? Will it be a "responsible stakeholder" in the international system?[3] Will it be a challenger seeking to transform the system, or will it be an adaptive power, adjusting itself to the system as it exists today?

While the newness of India's approach to the world outside is unquestionable, it is somewhat exaggerated and considerably misunderstood. I argue that India's foreign policy was "pragmatic" in the past and remains so now. But the *content* of this pragmatism has changed. Before 1990, India's approach to the external realm is best characterized as offensive-realist, while on the other side of the watershed it has become defensive-realist. In plain language, India before 1990 was a fearful state that saw itself as constantly under threat. It was prone to think of its security in terms of the usability of power, whether against it or by it. Today, although vestiges of that worldview remain, it is a more confident state that is far less inclined to view power as a primary instrument for the attainment of strategic ends, whether against it or by it. Accordingly, its foreign policy behavior has been greatly moderated and has assumed a more benign aspect.

From a theoretical perspective, the chapter examines Indian strategic behavior in terms of the dichotomy between offensive and defensive realism.[4] At a general level, this dichotomy has been the subject of considerable discussion in academia. Offensive realists have argued that the world is—and is seen by states as—one in which major powers try and maximize power because they will always be insecure until they have eliminated all threats to their security, which they can never really do—and that this is the fundamental "tragedy of great power politics."[5] Defensive realists, on the other hand, are more optimistic. In their view, states believe that—and act as if—the endless pursuit of power can be counterproductive, raising tensions and the risk of calamitous conflict without engendering real security. From this perspective, security can and should be obtained without maximizing power. Most of the writings on the subject tend to be static—that is, there is little effort to consider whether states at times shift from one type of realism to its opposite.[6]

The substance of my analysis is that Indian foreign policy in the period before 1990–91 was consistent with the tenets of offensive realism and that after 1990–91 it has been more in accord with the precepts of defensive realism. The change had to some extent already been conceived of in the 1980s by leaders who had learned from strategic experience but was actually triggered by systemic factors that created powerful incentives for a reversal. The chapter makes this case with respect to India's relationships with major powers in the international system. At the global level, India was and remains—despite the "rising power" label widely attached to it—a relatively weak state. Although its structural position has changed significantly in the two decades since the watershed moment, policy change began when it was still to develop its economic and military muscle. Despite its weakness, it adopted a more confident and less fearful approach to the international system, which it retains. This newfound confidence arose not only from its new pragmatism but also from the readiness of the major powers to engage with it and accommodate its rise rather than resist it, as other chapters in this volume show.

In the next section, I develop the theoretical framework for this chapter. I first delineate the differences between strong-power and weak-power behavior within a general realist framework and then show the essential divergence corresponding to the offensive/defensive dichotomy. The section that follows outlines the offensive-realist phase in India's external relations until 1990–91. The subsequent section delineates India's foreign policy shift from offensive to defensive realism in the global system. Thereafter, the dynamics of the shift are explained. The chapter concludes with a review of the findings and an assessment of their policy and theoretical implications.

Theorizing the Shift from Offensive to Defensive Realism

For a starting point, I accept the validity of the realist perspective on the behavior of states, which—as it stands today—incorporates both systemic and domestic political factors as explanatory variables. The now standard approach with regard to the former is structural realism. This school holds that the key drivers of state behavior are anarchy or the absence of a sovereign power above states, which places a premium on self-interest and power in what is a self-help system, and the distribution of power, which provides incentives to engage in the accumulation of armaments, balancing, and war.[7] The broad foreign policy strategies that states follow reflect their relative positions in the distribution of power.[8] Strong states show three preferences, all aimed at drawing advantage from their strength: (1) They prefer bilateral approaches to the resolution of disputes or disagreements; (2) they seek closer economic and cultural relations with weaker powers; and (3) from time to time, they tend to utilize power through action or threat of action as an instrument to attain strategic objectives. Weak states tend to do the opposite: (1) They prefer multilateral approaches to resolving disputes and disagreements (seeking strength through numbers); (2) they try to avoid economic and cultural integration, since this leaves them vulnerable to bigger powers' strengths, and instead attempt strategies of moat building or distancing to keep the big powers at bay; and (3) they try and resist big powers' intervention by means of balancing, both internal (building their own strength) and external (drawing on others' strength through alliances or like arrangements).

In practice, the degree to which states adopt such foreign policy strategies is variable, since they are influenced in their choices not only by structural incentives but also by domestic pressures. Here the divergence between offensive and defensive realism becomes relevant.[9] Offensive realism is the simpler of the two. It holds that states are always insecure in the anarchic system and try to maximize power to the extent they can. There is no such thing as trust. Cooperation, in this view, is tactical and invariably temporary. Hence, states engage in arms buildups and constantly seek to take advantage of the weaknesses of others. Defensive realism, in contrast, believes that the accumulation of power can be counterproductive since it tends to produce spiraling competition that is both costly and risk-laden without bringing real security. States often have common interests in regulating their competition through self-restraint and cooperation. This is particularly true when they gauge adversaries to be fundamentally security-seeking rather than greedy.

The offensive/defensive divide, in conjunction with the strong/weak state divide, produces certain predictable patterns in state behavior. Strong states with an offensive-realist worldview tend to be assertive, intolerant of weak states that do not accept their preferences, and prone to intervene and utilize other forms of force against them. Strong states that are defensive-realist in character are more tolerant of weaker states' adverse policies, avoid applying power against them, and try to exercise leadership or at least to offer to weak states significant incentives for cooperation. Weak states also differ significantly depending on whether they are offensive-realist or defensive-realist in their orientation. The former try to resist bigger powers through internal and external balancing and distancing; the latter are open to bandwagoning—that is, obtaining advantage from close relations. In the present case, we see that India has undertaken a shift as a relatively weak state at the global level, with 1990–91 as the watershed. It goes without saying that the patterns outlined above are in the nature of ideal types rather than very precise descriptions. For instance, India before 1990 was not quite an isolationist state in world politics in spite of its fear of dependence on the great powers. Rather, it tried to carve out a leadership role for itself vis-à-vis the Third World through the Non-Aligned Movement (NAM), United Nations peacekeeping, and the Group of Seventy-Seven (G77) developing countries. But, on balance, it largely conformed to the weak-power pattern outlined above.

How is the shift to be explained? Realists point to material factors, which can be found at both the systemic and domestic political levels of analysis. Constructivists offer ideational explanations. The debate on the end of the Cold War, which marked a deliberate shift by Mikhail Gorbachev and his team from an oppositional to a cooperative approach to the United States, is illustrative of the two arguments.[10] Was the shift from offensive to defensive realism the consequence of the Soviet Union's exposure as a fundamentally weak state unable to cope with the dynamics of the postindustrial technological revolution? Or was it attributable primarily to a radical set of ideas on openness and restructuring that determined how the political elite at a particular juncture responded to conditions that were not new? Although both material and ideational sources of change are present in the Indian case, the weight of material factors appears to have been heavier. There was certainly awareness in the Indian elite that existing policy was not delivering the goods. Growing anomalies were the precursors of a possible "Kuhnian revolution"—that is, a fundamental reorientation of strategic thinking and policy.[11] For instance, the autarkic economic model adopted by Prime Minister Jawaharlal Nehru was clearly not yielding growth. But whereas the transition in the Soviet Union occurred without an exogenous crisis, the change in India's global orientation was set off by not one but two crises in its relationships with the external world.

The Offensive-Realist Phase

Although by no means a minnow, India around 1990 was a relatively weak power standing well below even the second-tier powers. Its gross national income per capita in 1989 was just US$400, as compared to Italy's US$16,590, Germany's US$19,140, and Japan's US$26,650.[12] Although it had begun to develop nuclear weapons at just about this time, it did so hesitantly and covertly, and its actual capacity for nuclear deterrence was uncertain. Its general behavior pattern, moreover, was that of a state that views the world around it in offensive-realist terms, fearful of the power of the major states, and seeking to carve out an autonomous zone around itself. As noted earlier, the key characteristics of weak state behavior are distancing or moat building, a preference for multilateralism, and a propensity for internal and external balancing, with a tendency to depend on the latter. India exhibited all of these features in abundance.

To a considerable degree, India's diffident approach to the world was the outcome of historical experience: a long period (some two hundred years) of colonial domination by Britain. Moreover, the empire and capitalism were associated with India's impoverishment and exploitation and thus viewed with considerable suspicion. As a consequence, Indian leaders were unwilling to integrate their newly independent country into the global economy as they worried about continuing vulnerability to what came to be known as "neocolonialism." The natural result was a preference for moat building. Under Nehru, the Indian economy from the mid-1950s shifted to an increasingly autarkic mode, seeking—with Soviet inspiration—to develop a heavy industrial base with extensive state control and investment and emphasizing import substitution. This was hardly unusual—even the United States in its formative years had adopted a policy of self-reliance.[13] During the 1970s, India played a significant role in building the G77 as an institution that represented the global "South" and attempted to bargain collectively with the global "North" for better terms of trade in the quest for a "New International Economic Order."

On the strategic side, India rejected the notion that the newly independent countries had to choose between the Cold War blocs and sought instead to create a "third force" that in the 1960s became NAM.[14] It was not about to forgo its hard-won independence and allow a bloc leader to dictate security policy. Membership of NAM, which pushed for postcolonial objectives such as universal decolonization and rejection of apartheid, as well as a degree of autonomy from Cold War politics, represented a strategy typical of weak states—that is, strength in numbers. It also offered the option of "balancing" (playing off) the United States and the Soviet Union. India was able to extract some gains from this, obtaining American assistance for agricultural development—the Green Revolution—and Soviet aid for the building of large capital-intensive industries such as steel, coal, and power. Fearing major power intervention, India was also stridently critical of American intervention around the world, notably in Vietnam. In December 1971, when India was at war with Pakistan, the United States sent ships from its Seventh Fleet, led by the USS *Enterprise*, into the Indian Ocean, in a show of force that had a powerful impact on the Indian strategic mind. The episode underlined Indian fears about the dangers of major-power intervention. Hence New Delhi demanded that the United

Nations declare the Indian Ocean a zone of peace, that the United States vacate its base at Diego Garcia, and that foreign ships leave the ocean's waters.

Turning to internal balancing, India also began to pay more attention to its navy, the weakest among the three military services, and by the 1980s had embarked on the quest for a blue-water force with two aircraft carriers, several new submarines, a leased Soviet nuclear submarine, and long-range maritime surveillance aircraft (the Soviet Tu-142M) with a range of over twelve thousand kilometers. India also developed "the heaviest combat airlift of any air force outside the United States Air Force or the [then] Soviet Air Force."[15] Although unwilling to build a nuclear arsenal, Prime Minister Indira Gandhi opened the door a little wider to a future arsenal by launching the Integrated Guided Missile Development Programme in 1983. But Indian efforts at building military capability domestically achieved limited success, and India had to depend on external balancing to strengthen its military sinews.

While the perceived threat from the United States was not imminent, that from China was a much greater worry after 1962 when the Indian Army received a severe drubbing at the hands of Chinese military power. New Delhi's anxieties were compounded when China crossed the nuclear weapons threshold with its first nuclear test two years later. At the cost of losing prestige as a leading nonaligned state, India resorted to external balancing by turning to the Soviet Union as a counterweight to China's power. In 1971, Mrs. Gandhi signed a twenty-year treaty of peace, friendship, and cooperation with Moscow to balance against Chinese power. Article 9 of the treaty—which specified that the two countries would enter into "mutual consultations" and "take appropriate measures" in the event either were attacked or threatened with attack—signified the virtual abandonment of the cardinal principle of India's nonalignment: nonparticipation in great-power military alliances.[16] In short order, the Soviet Union became India's predominant supplier of military hardware. Subsequently India sought to avoid overdependence on Moscow by making major purchases from other states: submarines from West Germany, Jaguar aircraft from the United Kingdom, Mirage aircraft from France, and long-range heavy artillery from Sweden, but the Soviet Union remained the chief source of foreign arms. With the augmentation of its military capabilities, India adopted a harder posture toward China, displaying a new willingness to challenge that country on the border. In 1986–87, a military confrontation that stretched out over several months but did not result in war was played out on the Himalayan border in the area known as Sumdorong Chu.[17] The Indian-Chinese relationship remained primarily a zero-sum, military-strategic one.

The Shift to Defensive Realism

Indian foreign policy's offensive-realist syndrome has diminished sharply since the early 1990s. First, the fear of the capitalist system has dissipated. Following a reversal of economic policy and a shift to economic liberalization and deregulation from 1991, its growth rate has picked up sharply, and the size of its economy has expanded hugely. India's gross domestic product (GDP), which had averaged an unremarkable 3–4 percent until the end of the 1980s, picked up pace, quickly reaching over 8 percent a year. In 2007, a Goldman Sachs report predicted that India's economy would overtake that of Japan by 2030 and that of the United States by about 2040.[18] By 2011, India had already passed Japan in purchasing-power parity terms.[19] Rapid growth enabled it to undertake an accelerated military modernization process without increasing its military spending as a proportion of GDP. In 1998 moreover, India ended a quarter-century of ambivalence, carried out a series of five nuclear tests, and declared that it was now a nuclear weapons power.

These developments have increased India's confidence, and it no longer displays the kind of anxiety-filled strategic behavior of earlier days. In the early 1990s, symptoms of the autarky that was officially being abandoned continued to be manifest. The Bharatiya Janata Party (BJP), a rising domestic political force that was soon to come to power, insisted on a preference for *swadeshi* (indigenous) goods and controls over investment. There was a strong domestic demand from both the political Right and the Left and from big industry to stay out of the new intellectual property rights regime being pushed at the World Trade Organization (WTO). By the early 2000s, the BJP had shed its *swadeshi* line, and India, while still resisting unpalatable changes in the WTO's Doha Round of negotiations, did so from the inside (in cooperation with China, no less) rather than display an inclination to become an outsider. Indian economic isolationism was history. A newly energized entrepreneurial class was not only pressing for deregulation of state controls and enhanced foreign direct investment but was also looking to expand both manufacturing and services abroad, notably in cutting-edge sectors such as information technology.

India's military-strategic behavior has also shifted from the prickly "hedgehog" attitude of the prewatershed years to a more confident and outward-looking approach.[20] The United States is no longer viewed with the kind of suspicion that it was earlier, although significant differences in interests and strategic outlook remain. On the contrary, New Delhi has quickly established a strong cooperative defense relationship with Washington.[21] This includes the purchase of weapon systems, joint exercises involving all three branches of the Indian military, and a regular strategic dialogue on defense and related issues. Is this a case of balancing or bandwagoning? From the standpoint of what observers have called the emerging strategic triangle of the United States, China, and India, it could be viewed as a balancing approach.[22] Both see each other as useful for hedging against Chinese power. But it is also a bandwagoning approach because India seeks to draw from it other advantages that are not directly related to the Indian-Chinese relationship. First, it seeks a seat at the table of the major powers with American support or at least acquiescence. And second, it aims at (and has partially succeeded in) obtaining help from the United States to break through the constraints imposed by the nuclear nonproliferation regime and, despite the limitations arising from the Nuclear Non-Proliferation Treaty, becoming a regime insider.

India's policy toward China is also less uneasy and more confident despite a number of aggravations in the relationship.[23] Although the process of change began in the prewatershed era, the trade relationship has registered a steep rise from the 1990s, and China today is one of India's largest trading partners. In the past decade, strategic tensions have risen appreciably over the undemarcated border and a growing perception of Chinese containment and Indian counter-containment. While China appears to have established potential strategic bridgeheads in Sri Lanka and Myanmar in addition to its close military relationship with Pakistan, India has begun to build significant security relationships not only with the United States but also with Japan, Mongolia, Singapore, South Korea, and Vietnam. Unlike in the past, when India looked entirely to a "superpower," the Soviet Union, for succor, it now participates in the competitive game with unprecedented confidence. Moreover, China's attitude toward it has changed, with a new readiness to engage it in both economic relations and strategic matters. In particular, China has accepted India's special status vis-à-vis the Nuclear Suppliers Group, engages regularly with India in forums such as BRICS (Brazil, Russia, India, China, South Africa) and BASIC (Brazil, South Africa, India, China), and has embarked on high-level exchanges and a degree of defense cooperation with it.

India's Look East policy, initially aimed at finding common as well as economic strategic ground with Southeast Asia, has now extended into Northeast Asia and places a new emphasis on the Indo-Pacific.[24] Its global strategic horizons are exemplified by the prominence it gives to such institutions as the G20 (Group of 20) finance ministers and central bank governors, IBSA (India, Brazil, South Africa), BRICS, and BASIC. Along with Brazil, Japan, and South Africa, it has also staked its claim to permanent membership of the United Nations Security Council. The combined effort had, by January 2012, yielded support in one form or another from as many as 138 states.[25] While these attempts to widen the base of influential states within and outside the United Nations may not have achieved as much influence as India and the other emerging powers would like them to, the point here is that India's frame of reference has clearly changed. The sustained interest in multilateralism would appear to be a continuation of the old strength-in-numbers approach. In part, this is true—India is still a relatively weak state. But there is a critical difference: Its aim is no longer to keep the global system's power centers at arm's length but rather to become an integral and influential part of those centers.

Explaining the Shift

Concern about the fundamentals of Indian foreign policy had emerged much before the 1990s. In 1977, the new coalition party that came to power—the Janata Party (of which the BJP is an offshoot)—had called in its election manifesto for "genuine nonalignment," implying that India's drift toward the Soviet Union and away from the United States would be corrected. In practice there was continuity, as India, still keen on nonalignment, was unable to attract much American interest. In 1980, Indira Gandhi returned to power and sought to build bridges with the United States—her first overseas visit was to Washington and not Moscow. But there was no significant movement toward either liberalization of the economy or foreign policy realignment; neither domestic nor international factors were conducive to a substantial change. Domestically Mrs. Gandhi's "socialist" ideology had become sufficiently well-embedded for her to find it difficult to abandon it in the absence of powerful incentives to do so. Externally the Cold War continued to dominate the strategic landscape, and India and the United States still had no major strategic interests in common. Moreover, India was still at the receiving end of nonproliferation pressures emanating from the US Congress in the wake of its 1974 nuclear test. Her son, Rajiv Gandhi, who was prime minister from 1984 to 1989, moved forward in both respects, introducing a modicum of economic deregulation and attempting to improve relations with the United States. But again the inertia of history prevailed: Domestic resistance to change remained strong, and the United States was preoccupied with the Cold War and, from the mid-1980s, its impending conclusion. To hark back to the analogy with Thomas Kuhn's explanation of scientific revolutions, there was a growing awareness of the failings of the existing system—the slowness of economic growth and the persistence of poverty, the hollowness of Indian military power (see below), and the contradiction in fearing the very country that was the chief destination of elites wanting to migrate for better economic prospects. But there was neither structural incentive nor domestic compulsion to encourage the leadership to break with embedded belief systems and practices.

The turning point came from a combination of three more or less simultaneous systemic pressures.[26] First, a serious balance-of-payments problem, developing from around 1985, produced by 1990 a crisis that involved a huge current-account deficit and a depleted foreign-exchange reserve adequate for only three weeks' imports. India had to approach the International Monetary Fund for a bailout and was forced to agree to a structural adjustment that launched the deregulation of the economy, a new openness to foreign investment and technology, and steady integration with the world economy. The changes introduced as a result of the crisis unleashed economic energies that set in motion accelerated growth, which completely altered the image of India both within and outside the country. Domestically the change produced a new sense of confidence; externally it brought unprecedented interest in India not only as a source of profit but also as a player of considerable import on the strategic chessboard.

A second systemic change was that the Cold War, which began to unwind rapidly from around 1989, culminated in the dissolution of the Soviet Union in December 1991. This meant that India suddenly found itself in an altogether new strategic environment. First, the linchpin of Indian foreign policy, nonalignment, became redundant: There were no alliances in confrontation to stay out of. Second, the demise of the Soviet Union took away India's chief instrument for balancing against the Chinese threat, leaving it with a deep sense of isolation. And third, the United States, once the excitement and novelty of the "unipolar moment" had begun to fade, was disposed to look for new friends to hedge against the rise of China. A newly galvanized India was an attractive prospect. In effect, while the old bases of Indian strategy had crumbled, the United States was the only major power with the capacity and the interest to help India balance or at least hedge against rapidly rising Chinese power. After an initial period of uncertainty, the two drew closer, and during the presidency of George W. Bush the relationship improved rapidly.

A third systemic source of change was also associated with the end of the Cold War. The collapse of the Soviet Union and of the associated nuclear threat to the United States initially led Washington to try to tighten the nonproliferation regime with renewed vigor. Ironically India had already begun to build a nuclear arsenal at precisely this time (1989–90) in response to the Pakistani nuclear weapons program, which the United States had ignored owing to the exigencies of the Cold War. Still more ironically, the intensifying nonproliferation pressure on India ultimately led it to break out of its restraint and test its weapons in the summer of 1998.[27] The ultimate irony, though, was to follow. After the expected admonitions, Washington came to terms with New Delhi, retracted sanctions, and decided that India, as an emerging power with both economic and military possibilities, was potentially a major player in global politics and hence a useful friend against the possibility of a recalcitrant China. India's nuclear coming-out—and American readiness to engage with New Delhi thereafter—thereby reinforced its confidence both in terms of internal balancing vis-à-vis Pakistan and China and in terms of external balancing by making it an attractive potential partner to counter China—a balancing game that Australia, Japan, Singapore, and others were soon to emulate to varying degrees.

These systemic developments were complemented by domestic factors. The leadership during the watershed period, chiefly Prime Minister Narasimha Rao, Finance Minister Manmohan Singh, and a handful of bureaucrats, grasped the nettle and turned the economic crisis into an opportunity to bring about a series of fundamental reforms that transformed the domestic economic environment. Like Gorbachev, they introduced changes from which there was no stepping back and that unleashed a cascading process of economic and strategic transformation. Unlike Gorbachev, they required a crisis to set the process of change in motion. As we have seen, a sense of dissatisfaction in the leadership had not been sufficient to trigger change. Yet it would be an exaggeration to attribute the change entirely to systemic pressure. While Gorbachev chose to introduce change where he need not have, Rao and his colleagues chose to go the distance and placed the Indian economy on an altogether new trajectory.[28] Similarly BJP prime minister Atal Bihari Vajpayee and his colleagues shed their preference for *swadeshi* and instead rode the wave of liberalization. Vajpayee, moreover, chose to tread where Rao had feared to on nuclear testing. Rao had ordered a test in 1995 but pulled back upon receiving a warning from the United States. Vajpayee anticipated the US reaction, calculated the potential risk, and went ahead regardless in 1998. Was Vajpayee driven by an offensive-realist approach to international politics? It is easy enough to trot out the "Hindu nationalist" image of the BJP to underline such a claim. But in fact Vajpayee as a leader had always been more complex than the label implies. In the 1970s, as minister for external affairs, he had opposed the development of the bomb.[29] And as a poet, he had wondered whether history would ever forgive those who produced it.[30]

In sum, the shift from an offensive-realist to a defensive-realist approach to foreign policy that occurred in 1990–91 was the result of a confluence of systemic and domestic factors. Learning had begun to take place much earlier, and there had been, under Indira and Rajiv Gandhi, efforts to alter the basics of foreign policy, but these could not make much headway as long as systemic and domestic factors were functioning in a business-as-usual mode. It was only when there was a drastic alteration of the external environment that Indian policy shifted its worldview to a defensive-realist framework. No doubt leadership was critical to sustaining the change and to giving it the form it took, but that change took place at all must be attributed first to the impact of material and systemic factors rather than to ideational preferences and domestic learning.

Conclusion

This brief review shows that India has undergone a substantial change in its orientation toward the world. From being a relatively pessimistic and fearful state, it has become a more confident power. Two things are clear. First, India has not changed from an ideological to a pragmatic power. Its earlier fondness for lofty rhetoric should not be mistaken for lack of pragmatism, because (notwithstanding Nehru's misreading of China) it was always a pragmatic power but one with a sense of insecurity and weakness in an unfriendly world. The idealist-moralizing tone it often used—to which other states are hardly immune, as the democratic rhetoric of the United States shows—was merely a surface device adopted to clothe an essentially offensive-realist worldview born out of weakness. The new pragmatism is different, born of a self-assurance that rests on growth, the acquisition of real material power, an awareness that others look on it as a major player, and a desire to be an integral part of the international system rather than resist it as an outsider.

Second, the sources of the "new" India, although certainly shaped by domestic politics, were systemic in important ways. The triggers for change were the balance-of-payments crisis and the end of the Cold War. Subsequently India's position in the international system changed rapidly as a result of its accelerating pace of growth and its nuclear breakout, both markers of potential great-power status and indicators of its enhanced structural position. Above all, the rise of China, the widespread perception of American decline, and the readiness of the major and not-so-major powers to engage with India boosted its status and therefore its shift to a defensive-realist worldview.

Could there be a reversion to the India of old? Despite the widespread perception that liberal reform has fallen prey to the exigencies of coalition politics, resulting in policy paralysis, there is a high degree of path dependency involved in India's new openness to the world that will be extraordinarily hard to reverse. If one asks what *kind* of a power India is likely to be, the answer is that it will be one that seeks assimilation in a system with which it is in fundamental congruence regardless of dissatisfactions over the specifics of some institutions and rules. It no longer fights the system but bargains for a stronger place in it. In the past, it was loosely engaged with the global system, seeking close links with its neighbors and a safe distance from the big players (although it was compelled to depend strategically on the Soviet Union). In the twenty-first century, its confidence is boosted by its economic growth and by the fact that the big powers now treat it as an equal, both of which encourage it to integrate further into the global system. The chief driving force is clearly structural, for there is a remarkable continuity in foreign policy despite the vicissitudes of domestic politics.

With regard to international relations theory, this chapter has shown that a state need not always adhere to one kind of realism but may change its orientation without undergoing a drastic change in its internal makeup. In 1990–91, the government in New Delhi was reasonably strong under the Congress Party. Subsequently it has never been quite as solid, for all governments since the mid-1990s have been multiparty coalitions. But this has not affected the shift from offensive to defensive realism. The change has been largely structurally driven.

There are doubtless many things that neorealism cannot explain, but there are some things that it does, in this case remarkably well.

Notes

1. Some key and useful writings on this theme are John D. Ciorciari, "India's Approach to Great-Power Status," *Fletcher Forum of World Affairs* 35, no. 1 (2011); Stephen P. Cohen, *India: Emerging Power* (Washington, DC: Brookings Institution Press, 2001); Sumit Ganguly, ed., *India as an Emerging Power* (London: Frank Cass, 2003); Dinshaw Mistry, "A Theoretical and Empirical Assessment of India as an Emerging World Power," *India Review* 3, no. 1 (2004); Baldev Raj Nayar and T. V. Paul, *India in the World Order: Searching for Major-Power Status* (Cambridge: Cambridge University Press, 2003); Ashok Kapur, *India: From Regional to World Power* (New York: Routledge, 2006); and Arvind Panagariya, *India: The Emerging Giant* (New York: Oxford University Press, 2008). On the critical side, see, for example, Sumit Ganguly, "Think Again: India's Rise," *Foreign Policy*, July 5, 2012, www.foreignpolicy.com/articles/2012/07/05/think_again_india_s_rise (accessed July 6, 2012), and Amrita Narlikar, "All That Glitters Is Not Gold: India's Rise to Power," *Third World Quarterly* 28, no. 5 (2007): 983–96.

2. C. Raja Mohan, *Crossing the Rubicon: The Shaping of India's New Foreign Policy* (New York: Palgrave, 2003). See also Deepa Ollapally and Rajesh Rajagopalan, "The Pragmatic Challenge to Indian Foreign Policy," *Washington Quarterly* 34, no. 2 (2011): 145–62. For a much-discussed document on this issue—and an argument for persisting with nonalignment, albeit an updated version—see Sunil Khilnani et al., *Nonalignment 2.0: A Foreign and Strategic Policy for India in the Twenty First Century* (New Delhi: Centre for Policy Research, 2012).

3. Xenia Dormandy, "Is India, or Will It Be, a Responsible International Stakeholder?" *Washington Quarterly* 30, no. 3 (2007): 117–30.

4. See, for example, Thomas J. Christensen, *Useful Adversaries: Grand Strategy, Domestic Mobilization, and Sino-American Conflict, 1947–1958* (Princeton, NJ: Princeton University Press, 1996); Davide Fiammenghi, "The Security Curve and the Structure of International Politics: A Neorealist Synthesis," *International Security* 35, no. 4 (2011): 126–54; Charles L. Glaser, "Realists as Optimists: Cooperation as Self-Help," in *Realism: Restatements and Renewal*, ed. Benjamin Frankel (New York: Frank Cass, 1996), 122–63; Evan Braden Montgomery, "Breaking Out of the Security Dilemma: Realism, Reassurance, and the Problem of Uncertainty," *International Security* 31, no. 2 (2006): 151–85; Matthew Rendall, "Defensive Realism and the Concert of Europe," *Review of International Studies* 32, no. 3 (2006): 523–40; Keir A. Lieber, "The New History of World War I and What It Means for International Relations Theory," *International Security* 32, no. 2 (2007): 155–91; Glenn H. Snyder, "Mearsheimer's World: Offensive Realism and the Struggle for Security," *International Security* 27, no. 1 (2002): 149–73; Jack Snyder and Keir A. Lieber, "Correspondence: Defensive Realism and the 'New' History of World War I," *International Security* 33, no. 1 (2008): 174–94; Jeffrey W. Taliaferro, "Security Seeking under Anarchy: Defensive Realism Revisited," *International Security* 25, no. 3 (2000–1): 128–61; and Fareed Zakaria, *From Wealth*

to Power: The Unusual Origins of America's World Role (Princeton, NJ: Princeton University Press, 1998).

5. John. J. Mearsheimer, *The Tragedy of Great Power Politics* (New York: Norton, 2001).

6. A major exception is Tang Shiping's analysis of China's post–Mao Zedong shift from an offensive-realist to a defensive-realist strategy. See Shiping Tang, "From Offensive to Defensive Realism: A Social Evolutionary Interpretation of China's Security Strategy," in *China's Ascent: Power, Security, and the Future of International Politics*, ed. Robert S. Ross and Zhu Feng (Ithaca, NY: Cornell University Press, 2008), 141–62.

7. The standard text around which scholarship on this subject has been built is Kenneth N. Waltz, *Theory of International Politics* (New York: Random House, 1979). Other major texts are Robert Gilpin, *War and Change in World Politics* (New York: Cambridge University Press, 1981), and Mearsheimer, *Tragedy of Great Power Politics.*

8. Michael Mandelbaum, *The Fate of Nations: The Search for National Security in the Nineteenth and Twentieth Centuries* (New York: Cambridge University Press, 1988).

9. Considerable work has been done on the subject—too much to be fully cited here. For a detailed discussion of offensive and defensive realism that encompasses the greater part of the literature, see Shiping Tang, *A Theory of Security Strategy for Our Time: Defensive Realism* (New York: Palgrave Macmillan, 2010), esp. 9–32, 99–127.

10. Stephen G. Brooks and William C. Wohlforth, "Power, Globalization, and the End of the Cold War: Reevaluating a Landmark Case for Ideas," *International Security* 25, no. 3 (2000/01): 5–53; Robert D. English, "Power, Ideas, and New Evidence on the Cold War's End: A Reply to Brooks and Wohlforth," *International Security* 26, no. 4 (2002): 70–92; Margarita H. Petrova, "The End of the Cold War: A Battle or Bridging Ground between Rationalist and Ideational Approaches in International Relations?," *European Journal of International Relations* 9, no. 1 (2003): 115–63; and Robert S. Snyder, "Bridging the Realist/Constructivist Divide: The Case of the Counterrevolution in Soviet Foreign Policy at the End of the Cold War," *Foreign Policy Analysis* 1, no. 1 (2005): 55–71.

11. Thomas S. Kuhn, *The Structure of Scientific Revolutions*, 2nd ed. (Chicago: University of Chicago Press, 1970).

12. See IndexMundi, www.indexmundi.com/ (accessed October 10, 2013).

13. J. Ann Tickner, *Self-Reliance versus Power Politics: The American and Indian Experiences in Building Nation States* (New York: Columbia University Press, 1987), 183–99.

14. A. P. Rana, *The Imperatives of Nonalignment: A Conceptual Study of India's Foreign Policy Strategy in the Nehru Period* (Delhi: Macmillan, 1976).

15. Gregory Copley, "Inevitable India, Inevitable Power," *Defense and Foreign Affairs* 16, no. 12 (1988): 29, 52.

16. For the text of the treaty, see Surjit Mansingh, *India's Search for Power: Indira Gandhi's Foreign Policy, 1966–1982* (New Delhi: Sage, 1984), 387–89.

17. V. Natarajan, "The Sumdorong Chu Incident," *Bharat Rakshak Monitor* 3, no. 3 (2000), www.bharat-rakshak.com/MONITOR/ISSUE3–3/natarajan.html (accessed November 16, 2011).

18. Tushar Poddar and Eva Yi, "India's Rising Growth Potential," Global Economics Paper No. 152 (Goldman Sachs, January 2007).

19. Devika Banerji and Rishi Shah, "India Overtakes Japan to Become Third-Largest Economy in Purchasing Power Parity," *Economic Times*, April 19, 2012.

20. Mohan, *Crossing the Rubicon.*

21. S. Paul Kapur, "India and the United States from World War II to the Present: A Relationship Transformed," in *India's Foreign Policy: Retrospect and Prospect*, ed. Sumit Ganguly (New Delhi: Oxford University Press, 2010), 251–74; Daniel Twining and Richard Fontaine, "The Ties that Bind? US-Indian Values-Based Cooperation," *Washington Quarterly* 34, no. 2 (2011): 193–205; and Robert D. Blackwill, Naresh Chandra, and Christopher Clary, *The United States and India: A Shared Strategic Future*, Joint Study Group Report (New York: Aspen Institute India and Council on Foreign Relations, 2011).

22. Stephen Blank, "The Geostrategic Implications of the Indo-American Strategic Partnership," *India Review* 6, no. 1 (2007): 1–24.

23. Amardeep Athwal, *China-India Relations: Contemporary Dynamics* (New York: Routledge, 2008); Sujit Dutta, "Managing and Engaging Rising China: India's Evolving Posture," *Washington Quarterly* 34, no. 2 (2011): 127–44; Jonathan Holslag, "The Persistent Military Security Dilemma between China and India," *Journal of Strategic Studies* 32, no. 6 (2009): 811–40; and Mohan Malik, *China and India: Great Power Rivals* (Boulder, CO: FirstForumPress, 2011).

24. C. Raja Mohan, "India and Australia: Maritime Partners in the Indo-Pacific," *Asialink Essays* 3, no. 6 (2011), www.asialink.unimelb.edu.au/__data/assets/pdf_file/0008/505628/Maritime_Partners_in_the_Indo-Pacific.pdf (accessed November 16, 2011), and Shyam Saran, "Mapping the Indo-Pacific," *Indian Express*, October 29, 2011.

25. "Solid Support for Resolution on UNSC Expansion: Puri," *The Hindu*, January 28, 2012.

26. Sumit Ganguly and Rahul Mukherji, *India since 1980* (New York: Cambridge University Press, 2011), esp. 80–84 and 22–24.

27. Jyotika Saksena, "Regime Design Matters: The CTBT and India's Nuclear Dilemma," *Comparative Strategy* 25, no. 3 (2006): 209–29.

28. Rahul Mukherji, "Political Economy of Reforms," in *Oxford Companion to Politics in India*, ed. Niraja Gopal Jayal and Pratap Bhanu Mehta (New Delhi: Oxford University Press, 2010): 483–98.

29. K. Subrahmanyam, "Politics of Security: When Vajpayee Said 'No' to Going Nuclear," *Times of India*, April 10, 2004.

30. Cited in "Impact of a Nuclear Strike," *BBC News*, May 29, 2002, http://news.bbc.co.uk/2/hi/south_asia/2012543.stm (accessed November 13, 2011).

CHAPTER 10

CONCLUSION

Engagement, India, and the Changing International Order

Nick Bisley

INDIA HAS GONE from being a marginal and marginalized member of international society to one actively and assiduously courted by powerful states. The chapters in this book have examined some of the most important of these engagement efforts. Fundamental to all these is the sense that the international system is experiencing a period of "power transition."[1] These are periods that international history suggests are dangerous. In the past when dominant powers waned and new players have ascended, these shifts have created permissive contexts for war. In classical history, the Peloponnesian War, as recounted by Thucydides, famously had as its starting point the rise of Athenian power and the fear that this caused in Sparta, then the dominant power.[2] The Habsburg decline and the rise of Bourbon France are seen by many as the underlying cause of the Thirty Years' War in the seventeenth century.[3] Germany's rise, Britain's relative decline, and the destabilization this caused a decaying European order produced the First World War. From classical antiquity to the turn of the twentieth century, international history suggests that rising powers upset existing orders and tip international systems into convulsive war.

International relations theory also gives cause for concern. Structural realists believe that shifts in the relative power of states increase the prospect of conflict.[4] More rationalist analysts see periods of power transition as changing the calculations of threat and risk that states make, prompting new security dilemmas as rising powers expend their newfound resources on military modernization.

The current era seems to have all the hallmarks of such a dangerous period. The dominant power, the United States, continues to see its share of global output shrink; it has suffered significant strategic setbacks in Iraq and Afghanistan, and the financial crisis has produced a long-lasting recession and fiscal deficits that are likely to erode America's relative military power into the future. Arrayed on the international stage are a range of emerging powers that have enjoyed striking economic success. They are physically and demographically large, strategically located in key regions, and have ambition to participate in international politics at the highest level. China is by far the most advanced of these emerging powers, but India, Brazil, and Russia are taking steps that may well allow them, over time, to play the game of international politics at the top table. Not since 1939, perhaps even 1914, have the contours of world politics been shaped by so many great and aspirant great powers. International relations scholarship suggests that under such circumstances we should be very gloomy indeed.

Oddly, India's rise has not been met with pessimism. Many key powers are keen to engage with a rising India, seeing opportunities to advance their interests, values, and ambitions. In turn, India is also undertaking a range of engagements of its own. From the transformation of its relations with the United States to its desire to expand its sphere of influence, India's rising power is providing it with the material wherewithal to make good its long-held ambition not only to be a "heavyweight" in the international system but also to shape the system itself.

The aim of this concluding chapter is to reflect on the engagements of and by India and to examine what they imply for the conduct of international relations and international order. It has two sections. The first uses the peculiar case of India's engagements to make a number of broader points about engagement as a distinctive policy option. The second steps back from the particulars of engagement to make a number of broader points about the prospects of transformation to the current order and how India's engagements relate to that larger process.

Engagement and India

As Ian Hall makes clear in chapter 1, engagement is a particular form of bilateral interaction in which the engaging states seek to shape the behavior of others through noncoercive means.[5] Traditionally it is an approach that is used by interlocutors who are explicitly seeking to drive change in states that have been at odds with international society. Thus states that are undergoing a political transformation (such as Myanmar) or a rapid increase in their wealth (such as China) have been the focus of recent engagement efforts.[6] Engagement is generally associated with shaping outcomes within a target state and in turn influencing its behavior within the international system. In the case of a potential great power, most obviously China, the desire to have some impact upon how it carries itself in international society is also colored by the recognition of the consequences for the system that the behavior of great powers has. Engagement is a distinctive form of diplomacy that, as the term implies, entails something qualitatively distinct from ordinary bilateral diplomatic dealings. The forms this takes can vary. It might involve direct provision of material incentives to reward particular choices by the target state—this is exchange engagement. Or engaging states might use a catalytic strategy, seeking, for example, to generate circumstances that are conducive to long-term structural changes. This occurred in Eastern and Central Europe when Western powers admitted former Warsaw Pact and Soviet republics to the North Atlantic Treaty Organization and the European Union after the end of communism.

It is precisely because India is not, at first glance, typical of the kinds of pariah or transitioning states that are normally subject to engagement that makes it such an interesting case. India is a relatively stable democracy; it does not overtly contest either the balance of power or the normative underpinnings of the international order. Its political system, while not without blemishes, has been in place since independence, apart from a brief period in the mid-1970s, and shows no sign of radical change in the near future. It has been experiencing relatively rapid economic growth, although it remains a long way behind both the rates of growth and aggregate output levels of China. And just as India does not seem to fit into the standard mold of a state in need of engagement, the forms that the engagement of India has taken similarly do not fit into neat categories. This derives in part from what it is that states seek in their engagements with India and in part from India's distinctive attributes.

Why Engage India?

Perhaps the most striking feature of the varied efforts to engage India analyzed here is the diverse range of goals of the engaging states. Some seek immediate prospects for advantage, most obviously in commercial exchange, due to India's size and the rapid growth of its burgeoning middle class. But most seek long-term benefits by persuading India to support particular visions of international order. In the eyes of many, India is a state of such potential weight and influence that it can advance longer-term aims about the international order and one's place within it. That the United States, Japan, Russia, and even China see in India a potential partner that can advance their conception of an international order is notable indeed. For these states and others, engaging India is about shaping its destiny in such a way as to persuade India's elite and India's people to back certain visions of international order.

What is it about India that the powers surveyed in this book find so appealing? First, there is India's enormous population. As home to the world's second largest population, and one that will in all likelihood become the largest on the planet by the middle of the twenty-first century, India has an obvious demographic appeal.[7] Although in the past its scale was seen as a liability, particularly in terms of its poverty and squalor, today it presents an enticing prospect of millions of young, middle-class consumers. The economic success of India and China in recent years has shown that huge societies can develop rapidly and that scale presents, in a very basic sense, the foundation stone for genuine global weight.

Second, India is physically very large, accounting for the world's seventh largest territorial holdings that are located in a vital strategic zone. Notwithstanding the considerable security challenges it faces on its borders, India is preeminently placed with regard to the Indian Ocean, one of the world's most vital sea lanes, regarded by some as the center stage of world politics in the coming century.[8] It is physically contiguous to China, although protected by the Himalayas, and proximate to the growth areas of Southeast Asia, the Persian Gulf, and the potentially dynamic East African coast. Together, India's population, scope for economic growth, and geographic good fortune provide a strong material foundation for building profitable relations in the short term and broader systemic benefits in the long term.

Third, India has the material potential to become a great power. Great powers are unusual members of international society. They matter much more than ordinary states not only because of their sheer size and concentration of power but also because they have special privileges and obligations to international society.[9] They are unusual also because they are rare. The rise of states that are of such sufficient heft that they have a gravitational pull on the structures of the international system does not happen very often. Since the end of the Cold War, the United States has been the only state with that kind of wherewithal. But with the economic success of the emerging powers and the relative economic decline of the Western powers, many think that the timeless rhythm of modern international relations—the rise and fall of great powers—is reasserting itself.[10] China is the most obvious candidate in this sense, but many see a great power of the future in the potential of India's material attributes. Whether or not it is able to make good on this potential, India as a prospective great power has prompted engagement.[11]

Fourth, India's identity and its underlying values and political structure are important. As many authors in this book discuss, India adopted nonalignment as its foreign policy lodestar for the bulk of the period after independence. And although it ended up closely linked to the Soviet Union, its Nehruvian approach, its avowedly non-Western outlook, and its ambition for leadership established for India a distinctive identity as a state at some remove from the Western-dominated order. As Rajesh Basrur argued in chapter 9, often too much is made about the "pragmatic turn" in Indian foreign policy in the 1990s. India has always been pragmatic to some degree, but it has recently changed how it conceives of interests and its approach to advance those interests in the international system. Basrur argued that India used to fight against a system that it perceived as rigged against it; now it works to better position itself within that system. As a recent influential think-tank report makes plain, India's policy elite is keen to maintain aspects of nonalignment but is developing an explicitly interest-driven approach that is content with the core components of the existing system.[12] India has thus cultivated an unusual double identity. The echoes of its Nehruvian, anti-Western past linger in the minds of Indian elites and their international partners, while a more hard-headed interest approach is palpably evident.

This new, emerging, and complex international identity arguably makes engaging India easier, as potential suitors see elements within its different components that they wish to nurture. Thus, as Daniel Twining, H. D. P. Envall, and Ian Hall showed, the United States, Japan, and Australia see in a rising India a force that can potentially help to balance Chinese power and influence in the Asia-Pacific. As Lavina Lee showed in chapter 4, Russia sees an India that is still infused with a desire to dilute or transform the United States–dominated system into one that can help Russia and other like-minded states bring about a genuinely multipolar and non-Western order. Even China sees in India elements of thought and practice with which its elite believes it can engage, as Louise Merrington and Harsh Pant demonstrated in chapters 5 and 6, respectively.

Last but my no means least, many states are seeking to engage India because it is the world's largest democracy. With the exception of the Emergency period, it has functioned as such for the duration of its postcolonial life, and this is a considerable source of Indian pride that feeds into an important sense of itself. That this non-Western, potential great power that is capable of navigating the international system with a degree of Kissingerian hard-headedness is a democracy makes India unique. Thus even though India may be cultivating relations with Russia, buying European instead of American warplanes, and defying Washington's requests about Iran, the United States still sees an alluring partner in democratic India. India could become, in Twining's words, a key part of "a global balance of capabilities and ideas tilted toward freedom."[13] India is valuable to would-be engaging states because of its scale and capacity to shape the balance of power and because it is an open society with a robust commitment to democratic political principles.

Effective Engagement?

This book has explored how different states are engaging India with a range of different strategies. Some, notably China, are utilizing an exchange strategy in an effort to extract specific concessions from India and to draw it into a condition of economic interdependence. Others, notably Japan, are utilizing something closer to a pure catalytic strategy, aiming to cultivate India's elite over the medium to long term and shift it, over time, toward beliefs and practices more conducive to Japanese interests, especially with regard to China. And then there are players such as the United States, and, to a lesser extent and in different ways, Australia and Russia, that over time have used both exchange and catalytic strategies to gain specific deals and to transform the outlook of India's elite and its people more broadly. For the United States, the objective of this blended strategy is to shift India toward becoming a stakeholder in a democratic international order. For Russia, the objectives are different. On the one hand, Russia wants India to remain in a state of "co-dependence," as Lee puts it, with regard to Russian weapons and energy resources. On the other, Russia would like India to become a stakeholder in a more multipolar international order.

While it may be too early to draw any definitive conclusions about the success or otherwise of these various engagement strategies, some tentative conclusions can be drawn. First, India has proven to be far more receptive to defense and security arrangements than those relating to the economy. Although Japan's experiences with the Comprehensive Economic Partnership Agreement are a notable exception, American, Australian, Chinese, and even Russian attempts to improve commercial links have not been especially successful. India and China have some good economic complementarities, but these continue to be offset by areas in which they compete, most notably textiles and energy. The United States has thus far been unsuccessful in pushing India to further liberalize its economy, while Russia, the state with which India has its longest and arguably best relationship, is also unable to improve links beyond the defense and energy sectors. Those using engagement to advance short-term instrumental ends in the economic sphere have not been particularly effective.

In the defense and security sphere, engagement has accrued reasonable benefits to Russia and the United States in particular. The United States and India have extensive defense links, including close ties between the two defense forces created by the cooperation agreement and frequent exercises. The United States is now a top supplier of defense equipment to the world's largest arms consumer.[14] Unusually for an arms consumer, India has a diversified supplier base. Not only does the relationship with Russia generate high levels of sales, but, as Lee argues, Russia is also prepared to sell India sensitive technology, including a nuclear-powered submarine and an aircraft carrier. It also allows levels of technology transfer that others do not, and the two undertake joint development of new systems, most notably the BrahMos missile. This gives that relationship a particular significance.

That India is more open to defense and security engagement than economic engagement is not entirely surprising given its internal limitations on the defense-technology front and its perceived security needs. Moreover, it is also testimony to the underlying reality that the success of engagement is always ultimately contingent upon the target state and the extent to which it is willing or not to reciprocate. India has shown a reluctance to expose itself too much to external pressure on its domestic economy. Even in the area in which it has been more responsive—defense cooperation and the arms trade—it has still sought at times to remain aloof. Collaborating with Russia and the United States at the same time, while keeping each on its toes (such as with the decision not to purchase an American fifth-generation fighter) is intended to ensure that India's much prized autonomy is maintained even while it builds deeper links with external partners. On the broader question of the structural or systemic ambitions of the engaging states, it is simply too early to tell, as much depends on the way in which India develops and the extent to which it makes good on its potential.

That said, at least one observation can be made. Although India has shown a much greater degree of comfort with the dominant order and has moved away from its shrill denunciations of the past, it will attempt to carve out a distinct path for itself as the international order evolves. America and its allies are calling for it to join them as an ally in all but name, while Russia and China see India as a counterweight to American power and influence and as a state that can help bring about a world order without Western domination. As the chapters in this book showed, India is as uneasy about closer relations with America as it is about being part of a Russian- or Chinese-led system. The importance of retaining autonomy in its international dealings is such that engagement for structural ends will always have its limits. India will not become a quasi-ally of the United States, nor will it join a strategic club with Russia and China. This does not mean engagement is without purpose but that interlocutors must recognize that barring some kind of radical transformation in thinking in New Delhi, such policies will only get you so far.

India's Engagements

All of this supports the basic but important point that engagement is a dynamic two-way process in which outcomes are shaped by the way the approaches of the two sides interact. This being the case, it is also important to consider the other side of the engagement question: India's own attempts to engage great powers and players in its region. Here we can see that, like the engagers of India, India has both instrumental aims over the short term and more structural or systemic goals over the long term, which it is seeking to fulfill by the use of both exchange and catalytic strategies.

As Merrington and David Brewster showed, India seeks short-term economic advantages in trying to build links to economically dynamic regions and improving access to energy resources. In areas where there are complementarities, this has proven to be successful, notably the financial links with Singapore and the coal trade with Indonesia. Yet where there are more complex issues to be overcome, progress has been less evident. This includes geography and indecision with regard to Central Asian energy markets and a lack of competitiveness in relation to other economic partners in Southeast Asia.

The other side of India's engagements relates to its broader ambitions for the international system. Although there is clear ambition to sit at the "high table" of international relations at some point in the future, this has not yet manifested itself in concrete policy. Rather, India's systemic aims in its engagements are to expand its sphere of influence and more specifically advance its efforts to balance Chinese influence in its broader region. It has been reasonably successful at utilizing catalytic strategies for building diplomatic and military influence in Southeast Asia and in particular developing good relations with Vietnam, but it has been hamstrung in Central Asia. More generally, India's engagement efforts have been constrained by limited resources and unclear strategies rather than by any particular reticence among its target states.

India and the Transformation of International Order

The major order transformations of the modern period have come in the wake of wars and convulsive violent shocks.[15] In the aftermath of violence and conflict, orders have been remade; in more recent times this has entailed formal conference diplomacy and institution building.[16] Disputes abounded as to how order should be built, the ideas that it should advance and protect, and how it should be maintained. But order simply had to be reconstructed as the old setting had been destroyed.

The extent to which order is changing in the current era is unclear due to its more benign conditions. The contemporary period is notable not only for the unusual concentration of power in the hands of the United States but also for the number of powers arrayed on the international scene that have the potential and ambition to be powers of the first rank.[17] India is a crucial part of this drama, and the efforts to engage India are suffused with a belief that the current period is a time of transformation. How open is the current system to such change, and what will be the product of, as Hall identified in the opening chapter, the dynamic "interactions between India and other states" and the international order more broadly?

International Orders and Change

Like all significant ideas in the social sciences, international order is a contested concept.[18] For the purposes of this chapter, by international order I mean the set of arrangements that exist to manage relations between distinct political entities. They comprise a range of elements that together establish the parameters of acceptable conduct among different political communities. These may include forms of power, institutions established to manage common problems, and shared values. In different periods and places, international orders vary in the form and function of these elements, producing orders with quite varied structural attributes that mean some orders can be adjusted more easily than others.

While they vary in their precise form, there are a set of common components of which modern international orders have been composed. The gap between the principle of formal equality and the substantive inequalities among states has always been very considerable. Thus the first aspect of any order relates to the particular role carved out for powerful states within the system and the manner in which it seeks to contain or harness power inequalities. The second aspect is the role played by institutions. Here institutions are understood in a traditional sense; they are made up of groups of states that adhere to formal rules and procedures to regulate actions within a specified sphere of conduct.[19] This relates to and, in some cases, incorporates the third element: the animating ideas of the order—that is, both the underlying values that the order protects and advances and the principles and rules that govern conduct.

International orders are only able to produce stability in international politics when there is a degree of consent toward, or at the very least acceptance of, these underlying values. Variation in the forms of order depends on the ease with which change can be accommodated within the particular form these elements take. Order is thus a process through which the tensions that arise among divergent political forms and uneven distributions of power are managed and the conflicts that inevitably arise are prevented from leading to systemic breakdown. Yet, as Henry Kissinger writes, "the bane of stable international systems is their nearly total inability to envision mortal challenge."[20]

The European order established after the defeat of Napoleon and that operated very effectively through much of the nineteenth century was intended to achieve three aims: the prevention of revolution, the maintenance of strategic equilibrium in Europe, and the prevention of systemic conflict. This was achieved by giving the great powers prerogatives to manage the system. As such it tied the interests of the powerful to the system, because the order served specific political ends about which the powerful agreed and because it was perceived to be legitimate.[21] Beyond the obvious fact that the order achieved its primary aims—the threat of revolution was averted, the map of Europe remained unchanged in its key elements for about sixty years, and systemwide war was avoided for nearly a hundred years—the order had several features worth drawing out in the context of the current period of power transition and potential order transformation.

First, the system included all the plausible major powers and recognized their standing (including defeated France and emerging Prussia, both of which, at least for a generation, were clearly not powers of the top rank). This meant that as Prussia became more prosperous, its interests could be incorporated into the setting. Second, the system could accept change provided it could be accommodated within the broader parameters of the order's main purpose. In ensuring minor changes at the margins of European power did not spiral out of control, the order was a striking success. And if ideas or actions were perceived by the powerful to conflict with the aims, then concerted action to snuff them out was undertaken. Third, the system promoted restraint among the powerful. Their interests were harnessed to system stability, and this was underpinned by the consensus that existed among the great powers as to the moral purpose of the order—the protection of a conservative political order in Europe.

After the unification of Germany, and in particular after the fall of Otto von Bismarck, the order began to break down. An unrestrained realpolitik replaced the balance of equilibrium and legitimacy that had been so crucial to the success of the old order. In the years prior to the First World War, there was no consensus about the purpose of international order, and change was managed through a process of shifting alliances and military commitments. The system at that time was potentially more accommodating because the rights and privileges of the powerful had all but disappeared. Crucially, however, the character of relations among the states became increasingly ossified around two blocs. The flexibility that was needed to manage the competing interests of five or six powerful states was not possible as the consensus around moral purpose and the overarching virtue of stability was replaced by hardened alliance frameworks and zero-sum competitive strategies. These mechanisms proved decreasingly able to restrain the powerful, opening the door for the First World War.

The international order established in 1945 articulated a distinctive vision of how relations between states should be organized. The order was strongly institutionalized and encapsulated a wide-ranging vision of the relations that it should oversee, incorporating not only traditional high-politics concerns of war and peace but also matters of economic interaction, linked as it was to the Bretton Woods multilateral economic institutions. In matters of international peace and security, it enshrined the special prerogatives of great power managerialism into its charter—in permanently giving five ostensible great powers a veto over decisions that were in turn binding on all members—and explicitly circumscribed the use of force. More broadly, the underlying principles of the order were the impersonal application of international law to govern relations between states. For the first time, the rules of the game were written down, given the status of law, and formalized in an institution that had a coercive mechanism that could swing into action in case members broke those rules.

This was a remarkable break with the past. Yet, for example, where the Congress of Vienna settlement rested on a thick sense of the moral purpose of international society, the United Nations (UN) order had a very thin normative consensus that was rooted in a distinctly international understanding of that society and not one in which international order served a broader political and social purpose. There has never been a clear sense of "for whom" and "for what" the order exists, beyond the basic interests of the states themselves, with tensions existing almost from the outset about these very issues. Indeed from the perspective of India and many other newly independent states, the order appeared heavily skewed in favor of the West. Whether in contests over the ideological and geopolitical consequences of decolonization or in the creation of a set of international instruments about individual rights, the UN-centered order has an ultimately unclear moral foundation and a weak basis in the social fabric of its constituent societies, with many states, including India, at odds with key components from its very beginning.

Transformation and the Current Order

While it has evolved after the Second World War in key ways, the underlying structures of the UN-led order remain largely in place. Given the challenge of emerging powers, how open to change is this system? From one perspective, the current order is flexible, relatively open, and provides an array of channels through which rising powers can be integrated into the existing setting. The complex layers of governance and rules embodied in the many multilateral institutions that are central to the current order are thought to be an important part of this flexibility.[22] These institutions provide the means through which economic interests can be advanced and protected, through which new locations of authority can be represented, and in which the standing and prestige of new powers can be recognized. John Ikenberry, the most prominent supporter of this view, argues that the existing order is easy to join and very hard to overturn, making the costs of accepting the order cheap and challenges to the order expensive.[23]

It is certainly the case that institutions such as the World Trade Organization provide the means for members to protect their interests and that bodies such as the International Monetary Fund (IMF) can be, and indeed have been, reorganized to some degree to reflect new distributions of economic power. Accommodation to change is most certainly possible.

Notwithstanding this claim, not all institutions have this requisite flexibility. The UN Security Council is perhaps the most obvious, and most important, outlier. Equally, the kinds of changes seen so far have only been fairly marginal in many institutions. The palpably dated notions that the head of the World Bank must be an American and that the head of the IMF must be a European (once again pursued following the fall of Dominique Strauss-Kahn) are typical of the institutional inertia of the current setting. But it is not just membership of elite clubs to which emerging powers aspire. They also seek recognition. Randall Schweller argues that in the main, rising powers can be distinguished between revisionist powers with aims that are revolutionary and those that have more limited concerns with the prevailing order.[24] Yet not all rising powers are explicitly and self-consciously revisionist in the sense that they are overtly seeking a substantive transformation of existing arrangements. It is here that India represents a distinctive challenge to the existing setting. It does not seek a fundamental transformation of the system or a radical expansion of its power, as did Nazi Germany and Imperial Japan. Instead it seeks both recognition from and standing within the system, but it also wants to ensure that this neither compromises closely held values nor further reinforces the existing power and influence of the West.

This desire for status, prestige, and influence, while not representing a fundamental challenge, will nonetheless test the existing order very considerably. It will do so because the capacity of the current order to bestow status, the privileges that it entails, and the cost that such action may impose on those who already have status is very significant. And it is very difficult to see ambition finding satisfaction without relatively painful change.

Beyond these institutional dimensions, the values and principles of the current order have an array of tensions and contradictions. First, there is not a clear and consistent sense of "for whom" the order exists. In some aspects the order is intended to advance the interests, rights, and prerogatives of states, but in others it is premised on a more explicitly liberal conception of the individual as its purpose. As Edward Keene notes, the world now "possess[es] a single, global structure of political and legal order but is riven by contradictions because we have not resolved the fundamental modern dichotomy about what order in world politics is for."[25] The contradiction between its more liberal tendencies and the more conservative elements makes the functioning of order complex, but it also provides an opportunity for emerging powers to shape the order in a decidedly illiberal fashion. States such as China and Russia are openly dismissive of many liberal norms; they take advantage of these tensions for their ends, but, if they were so inclined, they could also use the lack of consensus about the purpose of order to generate an alternative moral foundation for international order. Equally, India is potentially torn between its support for liberal principles and its unease about the institutional setting in which they reside at the international level.

In short, the liberal system may not be as flexible as some think and not as deeply entrenched as many imagine. The emergence of rising powers is exposing the problems at the heart of the current arrangements that are especially acute for India and that appear to give it such an important part to play. From an order-determining point of view, it could become the key swing state. It may well be that how India goes will determine how the order itself goes. Russia and China, and indeed elements in India, want an order that not only weakens American power and influence but that also protects a more traditional conception of sovereign independence. If India opts to side with such a view, then the liberal principles of the current period may well be at risk. If it does not, then trying to advance such an aim will be decidedly more difficult for Moscow and Beijing.

A second reason to think that the existing order will find it difficult to accommodate the emergence of a range of new powers is the lack of consensus about just what it is that powerful states ought to do in the international system. In the past, most obviously in nineteenth-century Europe's system but equally in the UN system (at least as it was intended to operate), powerful states had a distinct role to manage international order based on a tradeoff of rights and responsibilities. In the current setting, the consensus about what powerful states ought to do has been badly eroded. Indeed, many emerging powers are leery about taking on the sorts of responsibilities that some feel they ought to begin to bear. The United States increasingly articulates the view that China, as the world's second-largest economy, ought to begin to contribute to global public goods in the way that the United States does. China is very uneasy about this, not just because of the financial implications of such action but also because of a deeper skepticism about the utility of such action to its interests. Equally, while all of the emerging powers are ambitious to take on a greater role in international affairs, it is striking that none has even the most remote interest in taking on large-scale international obligations at any time in the foreseeable future. Different views about what it means to be a powerful state, and the expectations about influence and obligation that this generates, are likely to hinder the accommodation of these new powers. These tensions between ambition, responsibility, and resources are evident in India's approach to the international system and are in part responsible for the often stuttering forms of engagement that it has undertaken.

The emerging powers are clearly ambitious and have achieved remarkable success in recent years, but one must recognize that each faces very considerable domestic challenges to fulfill its potential. For example, China faces the real prospect of being caught in the middle-income trap,[26] as well as significant environmental, demographic, and governance problems. As many in India point out, its long-term success is by no means assured, a point also made regularly by the authors in this book. The political paralysis of recent years is only one among many problems, which also include domestic security challenges and infrastructure and governance concerns. These are all likely to continue to put a brake on economic growth and will reduce its capacity to translate its scale and ambition into genuine global heft. India, like China and the other emerging powers, is likely to become a significant global player, but it will be hampered by its domestic circumstances and limitations, and it will be continually focusing on its many domestic challenges. Even the optimistic Goldman Sachs economist Jim O'Neill argues that while China is likely to be the world's largest developed economy by 2050, it will still be significantly poorer than most other rich states.[27] We are likely to be faced with an unusual situation—that of powerful states that lack the ability to perform the kinds of roles that great powers have played in the past.

The rise of new powers is straining the existing international setting, and if they continue to develop as anticipated, then we can expect some change to the existing order. This does not mean that conflict is inevitable or that the order will be completely overturned. In contrast to gloomy international relations scholarship such as power transition theory,[28] the chapters in this book demonstrated that states do not only respond to the rise of new powers by turning to military means—they have a broader menu of choice when attempting to manage such states. The engagement strategies detailed in the preceding chapters come from this menu. The world is not girding its loins for inevitable conflict. Indeed, there is a wide array of views as to how the process of order transformation may occur. Conflict and contestation are only relatively unlikely possibilities.

Conclusion

What does India's engagement tell us about how international order may develop? The Western powers, led by the United States, believe that the existing order can accommodate India without too much damage to its underlying structures. Indeed, for some in the United States, the successful incorporation of India into the order is crucial, as liberal aspects are likely to come under pressure due to the successes of authoritarian and illiberal states. Yet there remain obstacles for a successful moderation of the order, beyond the obvious question of whether India can make good on its potential. It is not entirely clear that India will be content with the kind of view that America and its allies have of its role in the system. Nor can one be confident that even a prosperous, powerful, and broadly liberal India would not by dint of weight and influence produce a significantly different international system than the one we have. Finally, one cannot be confident that China would accept such a development. A liberal order anchored by an America resident in Asia and an activist great-power India is likely to reinforce those tendencies in Beijing to see the world arrayed against it and whoever wishes to contest and challenge that order. However it evolves, it is clear that those engaging with India recognize the potential importance of its growth not only for their interests but for the system more generally.

The rise of India, occurring as it does at a time of dynamic transformation in the system as a whole, has prompted many to think about broader changes to the international order. This book has shown how some states are trying to shape this process or position themselves in relation to it. Yet managing change of this magnitude is highly complex. The number of variables at play—the attitudes and ambitions of the rising powers, the response of the dominant power, the qualities of the dominant order, its scope for change and adaption, and the broader function of power and principle—is enormous, to say nothing of the political sensitivities at play. Even assuming one could keep egos in check in an exercise of Bismarckian diplomatic juggling, simply coordinating the process would be inordinately challenging. In the current period with the historical return of China, the striking growth of India, and the success of a wide array of emerging economies, as well as the senescence of the established North Atlantic powers, it is imperative that this challenge be met. The engagement of India shows how some states have begun to take up this challenge. It reveals just how open and as yet undetermined the future remains.

Notes

1. On which, see Nick Bisley, "Emerging Powers and the Changing Landscape of World Politics," in *Issues in 21st Century World Politics*, 2nd ed., ed. Mark Beeson and Nick Bisley (Basingstoke: Palgrave Macmillan, 2013).

2. Thucydides, *History of the Peloponnesian War*, ed. M. I. Finley (London: Penguin, 1954).

3. On which, see Peter H. Wilson, *The Thirty Years War: Europe's Tragedy* (Cambridge, MA: Harvard University Press, 2009).

4. Kenneth N. Waltz, *Theory of International Politics* (New York: Random House, 1979).

5. See Miroslav Nincic, *The Logic of Positive Engagement* (Ithaca, NY: Cornell University Press, 2011).

6. On Myanmar, see Jürgen Haacke, "ASEAN and Political Change in Myanmar: Towards a Regional Initiative?" *Contemporary Southeast Asia* 30, no. 3 (2008): 351–78. On China, see Alastair Iain Johnston and Robert S. Ross, eds., *Engaging China: The Management of an Emerging Power* (London: Routledge, 1999).

7. For data on populations, see United Nations, *World Population Prospects: The 2010 Revision, Volume II: Demographic Profiles* (New York: UN Department of Economic and Social Affairs, Population Division, 2011), http://esa.un.org/unpd/wpp/index.htm (accessed August 21, 2013).

8. Robert Kaplan, "Center Stage for the 21st Century: Power Plays in the Indian Ocean," *Foreign Affairs* 88, no. 2 (2009): 16–32.

9. See especially Mlada Bukovansky et al., *Special Responsibilities: Global Problems and American Power* (Cambridge: Cambridge University Press, 2012).

10. Christopher Layne, "The Unipolar Illusion Revisited: The Coming End of the United States' Unipolar Moment," *International Security* 31, no. 2 (2006): 7–41.

11. For a skeptical view, see "India as a Great Power: Know Your Own Strength," *Economist*, March 30, 2013.

12. Sunil Khilnani et al., *Non-Alignment 2.0: A Foreign and Strategic Policy for India in the Twenty-First Century* (New Delhi: Centre for Policy Research, 2012).

13. Daniel Twining, chapter 2 in this volume, 29.

14. Of the world's major militaries, India is by far the most dependent on importing military equipment, importing around two-thirds of equipment in 2012. See International Institute for Strategic Studies, *The Military Balance, 2013* (London: Routledge for IISS, 2013), 262.

15. See generally Andrew Phillips, *War, Religion, and Empire: The Transformation of International Order* (Cambridge: Cambridge University Press, 2011).

16. See K. J. Holsti, *Peace and War: Armed Conflicts and International Order, 1648–1989* (Cambridge: Cambridge University Press, 1991).

17. See Charles A. Kupchan, *No One's World: The West, the Rising Rest, and the Coming Global Turn* (New York: Oxford University Press for the Council on Foreign Relations, 2012).

18. For examples of the different ways in which the term is used, see G. John Ikenberry, *Liberal Leviathan: The Origins, Crisis, and Transformation of the American World Order* (Princeton, NJ: Princeton University Press, 2011), and Andrew Hurrell, *On Global Order: Power, Values, and the Constitution of International Society* (Oxford: Oxford University Press, 2007).

19. David Armstrong, Lorna Lloyd, and John Redmond, *International Organisation in World Politics*, 3rd ed. (Basingstoke, UK: Palgrave Macmillan, 2004).

20. Henry Kissinger, *Diplomacy* (New York: Doubleday, 1994), 133.

21. For more on this, see Nick Bisley, *Great Powers in a Changing International Order* (Boulder, CO: Lynne Rienner, 2012), 27–35; Paul W. Schroeder, "The 19th-Century International System: Changes in the Structure," *World Politics* 39, no. 1 (1986): 1–26; and Louise Richardson, "The Concert of Europe and Security Management in the Nineteenth Century,"

in *Imperfect Unions: Security Institutions over Time and Space*, ed. Helga Haftendorn, Robert O. Keohane, and Celeste A. Wallander (Oxford: Oxford University Press, 1999), 48–79.

22. G. John Ikenberry and Thomas Wright, *Rising Powers and Global Institutions* (New York: The Century Foundation, 2008), http://72.32.39.237:8080/Plone/publications/pdfs/pb635/ikenberry.pdf (accessed November 23, 2013).

23. Ikenberry, *Liberal Leviathan*.

24. Randall L. Schweller, "Managing the Rise of Great Powers: History and Theory," in Johnston and Ross, *Engaging China*, 18–19.

25. Edward Keene, *Beyond the Anarchical Society: Grotius, Colonialism and Order in World Politics* (Cambridge: Cambridge University Press, 2002), 143.

26. John O'Sullivan, "A Game of Catch Up: Special Report on the World Economy," *Economist*, September 24–30, 2011.

27. Jim O'Neill, *The Growth Map: Economic Opportunity in the BRICs and Beyond* (New York: Portfolio, 2011).

28. For the classic statement of power transition theory, see A. F. K. Organski, *World Politics* (New York: Knopf, 1958).

CONTRIBUTORS

Rajesh Basrur is a professor at the S. Rajaratnam School of International Studies at Nanyang Technological University, Singapore.

Nick Bisley is a professor of international relations at La Trobe University, Melbourne, Australia.

David Brewster is a visiting fellow at the Strategic and Defence Studies Centre, College of Asia and the Pacific at the Australian National University, Canberra.

H. D. P. Envall is a research fellow in the Department of International Relations, College of Asia and the Pacific at the Australian National University, Canberra.

Ian Hall is a senior fellow in the Department of International Relations, College of Asia and the Pacific at the Australian National University, Canberra.

Lavina Lee is a lecturer in international relations at Macquarie University, Sydney, Australia.

Louise Merrington recently completed her doctoral studies in the Department of Political and Social Change, College of Asia and the Pacific at the Australian National University, Canberra.

Harsh V. Pant is a reader in international relations at the Defence Studies Department, King's College, London.

Daniel Twining is a senior fellow for Asia at the German Marshall Fund of the United States, Washington, DC.

INDEX

5B
19|1|15
APP709.

Rs625/-